D1034193

THE
PLUNGERS
AND THE
PEACOCKS

OTHER BOOKS BY DANA L. THOMAS

THE MEDIA MOGULS:
THEIR LIVES AND BOISTEROUS TIMES

THE MONEY CROWD: WHO THEY ARE AND HOW
THEY OPERATE IN OUR FINANCIAL REVOLUTION

LORDS OF THE LAND: THE TRIUMPHS AND SCANDALS
OF AMERICA'S REAL ESTATE BARONS

THE STORY OF AMERICAN STATEHOOD

CRUSADERS FOR GOD

LET THE CHIPS FALL: A POLITICAL HISTORY OF NEW YORK
(WRITTEN WITH NEWBOLD MORRIS)

LIVING BIOGRAPHIES OF GREAT PHILOSOPHERS:
FROM SOCRATES TO SANTAYANA
(WRITTEN WITH HENRY THOMAS)

HOW TO INCREASE YOUR INCOME
DURING YOUR RETIREMENT

THE
PLUNGERS
AND THE
PEACOCKS

AN UPDATE OF THE CLASSIC HISTORY OF THE STOCK MARKET

DANA L. THOMAS

WILLIAM MORROW AND COMPANY, INC. NEW YORK

Copyright © 1967, 1989 by Dana L. Thomas

All rights reserved. No part of this book may be reproduced or utilized in any form or by any means, electronic or mechanical, including photocopying, recording or by any information storage and retrieval system, without permission in writing from the Publisher. Inquiries should be addressed to Permissions Department, William Morrow and Company, Inc., 105 Madison Ave., New York, N.Y. 10016.

Library of Congress Cataloging-in-Publication Data

Thomas, Dana Lee, 1918–
    The plungers and the peacocks : an update of the classic history
of the stock market / Dana L. Thomas. —Rev. ed.
        p.   cm.
    Includes index.
    ISBN 0-688-08136-3
    1. Wall Street—History.   I. Title.
HG4572.T46   1989
332.64'273—dc19   88-26056
                                                                    CIP

Printed in the United States of America

First Revised Edition

1 2 3 4 5 6 7 8 9 10

BOOK DESIGN BY JAYE ZIMET

FOR RUTH, WHO, THOUGH HANDICAPPED,
SERVED OTHERS WITH COURAGE AND COMPASSION

CONTENTS

INTRODUCTION

$\mathbf{M}$y original version of *The Plungers and the Peacocks* appeared in 1967. It traced the story of Wall Street from the beginning of our nation through the first two decades following the Second World War. Ever since my book first found an enthusiastic audience I have been urged to bring it up to date to cover more recent developments. The madcap stock market boom of the 1980s culminating in the 1987 Crash convinced me that the time had finally arrived to do this.

In researching Wall Street's fascinating past I have had access to a treasure trove of unpublished as well as privately published documents, including memoirs, diaries, letters, articles, books by leading stock market traders, speculators, investment bankers, brokers, financial historians and journalists. In addition I interviewed a number of historically important old-timers who had been witnesses to dramatic events going back half a century and more.

Some of my material relating to the period after the Second World War is partially derived from articles I wrote during the many years I covered Wall Street and the business scene as a financial journalist and associate editor of *Barron's,* dealing, among other subjects, with the computer revolution on Wall Street and the emergence of electronic stock trading; the buying and selling of gold; the growth of conglomerate building; the rise of the real estate mortgage trusts; offshore funds and other tax shelter operations; sugar industry lobby-ists; the relationship of hyper-inflation to the collapse of cur-rencies and political upheavals. (See Bibliography.)

I wish to give special thanks to my wife, Melba, for her editorial advice and support in the preparation of this book and to Irv Settel, a former professor, publisher, and himself an author, who finally persuaded me to update this work in the hope that today's readers would find in my exploration of Wall Street's past and its present some insights into how it will evolve tomorrow.

—DANA L. THOMAS
New York City, 1988

THE
PLUNGERS
AND THE
PEACOCKS

1
"SPECULATION WIPED A TEAR..."

THE FOUNDING FATHERS HATCH A DEAL AND WALL STREET IS BORN

Today everyone is concerned about what lies ahead. The ups and downs of Wall Street and the stock market will have an impact on all of us whether we are investors or merely bystanders. A booming market has frequently been the signal for widespread economic prosperity; a severe drop in the market has often led to a business slowdown, a loss of jobs, a plunge into a recession or worse. The fortunes of each of us, whether we like it or not, are inextricably linked to the destiny of Wall Street. Uppermost in our minds are worrisome questions. Will there be another severe market crash, and, if so, when? Are we headed for a great depression? How can we, any more than our predecessors, recognize the signs of a coming disaster and act in time to prevent it? Indeed, how will the stock market look and act in the year 2000 and beyond?

Aesop, the Greek spinner of fables, tells how one day a farmer discovered lying in the nest of his goose a glittering yellow egg. His first thought was to throw it away because he felt it was inedible. But upon examining it more closely he discovered it was an egg of the purest gold. Every morning thereafter, the farmer found a new golden egg glittering in the goose nest. Before long he became fabulously wealthy from these eggs, and he was seized with an idea. Why wait, he thought, for the goose to lay eggs one by one? If he killed the bird and opened it up, he would be able to get his hands immediately on all the gold it had to offer. So the farmer slaughtered his goose, ripped open its belly and found— nothing.

Wall Street is a goose that has been laying golden eggs since the birth of the Republic in the days of President Washington, when a handful of brokers met under a buttonwood tree and began trading in stocks and bonds. As the nation evolved from a handful of struggling, sparsely populated states into the richest society on earth, the stock market has served as the heart pumping the lifeblood for its economic growth. Wall Street raised the money to build the railroads linking the nation from coast to coast, made possible the launching of its steel and auto industries, the digging of its copper mines and oil wells, the development of the telegraph, of electricity, of the telephone; the financing of America's far-flung chain of retailing enterprises.

Yet despite these historic contributions, the stock market has at times caused great anguish for the American people. It has precipitated financial panics and market crashes, has triggered mass unemployment and depressions. It has served as the stage for wholesale thievery and double-dealing.

Recently we have had a highly traumatic experience with a bout of reckless speculation that brought on still another Wall Street disaster, the 1987 Crash. And voices have been raised again, as so often in the past, to apply new regulations to reform the market.

The major problem facing Wall Street and the rest of America today is nothing less than the healthy survival of our free-enterprise system. A way must be found to restore the stock market to its necessary function of providing the equity funds and liquidity so urgently needed for America's well-being without destroying the legitimate element of speculation that is so essential an ingredient of the investment game. The question is, when is financial speculation useful and when is it excessive and harmful? How can the greedy motivations of individuals be rechanneled into socially beneficial results? In short, how can we avoid killing the goose that lays the golden eggs?

This book has been written in the firm conviction that for us to assess the future accurately it is necessary to know the past. In no other field of endeavor has the past so significantly repeated itself as in the stock market. Although the players today are different and their environment has changed, human nature has remained the same and so have the basic dynamics of market investment. As Arnold Bernhard, the founder of *Value Line* put it, "The market, to a large degree, is a captive of the past as well as an anticipation of the future." In the case of Wall Street, history is the key to unlocking the future.

Let us cite merely one dramatic example. We cannot begin to measure fully the extent of the recent disaster that befell the nation—the 1987 Crash—without going back, as we shall do in this book, to Wall Street's greatest previous catastrophe, the market crash in October 1929. Although there are differences in the causes and results, there are also startling parallels—in investor psychology, in the grim working out of wrong-headed monetary policies, in the consequences of mindless speculation. And these must be fully understood if we wish to evaluate what lies ahead.

Investor psychology has not changed much through the ages. The strategies and tactics being employed for striking it rich today were used in all their basics a century ago. It is highly revealing to return to the great risk takers of the past and examine their ingenious stratagems for scoring financial killings. Some of their coups changed the course of American history. We shall disclose the remarkable story of these audacious swingers as well as the Plungers and Peacocks of our own era, the exuberant successors of J. P. Morgan, Edward Harriman, Jesse Livermore. We will also take a look at the stock market of tomorrow, assessing what role it is likely to play in the year 2000 and beyond.

The history of Wall Street is a rich, fascinating story of irresistible high drama. But it is much more. If we refuse to learn the lessons of history, the past will surely return to haunt us. People today, especially the young, are suffering from an absence of historical memory. And as one leading social historian warned, "The loss of this memory is dangerous for the civilized world."

So we begin.

In 1848 William Makepeace Thackeray wrote in an introduction for a new novel he was about to publish, *Vanity Fair*: "As the manager of the Performance sits before the curtain on the boards and looks into the Fair, a feeling of profound melancholy comes over him in his survey of the bustling place. There is a great quantity of eating and drinking, making love and jilting, laughing and the contrary, smoking, cheating, fighting, dancing and fiddling; there are bullies pushing about, bucks ogling the women, knaves picking pockets, policemen on the lookout, quacks ... bawling in front of their booths, and yokels looking up at the tinselled dancers and poor old rouged tumblers, while the light-fingered folk are operating upon their pockets behind. Yes, this is VANITY FAIR; not a moral place, certainly; nor a merry one, though very noisy. Look at the faces of the actors and buffoons when they come off from their business; and Tom Fool washing the paint off his cheeks before he sits down to dinner with his wife and the little Jack Puddings behind the canvas. The curtain will be up presently, and he will be turning over head and heels, and crying 'How are you?'.... I have no other moral than this to tag to the present story of 'Vanity Fair.' Some people consider Fairs immoral altogether, and eschew such, with their servants and families; very likely they are right. But persons who think otherwise, and are of a lazy, or a benevolent, or a sarcastic mood, may perhaps like to step in for half an hour, and look at the performances. There are scenes of all sorts; some dreadful combats, some grand and lofty horse-riding, some scenes of high life, and some of very middling indeed; some love-making for the sentimental, and some light comic business; the whole accompanied by appropriate scenery and brilliantly illuminated with the Author's own candles."

Some irreverent readers will think this is as appropriate a way as any to begin a story of Wall Street. For the hurly-burly spirit of the carnival, the Fools and Jack Puddings, the cheaters, the fiddlers and the mischief-makers have historically never been more in evidence than along those few acres of land lying in lower Manhattan between Trinity Church and the East River. But to call Wall Street Vanity Fair is a gross oversimplification, unless one is quick to point out that the story of the Street has been permeated with overtones of tragic irony far beyond the glitter of a puppet show.

The finicky-minded have looked upon financial speculation with misgivings. It has been classified along with gambling as one of man's more deplorable vices. Yet speculation has been the historic catalyst of the American economy. The willingness to take a risk was what caused the United States to expand across a continent, to develop its long-distance communications, to build cities that astonished mankind. The iron rails that spanned America were launched on outright speculation. General Motors, one of the world's largest corporations, was founded by a stock market operator, Billy Durant. The United States Steel Corporation was organized with heavily watered stock and unloaded onto the public by speculators. The telephone was little more than a gleam in the mind of its inventor until a group of Boston stock manipulators decided to take a flyer and turned it into reality.

The spirit of risk-taking lies deep within human nature. The hope of hitting the jackpot is what has differentiated the human race from an ant heap. For all his trickery, his tragic and comic misadventures, the speculator has been a vital mainspring of the human experience.

The stage upon which America's early master speculators bedazzled their peers had modest enough origins. When the Colonial Dutch inhabited New York, one early governor put a fence around pastureland located in what is now the Battery to keep the livestock from straying off. Peter Stuyvesant, his successor, turned the pen into something more permanent —a wall. And that is how this grazing land, ploughed up by succeeding generations of bulls and bears, received its name.

Wall Street has always been partial to resourceful enterprise. In Colonial times, before stocks and bonds were peddled, Captain William Kidd took up residence on the Street. This was before he became a pirate of repute, but he managed to make ends meet by living off the income of a wealthy widow and speculating in the auction marts, bartering Negro slaves from Africa. Kidd's career as a buccaneer was terminated when he was hanged from a yardarm; and ever since, fortune hunters have searched along the banks of the Hudson where rumors indicated Kidd had hid a fortune in gold. This search has been fruitless; but it has been no more of a wild-goose chase than many a quest along Broad and Wall streets.

Wall Street is embedded in the major events of American history. At the head of Broad Street, where it empties into Wall, stood the pillory stocks and whipping posts where sinners did penance in Puritan times. During the Revolutionary War, the Continental Congress made its headquarters in City Hall, a few blocks from Wall Street. Washington was inaugurated President on the stairs of the Federal Hall that was built in 1788 and is the site of the former U.S. Subtreasury Building, which stands at the corner of Wall and Nassau streets.

Although it served as the location of slave auctions, Puritan chastisements and a Presidential inauguration, Wall Street really found its métier when it began trading in securities.

As a matter of fact, financial speculation took place even before the physical structure of the New York Stock Exchange was organized. A particularly exuberant burst was touched off by the Revolutionary War. To finance the Revolution, the Continental Congress printed paper money and scrip. Farmers, soldiers and businessmen carried on transactions in this paper, but as the years passed and Congress gave no indication that the Government would redeem it for hard money, its value tumbled to virtually zero. The phrase "not worth a Continental" became widely current. Most Americans resigned themselves to their losses and put their shoulders harder to the wheel. But Alexander Hamilton, upon being selected Secretary of the Treasury in the Washington Administration, insisted that the Government establish its credit at home and abroad by redeeming the Continentals. Rumors that Hamilton was pushing for redemption reached the merchants and banking fraternity of the Eastern Seaboard; but news traveled slowly in those days and it was many months before it penetrated into the interior. Those close to the situation—leading members of Congress and financiers—formed syndicates in Boston, New York and Philadelphia to buy up all the available paper money as quickly as possible. Two Congressmen chartered two fast vessels, which embarked loaded to the gunwales with cash. Their agents swooped down on village after village, purchasing the scrip from its original owners, who naïvely let it go at 15 to 20 cents on the dollar.

When Hamilton's bill reached the House, the first section, which called for the refunding by the Federal Government of certificates with bonds at par and bearing interest, ran into opposition on the part of Congressmen who argued that the original holders would suffer double jeopardy. They would not only be fleeced by surrendering their holdings at a fraction of their worth, but since a tax would have to be levied to pay the interest on the refunding, they would have to bear the brunt of the levy.

But, despite bitter opposition, the first section of the bill was passed, and attention was focused on getting the second part through, calling for the Government's assumption of the State as well as the Federal debt. Since many speculators held heavy amounts of State paper, their anxiety mounted as this feature of the bill ran into heavy going. Several of the Southern states whose indebtedness was much less than their neighbors' objected to being subjected to the leveling process of refunding.

A decision was finally reached, ironically, through the intervention of Thomas Jefferson, the leading patron of grass roots America. He had been abroad on a mission as Secretary of State when the fight first broke out, and upon returning to Washington, he lent an ear to Hamilton's pleas. Hamilton needed one vote in the Senate and five in the House to pass his bill. Jefferson was interested in a measure of his own. The original location of the Government at the time was New York City and a study was under way to determine where to locate it permanently. Jefferson wanted it located along the Potomac River as near as possible to his birthplace. So a bargain was struck between the nation's leading liberal and its top-ranking conservative to swap urgently needed votes. Jefferson got his capital in what became the District of Columbia; Hamilton obtained his redemption bill. And according to Senator William Maclay, a wry observer of the times, "Speculation wiped a tear from either eye."

Revolutionists are fond of saying that one can't make an omelette without breaking eggs. This held true for the American Revolution. While the refunding bill undoubtedly enriched the more astute at the expense of their simpler fellows, Hamilton's measures put the United States' credit on a solid basis, paving the way for the economic growth of the nation. Before Hamilton reared his monetary structure, merchants in need of funds had to borrow from one another. The medium of exchange consisted of guineas, doubloons, pistols—all minted in foreign treasuries. The simplest transaction provoked the utmost confusion.

One of the offshoots resulting from Hamilton's labors was the emergence of the New York Stock Exchange.* The redemption of Continentals by the Government resulted in the issuance of certificates which became the first stocks and bonds traded in the nation. There were at first no formal exchanges. Traffic in Government certificates was undertaken by merchants who met in the open air at the east end of Wall Street and acted as agents for the securities, while the coffeehouses that lined the Street reverberated with gossip about the prospects of this or that certificate the agents chose to push. These merchant-auctioneers peddled stocks as a side business without a commission. But enterprising individuals, seeing an opportunity to become full-time specialists and collect fees, set up their own broker establishments for dealing in securities. And they banded together into an organization that succeeded in driving the merchant-auctioneers out of the business.

In May, 1792, twenty-four of these brokers gathered under a buttonwood tree and drew up a written agreement to deal only with one another on a common commission basis. "We, the subscribers, brokers for the purchase and sale of public stocks, do hereby solemnly promise and pledge ourselves, to each other, that we will not buy or sell from this date for any person whatsoever any kind of public stocks at a less rate than one-quarter of one percent commission on the specie value, and that we will give a preference to each other in our negotiations. In testimony, whereof, we have set our hands on this seventeenth day of May at New York, 1792."

During the first years, trading was done primarily in Government certificates created by the refunding program. The

*In its early years it was known as the New York Stock and Exchange Board.

establishment of banks to meet the growing needs of American depositors touched off a new wave of securities buying. By 1803, forty banks were doing business in the thirteen states, and Wall Street was the financial midwife raising most of the funds to launch them. In 1815 the New York newspapers began the practice of carrying tables listing the prices of stocks traded during the previous day. The war of 1812 with England had enormously swelled the debt of the United States, compelling the issuance of a wave of Government bonds. This, together with America's vigorous commercial expansion, created a heady increase in securities trading. Industrial corporations began to be formed. And the public demand for shares in them burgeoned. In 1825, the Erie Canal was opened, linking the Eastern Seaboard to the Middle West, and New York forged ahead as the center of the nation's import and export business. America was booming. And the Stock Exchange was having a hard time keeping up.

In 1793, the year after its founders had met under the buttonwood tree, the group constructed for its trading arena the most pretentious building on Wall Street, the Tontine Coffee House. By 1817, the business of the Exchange had reached proportions that required a reorganization. The membership decided to adopt a set of formal rules embodied in a written constitution, providing for the election of officers, and setting forth the qualifications for admitting new members.

Over the next twenty years the scope of Stock Exchange trading grew by leaps and bounds. And yet it was still small by later standards. The Exchange did not make a continuous market in securities but continued to operate during periodic call periods until after the Civil War. On Tuesday, March 16, 1830, for instance, only 31 shares passed hands—5 shares of Morris Canal and Banking Company were traded at 75¼, and 26 shares of the United States Bank were exchanged at 119, to comprise what was undoubtedly the most sluggish session in the history of the Stock Exchange. *For a mere $3,470.25,*

REPRODUCTION OF AN OLD DRAWING SHOWING THE
FLOOR OF THE STOCK EXCHANGE IN 1851 DURING ONE
OF THE REGULAR "CALLS".
COURTESY OF THE NEW-YORK HISTORICAL SOCIETY, NEW YORK CITY

*an ambitious trader on that day could have bought up all
the stock being offered and monopolized the trading.* But
never again!

The members of the Exchange during this period were,
for the most part, elderly men, pillars of their community.
They were the merchants and bankers, the movers and the
shakers. They were pompous, and wore swallowtail coats and
tall stove-pipe hats. Each trader marched solemnly into the
board room before each call, followed by a youth who carried
a heavy book in which the transactions were recorded. During
the call, the president stood on a rostrum announcing the
trades, and members sat in their tall hats around a table on
two elevated platforms at the other end of the room. At this
time a "seat" on the Exchange was literally a chair and nothing
else. Not until 1870 would seats have monetary value. In

1871 one could buy a seat for $2,000. By 1928, the price would be over $600,000.

Until after the Civil War, the Board kept its proceedings secret from the public. The traders were an exclusive club of insiders. There were no exchange reporters or news agencies, and no one but the members had access to information on transactions. The nature of these occasioned a lively curiosity, and a group of outsiders, failing to be admitted into membership, hired a building adjacent to the Exchange, dug the bricks out of the wall and drilled a peephole so that they could see and hear what was going on. At each quote announced by the president of the Big Board, an eavesdropper stationed at the peephole shouted the price to his associates, and they would conduct their own market on the basis of this quote. When trading on the Big Board slackened, the peeper and his colleagues whiled away the time pitching half-dollars at a crack in the floor, laying bets on how close they could get to it. Then, when trading resumed on the Exchange, the watcher rushed back to his post.

In addition to this peephole fraternity, other informal trading associations sprang up along the Street. So long as the nation's economy boomed and stocks continued to climb, these ad hoc groups prospered. But in 1857, when a financial panic gripped the money market, it became painfully apparent that in a period of heavy selling only the existence of a formal exchange assured the stability necessary for the unloading of securities. And a number of brokers pleaded with the Big Board to enlarge its membership and let them in. When it refused to entertain the notion, some of the younger, more aggressive outsiders thought up resourceful stratagems to force their way in. One frustrated group formed an organization called "The Open Board of Brokers." Another started a Government Bond Department devoted exclusively to U.S. Government securities. Both went after the Big Board's business by cutting their commission rates. And they drew blood. The senior exchange was compelled to drop its insularity and negotiate an agreement with the insurgent groups, amalgamating with them into a single organization.

The merger took place in May, 1869. The brokers of the Open Board celebrated the "capitulation" of the Big Board by singing "Auld Lang Syne" when the last day's trading was completed under the old auspices. They hoisted their vice-president, George Henriques, onto their shoulders and carried him into Delmonico's restaurant, still seated in his official chair, wining and dining him and then hauling him triumphantly onto the trading floor of the Big Board.

A new era was about to be launched with a greatly strengthened Stock Exchange that for six decades—until the great Depression of the 1930s and President Roosevelt's New Deal—would have unchallenged sovereignty over America's financial affairs.

2

THE BLUE, THE GRAY AND THE GOLD

ABE LINCOLN BATTLES THE WALL STREET SABOTEURS

Henry Clews, a leading broker who wrote a classic book at the turn of the century on his fifty years' experience as a Wall Street trader, addressed one of his chapters to young apprentice traders under the title "How to Take Advantage of Periodical Panics in Order to Make Money." He pointed out that many Wall Street professionals, by the time they had gained sufficient experience as traders, had unfortunately become old enough to have one foot in the grave. "When this time comes these old veterans of the Street usually spend long intervals of repose at their comfortable homes, and in times of panic . . . these old fellows will be seen in Wall Street, hobbling down on their canes to their brokers' offices. Then they always buy good stocks to the extent of their bank balances, which have been permitted to accumulate for just such an emergency. The panic usually rages until enough of these cash purchases of stock is made to afford a big 'rake in.' When the panic has spent its force, these old fellows … deposit their profits with their bankers, or the surplus thereof, after purchasing more real estate that is on the upgrade, for permanent investment, and retire for another season to the quietude of their splendid homes and the bosoms of their happy families."

If the ambitious young trader, Clews pointed out, instead of listening to stock tips from amateurs only had the patience to watch for "the speculative signs of the times as manifested in the periodical egress of these old prophetic speculators from their shells of security," he would be in a position to make a barrel of money. "I say to the young speculators, therefore, watch the ominous visits to the Street of these old men. They are as certain to be seen on the eve of a panic as spiders creeping stealthily and noiselessly from their cobwebs just before rain."

Throughout the nineteenth century there were enough panics to sharpen the appetite of the most zestful speculator in hard times, and one of the biggest money crises in the history of the Street took place while the Stock Exchange was still in swaddling clothes—indeed just before the merger of the independents that was discussed in the last chapter. It was occasioned by the outbreak of the Civil War.

When hostilities erupted in 1861, the Lincoln Administration was heavily saddled with debts and unable to meet the expenses of the war. From a financial standpoint, the North could hardly have picked a worse time for a showdown with the South. After a brief period of surplus funds under the stewardship of the Buchanan Administration, the Government debt had been rising ominously. When Lincoln took office, it had reached a level of $64.8 million in long-term bonds and temporary loans, against a cash income of only $3.6 million. At one time it was gossiped in Washington that the Secretary of the Treasury, Howell Cobb, a politician from Georgia, in anticipation of the coming conflict, had deliberately mishandled U.S. financing in an act of outright sabotage.

Alexander H. Stephens, the secessionist leader, reported in a letter to a friend that one of his political colleagues, Robert Toombs, "... the other night in high glee ... told (Cobb) in company that he had done more for secession than any other man. He had deprived the enemy of the sinews of war and left them without a dollar in the Treasury. He did not even leave 'Old Buck' two quarters to put on his eyes when he died." Historians for the most part are convinced that Cobb did not act treacherously but that the financial policies he followed from 1857 on were the result of extremely poor judgment.

In any case, the condition of the Union when Lincoln took office was somber. And it steadily deteriorated as the war stepped up in tempo. Rather than levy a stiff income tax on the people, an extremely mild tax was introduced and the Government took the more politically palatable tactic of printing $450 million in paper money—greenbacks—to raise the bulk of the money needed. Since the worth of the money depended on the ability of Washington to make good on its promise to redeem the currency in hard cash at some future time, this became associated in the popular mind with the fortunes of the armies on the battlefield. In view of the uncertainty of the outcome, the only currency of certain value was gold—the gold salted away in the vaults of banks or hoarded under the mattress. Gold became a commodity in which to speculate heavily on the Exchange. Indeed, as the war grew grimmer, the entire economy of the North virtually became pegged to the gyrations of gold. Merchants, manufacturers, doctors and dentists watched the course of gold prices to use as a yardstick by which to set their own prices. Prices turned bullish or bearish on the strength of the war news. When the Yankee armies won, the prestige of the Union took an upward bound and the desirability of hoarding gold waned. But when the Confederates triumphed, the pendulum of psychology shifted; the price of gold skyrocketed. Most of the time the news of victory or defeat reached the professional speculators before it became public knowledge or was known even to the press, thanks to spies and informers planted by influential traders with the armies in the field.

Some of the biggest speculators were Government officials who got inside reports on the tide of battle from agents stationed in Baltimore and Louisville, near the front lines, and who wired heavy buy or sell recommendations to Washington. The orders were transmitted in code. A wire to Jay Cooke and Company, financiers, from an informant stationed with the Union armies, dated August 29, 1862, for instance, read: "Pope captures 6,000 cavalry at Warrenton." This really meant "Johnson buys 6,000 legal tenders of Fox and Company." And on September 18, while the Battle of Antietam was in progress, a Cooke telegram to a client read: "McClellan supplies help. Tremendous battle going on, result undetermined." Translated, this meant "Sweeny applies for more. Decided change in market and cannot reply positively."

But the speculation in Washington was pikerish compared to what went on in Wall Street. From the outset of the war, powerful financial circles in New York had been hostile to the Lincoln Government. Much of the money invested in the Street had been Southern money and this was withdrawn en masse with the declaration of hostilities. And many Northern business leaders, apprehensive of attacks on factories and railroads, were against going to war to settle the dispute. Indeed, three months before the conflict broke out, New York's mayor, Fernando Wood, addressed the city's Common Council expressing the views of these financial circles. He proposed, amidst thunderous applause, that if Lincoln went to war, New York should secede from the Union and form an independent nation. He even came up with a name for the new nation (to consist of Manhattan, Staten Island and Long Island)—Tri-Insula. More practical heads prevailed and New York remained in the Union.

Now with speculation in currency reaching febrile proportions, Wall Street became the mecca of the Goldbugs. The

Governors of the New York Stock Exchange refused to have anything to do with this gambling on the defeat of the Union armies, and they abolished trading in gold on the floor of the Exchange. But it flourished elsewhere. By January, 1862, Broad and New streets were lined with the shops of a new species of broker who exhibited gold in the window and attracted huge crowds of buyers. The traffic became so dense that the brokers rented sidewalk space in front of their shops to accommodate the overflow, and the police had to issue orders to keep people on the move.

Finally, thirty brokers who had been meeting in a neighborhood restaurant hired larger quarters on New Street, called Gilpin's Gold Room, and they ruled that anyone could become a member and trade there for a $100 annual fee. According to William Fowler, a contemporary broker, the Gold Room was a gloomy basement. "Its style of architecture reminded one of the shanties erected for the temporary accommodation of miners working from auriferous vein which may any hour be cut off by a fault and cease to be remunerative. . . . Inside this shell of a building were numerous cattycorners and nooks fenced off by iron railings. . . . Into these recesses the weary operators were wont to retire.and wait for prices to move and then sally forth. . . . Voices rose and fell in discordant chorus, and in the pauses a dull burr and rapid clicking, as of a small cotton factory, told that the telegraph was spitting out long rolls of paper ribbons marked with quotations from London, Frankfurt and Paris. The cast-iron figure in the center of the hall . . . threw up a shower of spray which fell into a basin, tinkling and clinking like coin of gold. The operators grouped around it . . . staring at each other through the drops as if they were interrogating the fountain respecting the success of their ventures." The room had an indicator that displayed the price at which each new transaction was made. One face of the indicator could be seen outside on New Street and since, as noted, the gyrations in gold regulated the prices of many goods, merchants began their day by hurrying to New Street to take a peek at the first quote through the window before repairing to their businesses to mark their merchandise up or down accordingly.

The speculators had one major hurdle to surmount—how to physically exchange the gold from seller to purchaser. Actually, the transfer was not necessary for every transaction, since a buyer would usually arrange for delivery sometime in the future, gambling that in the meantime the price would go up and he would be able to unload the gold on somebody else. A second, third and fourth buyer would speculate on a continued rise in price, so that title to a consignment of gold would change hands a number of times before it was actually delivered from the bank. Then, when the time could no longer be put off, the gold was loaded into sacks and delivered by messenger boys. The traders were sharp practitioners and they frequently shortchanged one another by mixing worthless materials in with the precious metal. Moreover, there was the constant threat of robbery. Messengers carrying gold-filled sacks were frequently set upon by thieves who tossed acid into their eyes, struck them to the ground and made off with the loot. After a number of such incidents, the brokers arranged for the issue of checks drawable upon deposit at the Bank of New York to be accepted in lieu of the gold. Traders were permitted to open these accounts for a charge of $1,000 and to draw upon them with checks, across the face of which GOLD was printed in large, bronze letters.

The operations of the gold traders provoked protests from shocked citizens throughout the North. Lincoln himself was infuriated with the Goldbugs. In 1864 he wrote the Governor of New York, "What do you think of those fellows in Wall Street who are gambling in gold at such a time as this? For my part, I wish every one of them had his devilish head shot off."

Congress tried to ban the speculation. In June, 1864, it passed a law declaring all trading in gold to be a penal offense unless it took place specifically in the office of the seller or purchaser. The aim was to eliminate such spurious ventures as Gilpin's Gold Room and other trading holes. But it didn't stop trading one whit. Locked out of the Gold Room, the traders negotiated on the sidewalk, using specious means of evasion.

As hopes of an early Union victory faded and the South continued to hold out stubbornly, speculation reached a feverish pitch. As early as April, 1862, gold at Gilpin's had skyrocketed to $120. (That is, it took $120 worth of greenbacks to purchase $100 worth of gold certificates.) In July, when McClellan's lethargic Peninsula drive drifted into a stalemate, gold climbed even higher. After the Union defeat at Fredericksburg, it reached $134, and in the following January, soared to $150. Grant's campaign in the Wilderness, which suffered heavy losses and failed of its aims, sent the price still higher. His failure to take Richmond boosted it to $185 on July 11.

Washington sought assiduously for countermeasures to curb the speculators. Since it was unable to kill the trading by decisive military action, it took action on the financial front, launching a massive campaign to sell war bonds and bind the rank and file citizen of the North to the support of the Government's credit. To administer the program, the Lincoln Administration turned to the investment house of Jay Cooke, offering it a commission on the funds raised. Cooke was one of the most prestigious investment houses in the nation, a specialist in merchandising financial schemes to the public. It had previously undertaken a variety of fund-raising projects for the Secretary of the Treasury, and Jay Cooke, the senior partner, plunged into this new venture with zest. The counterattack he launched was a meticulously planned one. To pave the way for high-powered publicity, Cooke hired Sam Wilkeson, an editor of the New York *Tribune* and a close associate of Horace Greeley, the publisher, to head up a press bureau; and he paid off an army of editorial writers and reporters to flood the nation's newspapers and magazines with articles lauding the war bond drive. While believers in the incorruptibility of the Third Estate undoubtedly raised a scandalized eyebrow at the way newsmen allowed themselves to be bought, Cooke at least handled the matter delicately. Through the New York advertising agency Shattuck, Peaslee and Co., Sam Wilkeson developed a package of publicity releases to be inserted in the press under the guise of news articles. And these were accompanied by memos providing journalists with guidance in their editorial writing. It required a nice sense of diplomacy to swing some newspapers into line. Wilkeson never explicitly sent an order or uttered a threat; but the newspaper or magazine publisher realized that when the request to insert a favorable editorial or article was passed along, he was expected to do his duty.

As for the news reporters who turned out their copy under Wilkeson's eye, they were rewarded on a nicely balanced scale. Cooke gave an especially meritorious journalist an option for sixty days to buy Government war bonds. If the right was exercised within the period, the newsman received the profits on the transaction minus the interest computed at 6 percent. If the price of the bonds rose to a point at which it was not feasible to exercise the option, Cooke obligingly extended the period. For their part, the writers dutifully sent in clippings of their articles and editorials to Cooke's headquarters. No important newspaper in the North was overlooked by Cooke. Financial editors, associate editors and lead-article writers received attentions on a scale which, according to a historian of the period, "it is safe to say that the rank and file of American newspaper men have never since enjoyed." In addition to paying off in cash, Cooke sweetened the palates of the more important editors with gifts of wine and duck. On some days, fifty cases of wine, specially packed in ice, went out in a single shipment charged to the war bond's advertising account.

This lavish investment in feeding the flock paid off handsomely. The Niagara of stories that spewed forth from Cooke's press corps aroused many people of the North against the wheeling and dealing of the Goldbugs. They were determined to show the cynical foxes of Wall Street how *they* felt about the nation's future. And the press assiduously reported on every nuance of this grass-roots response.

Stories in the New York *Tribune* described how men and women poured into the headquarters of Jay Cooke in Philadelphia to press their hard-earned savings on Cooke's agents in exchange for war bonds. Wilkeson himself wrote in the *Tribune*, quivering with histrionic ardor, "It is noon at Jay Cooke & Company. Inside the parent front room of all these little back and side rooms, the narrow space between the counters and the wall is crowded with people ready to be waited on. They are of all classes and all degrees and of all colors. There are black men in Jay Cooke & Company and they hold money in their hands, and there is a soldier there, and there is an officer, lame, yet with an unmistakable air of command and of guardianship; and there are Quakers who look annuity and coupons and peace and goodness all over them; and there is a clergyman, and a woman that sews . . . and three women who sew not, neither do they spin, but who make investments, and there are mechanics, one with his dinner pail. . . ."

All over the North men and women trekked to the network of Cooke offices to hand in their money, and Cooke's hired journalists squeezed every last ounce of human interest from the situation. "There was the little old Irish woman with a wrinkled face and white hair," reported one correspondent, "who trudged into one office to buy $1,200 worth of bonds. 'I want to subscribe $1,200 to the Government loan. All that I am worth I acquired here. I had not one cent when I came to this country, nor had any of my friends. I take this much for old Abe and the country, and if more is necessary they shall have it.' "

There was the elderly widow whose husband had died years before, leaving her, so everybody supposed, destitute.

She walked into a bank and, asking for bonds, drew from an old handkerchief $1,200 in bills that had been lying so long and had become so musty the clerk almost fainted from the disagreeable smell. An order for bonds came from a group of cowpunchers and Mexicans in Santa Fe. A German walked thirty miles from his Iowa farm to the national bank in Dubuque. He was dressed in rags like a beggar to avoid being robbed on the road. He took out $13,000, part of which was his own cash, the rest money his neighbors had entrusted to him to buy them bonds. "Every dollar of the thirteen thousand had been dug by these Germans out of the soil with hard days' work," concluded the newspaper story.

Aggressively, Cooke, Wilkeson and Company pressed their advantage. Handbills, posters and broadsides were plastered on windows and walls all over the North. Wilkeson issued regular reports on the progress of the bond drive, presenting the latest figures on the amount of money subscribed on one side of a sheet and the words and music of "America," "Hail Columbia" and "John Brown's Body" on the other. On the masthead he printed an American eagle bearing a scroll in its beak inscribed, "Your sons and your money on your country's altar."

There was no limit to Cooke's exuberant audacity. He ordered his agents to follow the advancing Union armies and whenever a Southern town was taken to peddle Yankee war bonds among the rebel populace. Some skeptics felt that this was like trying to sell iceboxes to the Eskimos; but Cooke shrugged off the faint-hearted. In March, 1864, the Northern newspapers reported that the irrepressible financier had placed in Fortress Monroe, Grant's headquarters, a trunk marked "Richmond, Virginia," crammed with circulars for signing up subscriptions in the Confederate capital the moment it surrendered. "Mr. Cooke," wrote one reporter, "expects the way to Richmond to be opened shortly and he is ready to offer the inhabitants who remain a better investment for their money than Confederate bonds."

But in the final analysis, the only permanent answer to the speculation in gold was the decisive victory of the Union army. And Lincoln's generals strove to bring the war to an end as soon as possible. Some historians are inclined to believe that Grant's strategy in the Wilderness Campaign, when he made massive frontal attacks upon Confederate strongholds and suffered staggering losses, was shaped largely by the pressure put on him by Washington politicians who felt that a decisive military showdown was an absolute must to put a stop to the hemorrhage that was taking place in the Government's Treasury as a result of the gold speculation.

In any event it was only with the ending of hostilities that the chance to make a killing in gold was abruptly halted. And even so, the final departure of the Goldbugs was postponed by an unexpected event—the assassination of Lincoln. Jay Cooke was preparing to depart on Saturday morning, April 15, from his country home in Pennsylvania for the railroad station when he received a wire from his brother Henry, a Washington broker, informing him of the President's death. Fearful that the stock market might go into a tailspin, Cooke telegraphed his agents in New York City, ordering them to stand ready to purchase Government bonds in any amount necessary to sustain it, come what might. "It is all important that Government securities should stand like a rock." That Saturday morning, the dealers in Government bonds and the Governors of the Big Board closed their doors. "Everybody is much too horrified to think of business. We must wait for Monday," an agent reported to Cooke.

Not everybody. Minutes after the death of Lincoln was announced, a number of gold speculators could not overlook a chance to try their luck. They bought gold in heavy amounts, paying $153 and up. But the public refused to panic. On Monday the market opened calmly and Government agents were easily able to absorb the trickle of bonds that were cashed. Gold opened at $153 and tumbled to $148. Speculators sustained a loss of five to ten points, enough to wipe out their normal margin, and a number went bankrupt.

But many others, who had pulled in their horns in time, took millions out of Wall Street during the peak of gold speculation. The foundations of a number of fortunes that were to thrust their possessors into positions of noteworthy influence in postwar America were laid in Gilpin's.

The Civil War had another important impact. By setting off a speculation of unprecedented proportions, it brought about the first attempt by the Federal Government to extend its jurisdiction over the Street. It laid bare an issue that was to be posed time and again in subsequent years—who was to exercise the supreme power over the nation's financial destiny? While the routing of the Goldbugs was an important victory for Washington, there would be no further one of major significance for generations.

3

ULYSSES IN NIGHT TOWN

THE PLOT TO SEIZE THE NATION'S GOLD SUPPLY—THE RUIN OF AN EX-PRESIDENT

Thomas Carlyle once said that the great events of history crystallized as a result of the right men meeting with the right hour. Certainly the great speculators of history have succeeded not only by their own astuteness but through the happy confluence of historic conditions that have played into their hands.

Arthur Cutten, one of America's most successful commodity speculators, once had a chart prepared by George Broomhall, a British authority on statistics, to show the historic fluctuations in the price of wheat. In studying these, Cutten went back to the time when commodity prices were first recorded on the exchanges of the world. He discovered that the barometer of man's speculations read like a fever chart of social crisis; that one could actually follow the story of humanity's strife and struggles, its triumphs and disappointments—indeed the entire cyclorama of social history—

by analyzing the fluctuations of commodity prices. The greatest bullish force that skyrocketed the price of corn, wheat and barley to record levels was war; the major force that sent prices tumbling was the ending of war. Cutten prominently displayed Broomhall's chart in his office, tracing in great detail the fascinating zigzagging of the contours of price trends for the edification of his visitors.

In the year 1573, there was dollar wheat at Strasbourg, and before the year ended prices had climbed to $1.25—a record level for wheat in those times. But there was a grim reason—wheat was in short supply, and the great powers of Europe were locked in bloody religious wars. During the Thirty Years' War, prices zoomed to a peak of $3.11. When Napoleon's armies marched across Europe, the price levels of wheat resembled a cross section of the peaks and valleys of the Alps as they rose and fell with French victories and defeats. Everything that took place during the First World War, the munitions ships that were hit by mines and sunk in the icy waters of the North Atlantic, the passenger vessels that were torpedoed and wrecked, the peace offers alternating with the belligerent pronouncements of the diplomats— all of this was reflected in the prices of the wheat pit. To the traders bidding in Chicago or Liverpool, it was as if all these tragic happenings were mirrored in one another's eyes. The sharp tumble of quotations would be the first indication, before the news was made public, of a terrible German victory on the Somme front. A sudden huge buying order would be the first hint that a smashed square-rigger was slithering to the bottom of the ocean in a final gasp with her flags still flying and her hold bulging with grain. The zigzag of prices was a surer indication than detailed intelligence reports of the changing fortunes of combat. When Turkey joined the Central Powers, wheat rose sharply, for this meant that Russian grain would be cut off from Europe. Wheat tumbled when the British embarked for the Dardanelles. It dropped again with reports that President Wilson would place an embargo on grain shipments. Cutten assiduously learned how to read and profit from the fluctuations of human events limned in Broomhall's chart, and by the time he left the trading pit he had become many times a millionaire.

Throughout history astute speculators have made money by exploiting social and economic catastrophes. But in one notable case on Wall Street, a group of speculators went a step further; they actually engineered the catastrophe to exploit. The plot they generated in 1869, four years after the Civil War, was an effort to corner the nation's gold supply. It touched off one of the worst panics in the market and brought about a Congressional investigation, during which a President of the United States was accused of complicity in the conspiracy.

To appreciate the genesis of the plot, one must understand the nation's financial situation immediately after the Civil War. The theme that continued to run like a major nerve complex through America's economy was the currency situation. The North had issued millions of dollars in paper currency to carry on the war and the question arose as to how the debt would be paid. Shortly after Appomattox this debt had reached the enormous amount of $2.8 billion, or three-quarters of the entire debt of Great Britain. There was widespread skepticism among Americans about the Government's intention of redeeming its tenders in hard cash. Indeed, some economists and Washington politicians argued in a fashion reminiscent of later eras that a national debt was not at all a liability. It was not necessary for a nation to repay its obligations or to live solely within its income; the amount of money borrowed from the people in war bonds could be used for the people's advantage in other ways than refunding it. This kind of thinking, however, did not assuage millions of citizens who had been brought up in the belief that a nation, like a family, should not live beyond its income.

Gold continued to be a source of major concern. While the United States used greenbacks as a medium of exchange, the currencies of the major nations of Europe were based on gold and any business dealings with them had to be carried out in gold. The prices of American corn and wheat exported to Europe were pegged on gold, but the farmer's actual proceeds were in greenbacks. It was to his advantage, therefore, to export his grain when the price of gold was high, since his product would be purchased for a larger amount of greenbacks.

In 1869 American farmers produced a larger supply of crops than could be absorbed by domestic consumers. To get rid of the excess at a decent price, it would be necessary to export it overseas. The nation's farm groups, economists and businessmen, anxious for the price of gold to climb to bolster the farmers' export prices, urged the Government to refrain from selling the gold it normally carried in the Treasury vaults, whose sale, by swelling the floating supply of gold already available commercially, would send the price down.

Among the leading financiers who urged this policy on the Government was one highly gifted pioneer in the seamy byways of speculation, Jay Gould. He was a slight, sallow-faced fellow with rheumy eyes and an untidy black beard. A relative of his had invented a mousetrap, and Gould made a career out of mousetrapping his fellow men. After the war he found his métier in the railroad building boom that exploded from coast to coast, much of which was hasty, speculative and ill-advised.

Gould's operations followed a monotonous pattern. He'd buy up several financially overextended and shaky roads, amalgamate them and dress them up with a new corporate name. Then he would issue a doctored-up financial prospectus that indicated that the future was a positively scintillating one. Following this, he would unload the rails at an inflated price to a sanguine buyer. If the purchaser found he had a lemon on his hands and was faced with bankruptcy in a year or so, Jay Gould would pop up, ready to buy back the road at a distressed price. Then he would reorganize it, issue highly optimistic financial statements trumpeting its prospects anew and unload it again at a handsome price. He repeated this maneuver again and again, reaping a profit on each reorganization. A number of his victims were European investors, and he developed a rather malodorous reputation abroad. On one occasion when he visited the Continent he called on a member of the Rothschild family. When he sent up his card announcing himself, his host sent back a message declaring that "Europe is not for sale."

This was the manner of man who in 1869 turned his attention to the plight of the American farmer.

Not surprisingly, Gould's dedication to keeping Washington's gold locked up in the Treasury was not due to any compassion. An active Goldbug during the Civil War, and allied now with the New York political boss Jim Tweed, who made available to him for manipulative purposes large sums of city funds deposited in the banks, Gould had become extremely skillful in the science of manipulating currency. In 1869, in the New York money mart, which was the financial capital of the nation, the supply of Treasury gold did not exceed $25 million. Uncle Sam held less than $100 million —a quarter of which was in the form of special deposits represented by certificates, part of which were deposited in banks and the remainder circulating throughout the country.

Gould calculated that under prevailing conditions it would be possible for a resourceful trader to seize the nation's entire floating supply of gold; and, once it was cornered, to exact whatever price he chose for releasing it again. Stocks had been cornered by market operators; why not gold? he reasoned. What enhanced his chances for success was the fact that nobody had tried to do this before; the surprise element would be to his advantage. But one condition was essential for the success of the project. The Government could not be allowed to upset the applecart by selling gold from the Treasury in the commercial market, sending prices down. To prevent this from occurring, he envisaged a plan that was as arrogant as it was ambitious. He proposed to fix the President of the United States.

He had at hand a man ideally equipped for the job—Abel Corbin, an elderly political lobbyist who had married President Grant's middle-aged sister. Gould had met Corbin through previous business dealings and now he unfolded his plan, pointing out that a barrelful of money could be made if matters were handled properly.

Corbin was not one to allow such an opportunity to go begging. He offered to contact his brother-in-law, Grant, and impress upon him the importance of keeping a lid on Treasury gold to safeguard the nation's prosperity. The President was known to be naïve in financial matters. He had an exaggerated reverence for successful businessmen. He happened to be scheduled to attend a political ceremony in Boston, and Corbin suggested that he travel the final leg of the trip from New York by sea in the company of several of his business associates who had important advice to proffer. The fact that two of these associates happened to be Jay Gould and his business partner, Jim Fisk, financiers who were widely known for their stock manipulations, apparently did not alert Grant to trouble.

The President, accompanied by his Secretary of the Treasury, George Boutwell, arrived in New York and was escorted by the city militia to the *Providence*, which was sailing for Boston. The boat belonged to the Narragansett Line, one of Jim Fisk's properties. The President was conducted to the ship's parlor, where he was handed a cigar and put into an easy chair. As the vessel lifted anchor and moved down the Hudson, the conversation grew brisk and the smoke became heavy. The President's penchant for whiskey was legendary. It had got him through many a gloomy night on the battlefield. But if the Gould clique hoped that Grant's reserve on this occasion would be melted by a timely shot of bourbon, they were disappointed. Grant eschewed the drinks and confined himself to puffing on his cigar.

The talk turned to the question of the national economy

and the Government's fiscal policy. Jay Gould put forth the suggestion that it was essential for the Government to refrain from selling gold. He argued that as the price of gold was allowed to rise, the level of prosperity would go up with it. But if Washington dumped gold, this would bring about a severe recession. Riots would break out among the workers, businesses would collapse and even civil war might erupt, he hinted. Amidst the arguments, pro and con, voiced by the entourage, the President offered no opinion of his own. Pressed by the Gould clique, he finally declared in noncommittal fashion, "There is a certain amount of fictitiousness about the prosperity of the country and the bubble might as well be tapped in one way as another." This pronouncement was as inscrutable as President Coolidge's later statement, "I do not choose to run."

Actually, the President had for some time been hearing conflicting advice. While Gould was prepared to bull up the price of gold, and a number of brokers who had not lost their Goldbug habits were preparing to speculate along with him, there were pressures on the Government from other sources to sell gold and strengthen the value of the greenback by keeping the price of gold low in relation to it. This campaign was generated by Jay Cooke and other commercial bankers who had been active in buying millions of dollars worth of Government bonds during and after the war, and now had huge inflated profits that they were desirous of converting into sounder values. They campaigned in high Government circles for Washington to embark on a policy of deflation, to redeem legal tender in hard cash, based on the gold standard. Gould, who argued that the greenback was too expensive and must be cheapened, had to contend with the argument that it must be strengthened in value.

The Gould group realized that it was taking a risk but, convinced it could influence the President through the intercession of Corbin, it decided that the odds for success were excellent. And it pressed on with its plans, worming its way into the Presidential presence at every opportunity. Grant remained extremely gullible. He apparently was not in the least suspicious when at one social function after another, Jay Gould and Jim Fisk popped up at his elbow, squired by his ubiquitous brother-in-law Corbin. The President could scarcely turn around for a Corona Corona without the burly Fisk or the sallow Gould badgering him with the incessant warning "Don't sell gold." On one occasion when he visited Manhattan he attended, with his wife and daughter, the Fifth Avenue theater owned by Fisk, and he sat in a special box with Fisk, Jay Gould and brother-in-law Corbin. For this occasion, Josie Mansfield, a Broadway show girl who was Fisk's mistress, was hurriedly banished from her usual place in the box. It just didn't seem right even to Fisk to put his frolicsome partner next to the President of the United States. Josie was ostracized to a box opposite the Presidential one, and all night she glared at her consort as he fawned before the President.

In addition to placing a pipeline directly to the President in the person of Corbin, the Gould group made further preparations. When the Assistant United States Treasurer, H. H. Van Dyke, who was the top Treasury man in New York, resigned, Gould instructed Corbin to induce Grant to name a successor who would fall in with their plans. The individual Corbin initially proposed for the job turned out to be a man with some integrity. He refused to make money by betraying the President's confidence. But the second candidate, General Daniel Butterfield, was more pliable. It wasn't difficult to foist Butterfield on Grant since he had been a major fund-raiser for the Republican Party. And Grant was not one to turn the back of his hand to a political benefactor.

With Butterfield ensconsed, Gould and his friends began to buy gold in earnest. Thanks to a liberal disbursement of money, a number of publicists began planting articles in newspapers and magazines, warning the Government against selling gold. The economic life of the nation, the livelihood of millions, argued these soothsayers, depended on a continued rise in gold prices. Little squibs popped up in print all over; lecturers mounted the platform, and politicians appeared on the stump to hammer home the thesis.

One citadel of journalism that succumbed to the Gould offensive was the New York *Times*. Although its financial columns could not be bought, its editors were taken in nevertheless. Gould realized that an article favoring his economic policies carried by the *Times* would carry tremendous weight with Washington circles. When the *Times* spoke, even the President listened. Gould got Corbin to write an article summarizing the Gould plan for national prosperity, and he instructed Corbin to have the word passed around quietly that the article accurately reflected Grant's own thinking, as Corbin had gleaned it during private talks with the President. Corbin sounded out a business associate, James McHenry, who was a stockholder of the Erie Railroad, owned by Gould and Fisk, and who also happened to be a close friend of John Bigelow, the New York *Times*' financial editor. Lured by the prospect of making money in Gould's speculations, McHenry agreed to bring the article to the attention of Bigelow, pointing out that it had been written by someone close to Grant and represented his views. John Bigelow normally was a skeptical, tough-minded editor. But he had no reason to suspect his friend's assurances, and he had the article printed under the title "The Financial Policy of the Administration." It flatly predicted that the Government would not sell gold at least until the crops of the nation's farmers had been disposed of.

As the summer drew to an end, the plans of the Gould crowd were at the high-water mark. A large part of the nation's press was hammering away for the policy Gould espoused. The ring's own man, General Butterfield, was installed at the New York Treasury. Indeed, to bolster Butterfield's zeal for carrying out his task, Gould bought a million and a half dollars' worth of gold to be credited to Butterfield's account if and when the operation succeeded.

There was one final item to be attended to. When the trap

was sprung, it would be convenient to have the President as far from Washington as possible, so that there would be no chance for changing his mind. It was decided to induce Grant—through Corbin, as usual—to take a vacation and visit with an old friend, W. W. Smith, who was Mrs. Grant's cousin and who lived in Little Washington, a town in a remote corner of western Pennsylvania with a population of a few thousand and no telegraph facilities.

The unsuspecting President agreed that it would be nice for him to spend a few days with his old friend Smith, who had been a former military associate, and play croquet with him. He left Washington on September 13, riding in a luxurious railroad car owned by Gould's Erie line and usually reserved for the directors of the road.

Everything seemed propitious for the big steal. Affairs had been arranged down to the slightest detail; yet the conspirators were uneasy. The stakes were huge. The one unknown factor remained Grant's own attitude. He had not definitely revealed what his thinking was, and even though he had been trundled off to the hinterlands, the specter of some unexpected action by him continued to bedevil the Gould ring— to such an extent that it overplayed its hand.

The ring had bought close contracts for over $110 million worth of gold, and it was in a cold sweat as the moment for the coup approached. Feeling the need of further assurances, it decided to get through to the President once again word to resist any contrary advice and refrain from selling gold. Corbin gave a trusted Erie employee, W. O. Chapin, a letter to be delivered personally to the President. Chapin took the Pennsylvania Central and arrived at Pittsburgh in the evening after an all-day trip. He rode the final stretch on horseback, reaching Little Washington the next morning and was taken in to see the President. Grant was playing a game of croquet; he dropped the mallet, read Gould's letter and replied noncommittally that there would be no answer.

Actually Grant had done an about-face in his attitude. His

suspicions had at last been aroused by the pervasive efforts of Corbin, Butterfield and the others around him to induce him to keep gold in the Treasury vaults. He suspected that his brother-in-law was engaged in speculative ventures with Gould; and it now dawned on him that these might present a threat to the nation.

At his direction, Mrs. Grant wrote to her sister-in-law Jenny in New York, "Tell Mr. Corbin that the President is very much disturbed by your speculations and you must close them as quickly as you can." But the mail from Little Washington was slow. It was several days before the letter reached the Corbins informing them that the game was up. In the meantime the Gould ring went on serenely buying gold. During this massive buying spree, the Tenth National Bank in Manhattan, which was controlled by the city's political boss, Jim Tweed, placed its assets at the service of Gould, issuing him certified checks in virtually unlimited amounts against purchases of gold which were used as collateral. By mid-September Gould and his associates had committed themselves to over $100 million worth of gold.

The precipitous advance in the price of gold had by now excited the alarm of financial observers, who suspected that speculators were pushing it up. The Jay Cooke group, bent on strengthening the dollar by keeping the price of gold low, had become thoroughly aroused. Newspapers carried editorials advising the Government to curb the speculative advance. Amidst all this, Mrs. Corbin received Mrs. Grant's letter. Her husband showed it to Gould. The little financier grasped the implications instantly. If this letter were made public, it would break the price of gold, for the President had clearly indicated that he had caught on to the operation and was prepared to halt it.

Gould was in a dilemma. He and his associates had bought over $100 million, the bulk of it on heavy margin. Corbin, on whom he had counted to keep the President neutralized, had been unable to deliver. Gould's only chance was to get rid of his own holdings as quietly as possible without letting his colleagues know what he was doing. Indeed, it would be better if they could actually be kept in a state of euphoria and induced to buy more gold. Gould said nothing to his partners about Mrs. Grant's letter. Instead, he exuded a massive confidence, advising Fisk and his other associates to go on buying. Fisk, who was no novice himself in skullduggery, was hoodwinked. He strolled into the office of his brokers and placed orders for several more millions of dollars' worth of gold. In the meantime Gould began to unload his own holdings skillfully, in steps, taking care not to upset the bulling operations of his partners.

By now, their concentrated, obsessive buying operations were drying up most of the money on Wall Street normally available for stocks; and the prices of equities were tumbling. Money became so tight that the arteries of the nation's economy were hardening. Owners of businesses and workingmen from coast to coast felt the squeeze. The world's money marts eyed Wall Street anxiously. Grant returned to Washington to find the nation threatened with a severe financial crisis. Rumors spread that a clique in Wall Street was bulling up gold only because it had top officials in Washington secretly behind its efforts and iron-clad assurances that the Treasury would not sell. The New York *Times*, which had been tricked into printing the earlier misleading article, now demanded Government action to break the ring.

On Friday, September 24, henceforth known as "Black Friday," the gold room at Broad Street and Exchange Place was a scene of anxiety. In one corner Albert Speyer, Fisk's broker, bawled out offers for gold at $150, while simultaneously, in another part of the room, Gould's brokers unloaded gold at $136. Gould had instructed his brokers to sell. But he warned them to make sure that they didn't unload inadvertently on Fisk's brokers, tipping them off to his double cross.

Outside, the streets were packed with people. The National Guard stood by, ready to rush to Wall Street if rioting developed. Business from Maine to California had ground to a standstill. Everybody was on edge, waiting for the latest news from the Street. And still gold climbed—up and up. When it reached 160, men who had gone short and were unable to cover their holdings became frantic.

Then, just before noon, word was rushed from Washington to Butterfield in New York, and a bulletin was issued at the Subtreasury. "The Treasury will sell, at 12 o'clock tomorrow, four million gold and buy four million bonds. Proposals will be received in the usual form."

The sum of $4 million was not in itself large enough to break the market. It was the psychological effect of the President's action in informing the nation that the Government was prepared to take all necessary steps to protect it.

Within minutes the word was out, and the price began to tumble, skidding from 160 to 135. Pandemonium broke loose. Albert Speyer lost his head and continued buying up gold at a price of 25 points higher than it was being quoted by other brokers only a few feet away, constituting, in the words of Henry Clews, "one of the wildest and most ludicrous spectacles ever witnessed among men, not idiots." Awakening to the realization he had been wiped out, Speyer rushed about the floor shouting, "Here I am! Shoot me!"

Speyer was not the only broker to go to pieces during that gloomy day. Several killed themselves. With a terrible anger, the mob turned on the individual who had brought this tragedy upon it—Jay Gould. It surged down the street from the Gold Exchange toward the office of William Heath, one of the ringleaders, where Gould was hiding, intent upon stringing him up on the nearest lamppost. Only the quick arrival of deputy sheriffs, who formed a cordon around the office, prevented the lynching from taking place.

Gould and a few close associates cowered in Heath's office. After several hours, when the crowd began to disperse, Gould screwed up enough courage to try to escape through a back door. He looked quickly around and slunk off through a private passageway behind the building. Shortly afterward, Jim Fisk emerged, his face flushed with perspiration. In his excitement he took the wrong turn and nearly ran into Broad Street, where the bulk of the lynch mob was still waiting. But he discovered his mistake in time and followed Gould through the rear passageway. Finally William Belden, Gould's broker, came out with his eyes reddened, as if he had been weeping. "Which way have they gone?" he called out, and then he darted into a passageway and out of sight.

Each of the group dispersed into waiting carriages, seeking the safest available shelter. Fisk went into hiding behind massive oak doors. But the mob learned of his whereabouts and moved forward to force entrance. The police threw up a barricade around the building. Fisk seemed genuinely puzzled by the display of public anger toward him. After all, he reasoned, he too had been betrayed by the unexpected developments of Black Friday.

He gave an interview to a newspaper reporter, complaining that the anger of the public was directed at the wrong people. He and Gould would never have risked such a tremendous amount of money on the rise of gold, he argued, if they hadn't had absolute assurances from high Washington sources that they would be protected. Fisk insinuated that the President himself had been financially interested in the gold corner and stood to profit heavily by it. He pointed out that Grant had gone sailing in his boat, traveled in his private railroad car and sat in his box at the theater. It was only at the last moment, under heavy pressure, Fisk insisted, that the President had got cold feet and had dumped the gold.

The Banking and Finance Committee of the House of Representatives launched an investigation. Gould and Fisk appeared as witnesses and repeated their accusations of Grant's involvement. Evidence purporting to implicate Mrs. Grant through her brother-in-law, Abel Corbin, was also introduced. However, the President and his wife were exonerated by the committee. Grant's fault, it was implied, was not his lack of integrity but his naïveté. Corbin, however, was given a scathing going-over in the committee's report. Butterfield was forced to resign as Assistant Treasurer. Gould and Fisk were excoriated for their roles. But the report pointed out that they could not legally be punished. There was no law on the statute books that made it a crime for anybody to try to corner the nation's gold supply.

To this day, it has not definitely been established how the Gould clique came out financially. The evidence, however, strongly indicates that Gould got out from under his holdings in time not only to avert ruin but possibly to make a profit on the downward side as a bear. As for Jim Fisk, who had been tricked into buying gold up to the last moment, he seems to have escaped unscathed by repudiating his debts. He claimed that he had been buying the gold not for himself but for the account of the ring's broker, William Belden. And he produced a contract from Belden to support this. Belden went bankrupt in the amount of $50 million; and it is generally believed that Gould salved his wounds by settling a handsome sum on him.

The only ones who apparently took it on the chin were the clients of Belden's brokerage house, who were wiped out under the bankruptcy entered into by Belden. He repudiated the $50 million debt and not a penny was ever collected.

Perhaps the best commentary on the guilt to be apportioned to each member of the conspiracy was made by Jim Fisk during the Congressional investigation. As the malodorous evidence steadily mounted, the candid rascal put his fingers to his nostrils and said, "Let everybody carry out his own corpse."

The Gould conspiracy was the *reductio ad absurdum* of a drive to push currency manipulation to extreme lengths by neutralizing the influence of Government gold. In the twentieth century, Governments, as a matter of high political principle and for the most honorable reasons, would create the

THE BOTTOM OUT
EVERYTHING COMING DOWN
LITHOGRAPH PUBLISHED BY CURRIER & IVES IN 1870.
COURTESY OF THE NEW-YORK HISTORICAL SOCIETY, NEW YORK CITY

climate for currency manipulations of a less crude sort but having, in some cases, as damaging a result. By dropping the gold standard and creating as much paper money as political whims dictated, they would cause money to deteriorate in worth. It was Gould who shrewdly recognized that in a free economy the actual value of goods is determined not only by the supply and demand of things, but by the supply and demand for the currency with which they are equated. He tried to do in an unvarnished fashion what modern manipulators have succeeded in accomplishing on a grand scale— to tinker artificially with the supply and demand of money, leaving the populace to the tender mercy of shifting values.

President Grant emerged from the affair a sadder man. But destiny has an odd habit. It seems to pursue some people with a single-minded vindictiveness. Grant's involvement with Wall Street was not yet over. After serving two terms, he retired from the White House, and friends bought him a four-story home on East 66th Street in Manhattan. Although his Administration had been a controversial one under bitter attack by the Democrats, Grant was able to draw from the reserves of sentiment he had built up as a war hero and he was warmly received wherever he put in an appearance. He was feted at the Union League Club, accorded a standing ovation when he went to the theater. He became a familiar sight as he rode in Central Park in his carriage, puffing on his perennial cigar. His house contained the treasures he had received on his world travels and the souvenirs of his military campaigns. The most influential men in the city sought him out, and he spent his happiest moments playing cards with cronies and gossiping about horses, which were his passion.

But the serenity of Grant's life was brought to a halt. An operator in Wall Street, Ferdinand Ward, sizing up the General as an ideal front man, became friendly with Buck Grant, the General's son. Ward was introduced to the General through Buck, flattered the old man and suggested that he go into the brokerage business with him. The General was told that he need not do any work but simply lend the prestige of his name.

As soon as the brokerage firm of Grant & Ward was organized, Ward began using Grant's name as an open sesame to wangle influential connections. He went to New Yorkers who had substantial bank balances, offering them a chance to invest with him in ventures that would bring big profits but which, he hinted, were of a delicate nature. They had to be handled quietly because they involved Government contracts and quasi-political deals. Ward implied that Grant's influence in high Washington circles would bring home the bacon but that the General's role had to be kept in strict confidence since he could very possibly be nominated for a third term in the White House and the disclosure of these dealings would provide ammunition for his political enemies.

The story about Government deals was a fabrication. Ward was doing nothing more than putting his investors' money into ventures open to anybody without any political influence. For a time he did a profitable business, repaying his clients handsomely. But then he went into several unfortunate speculations; he lost heavily in Southern mining shares and West Shore bonds. And, finding it impossible to continue to pay dividends legitimately, he began borrowing money at exorbitant interest rates, hoping to make a big enough killing in the market to wipe out his debts. When this failed, he resorted to a shopworn device, paying his earlier investors out of the capital of later arrivals. The technique worked for two years, during which the Grant family, assuming that everything was on the level, put its entire capital into the brokerage firm. On the books, between April 18, 1882, and May 1, 1884, Grant & Ward showed a fictitious profit of $2.6 million. Actually it was careening toward bankruptcy. Grant's savings continued to be poured down the drain. And, in addition to his father's money, Buck sank his own and his wife's cash into the brokerage house. Then, he borrowed $500,000 from his father-in-law, ex-Senator Chaffee, of Colorado, to put into the leaky ship.

By the spring of 1884, Ward was in serious trouble. He had borrowed large sums on collateral and had been rehypothecating his securities. To raise capital he had been discounting the firm's notes, paying up to 30 percent in interest. To add to his difficulties, the stock market went into a slump, eliminating any chance he had of getting his money back. A number of his clients who had been squeezed heavily in the market asked for the cash they had deposited with him.

Ward was on the board of directors of the Marine National Bank, whose president, James Fish, had become involved with him, loaning him a major part of the bank's funds to try to shore him up. Now Fish was at the end of his tether.

Ward came to the ex-President and put matters to him casually so as not to alarm him. He said that the Marine National Bank was in temporary trouble; it was short of a few hundred thousand dollars in its cash reserves. If Grant could borrow $150,000, Ward said he would try to raise an equal amount and the pressure on the bank would be relieved.

Grant accepted at face value Ward's assurance that this was merely a temporary crisis; suspecting no fraud, he decided to visit his old friend William Vanderbilt, the son of the Commodore, who had amassed the greatest fortune in America up to that time, in railroad operations. Ushered into Vanderbilt's office, the General wasted no time in coming to the point. He told Vanderbilt he urgently needed a loan and he offered him as security his war medals and other souvenirs of the battlefield.

Vanderbilt shrugged and said, "I don't care anything about the Marine National Bank. It can fail without disturbing me. And as for Grant & Ward—what I've heard about that firm would not justify me in lending a dime." He paused. "But for you, General Grant, I'll give $150,000 personally—on your word alone."

Vanderbilt's check was unable to halt the disaster. On Tuesday morning, May 6, the Marine National Bank suddenly closed its doors on stunned depositors. It had lent Grant & Ward over $4 million—most of it on uncollectable notes. The brokerage firm was bankrupt, with assets of $67,000 against liabilities of $16.7 million. Grant's own share in the business, which had been carried on the books at $2.6 million, had been whittled away to nothing. The failure of the firm touched off a sharp drop in the stock market. A chain reaction of bankruptcies hit financial houses that had been dealing with Grant & Ward or the Marine National Bank.

Grant was astonished. Not till the very last moment, when the brokerage house was on the verge of declaring bankruptcy, had the ex-President learned the true state of affairs. He hurried down to the offices to examine the books and see for himself the extent to which he had been hoodwinked. A mob of reporters gathered outside to cover his visit.

The General presented a tragic sight. He had fallen on the sidewalk in front of his home several months earlier and he was walking on crutches. Alexander Dana Noyes, a financial writer of the times, reported afterward in his reminiscences: "What followed is perhaps the most vivid picture in my own memories of Wall Street. The outer door slammed open. It admitted General Grant, followed by his Negro servant. Moving rapidly across the room on crutches ... the General looked neither to the right nor the left. He made for the partners' private office, unaware that nobody was there. To me, it was a never-to-be forgotten picture ... here, on this strange occasion, there was passing before us in a flash the stocky figure with the grizzled beard and smoothed-down sandy hair which hundreds of magazine pictures had made as familiar as that of an everyday acquaintance. Probably all of us remembered at that moment the description, by every war correspondent, of the inevitable cigar at which the General puffed reflectively on the eve of a battle; for as he moved across the room ... (we noticed this at once) he held tightly clenched between his lips a cigar that had gone out. Nobody followed him or spoke to him, but everyone in the cynical, 'hard-boiled' group took off his hat as General Grant went by. I have always liked to think that this was not so much tribute of respect to a former Chief Magistrate as spontaneous recognition of the immense personal tragedy which was enacting itself before our eyes."

The Grants' savings were virtually wiped out. An old friend, the Mexican Ambassador, reading of the family's difficulties, paid a call and although Grant strenuously objected, left a check for $1,000. A stranger, Charley Wood, sent a check for $1,000, requesting "that this amount be accepted as a loan on account of my share for services ending in April 1865."

Worried about Vanderbilt's $150,000 loan, Grant called on the financier and insisted on signing over all his assets, including the deed to his house on East 66th Street, his farm in Missouri, the trophies he had collected during the war. Vanderbilt refused, urging the General to forget the debt. But Grant insisted and a compromise was worked out. At Vanderbilt's suggestion, he agreed to turn over his war trophies to the Smithsonian Institution for the benefit of the nation.

It was an unhappy day when the moving van arrived to haul away the General's souvenirs. They had been lugged down to the parlor for a final look. Here were buttons snipped from the General's uniform—one for each battle he had taken part in. Here were the epaulettes he had worn during the siege of Richmond; his sword; a replica of the table in the farmhouse at Appomattox where he and Lee had signed the treaty ending hostilities. Here was the pen he had used to write his field orders; a medal awarded him by Congress after the Battle of Vicksburg. Here was a collection of Oriental money and a gift of ivory tusks from Siamese royalty. As piece by piece these objects were carried from the parlor and placed in the van to be carted away, tears filled the eyes of Mrs. Grant, and the General bowed his head.

His life was changed now. Gone was the carriage with the

high-blooded horses, the retinue of servants and the other hallmarks of gracious living. The General brooded hour after hour over the tragedy he had inflicted on his family and the people who had invested with his firm. Whenever anyone visited him, he would take him aside and speak bitterly of Ward's betrayal. He lived it over and over again like a recurrent hallucination.

As he searched for opportunities to rehabilitate his finances, an unexpected one arose. The editor of the *Century* magazine suggested that he write his Civil War memoirs. And Grant, having no faith in his ability as a writer and believing with curious humility that no one would be interested in reading what he had to say about the war, accepted the offer.

Once the project was launched, he became fascinated with it. The editors suggested that the articles be expanded into a book. Mark Twain, who had recently become a publisher, hearing that the General was writing his memoirs, came to him with a substantially higher offer than the *Century*'s, and Grant, although he was reluctant to break with the *Century*, which had given him the opportunity to begin with, nevertheless consented, because he needed the money.

And so America was treated to the spectacle of one of the most unliterary of men, forced by a disaster on Wall Street, to turn to the only asset he had left—his experiences as commander-in-chief of the Union armies.

Shortly after he sat down to this project, he learned that it was to be his last. A few months previously he had bitten into a peach and developed pains in his throat that refused to go away. A consultation with a specialist disclosed he was suffering from cancer. There was no hope for him, since it had reached a stage beyond surgery.

He was set on finishing, for his debts weighed heavily on him. When he went to his physician for treatments, he insisted on going by streetcar to save the fare of a cab, although the doctor was several miles away. But as the weeks passed, the pain became excruciating and he allowed himself to be put into a cab. Slowly, the disease extended its grip. It became difficult for him to swallow food. Soon he was visiting the doctor twice a day for treatment. It became too exhausting to go out for a drive in Central Park and even to dress in the morning. He sat working in a bathrobe with a scarf tightly wrapped around his neck. Yet he pressed on with his writing. Although it was painful for him to open his mouth, he sat for hours dictating to a stenographer while his wife and sons looked up documents to reinforce his recollections of what had taken place on the battlefield. His family and friends were divided over the wisdom of letting him work. Some said it would hasten his death. But Julia, his wife, believed that the work was keeping him alive.

As the weeks passed, he shrank from over 200 to 130 pounds. He took morphine to ease the pain. He insisted on reading newspaper articles that described his losing battle with the cancer, and he went over every medical bulletin before it was issued by his doctors, studying each detail with the detached fascination of an outsider absorbed in an interesting clinical history.

He kept on dictating his memoirs. His voice, although not entirely gone, had become guttural and very indistinct. In order to save it for his dictation, he refused to speak at any other time, writing on a pad of paper his answers to questions.

His particular dread was the sleepless nights. The only way he could get rest was with morphine, but he was afraid of becoming addicted to the drug and he fought against having the dose increased.

One night while the patient tossed restlessly, Dr. Shrady, his physician, suggested, "Allow me to arrange your pillow and turn it on its cooler side, while you imagine yourself a boy again." And he added, "When you were a youngster, you were never bolstered up in that fashion. . . . Now, curl up your legs, lie over on your side, and bend your neck while I tuck the cover around your shoulders."

Docilely the General allowed himself to be positioned.

Dr. Shrady put Grant's hand under the pillow and patted him. The light was turned off and the doctor sat with Mrs. Grant beside the bed. In a few minutes the patient had drifted into a sound, peaceful sleep. "He rested," recalled Dr. Shrady, "as he must have done when a boy." The next night the General repeated this boy-fashion of sleeping and again got badly needed rest. Grant told the doctor afterward that he had not slept with his arm under a bolster and his knees curled up under his chin in that way since he first went to West Point, forty years before.

Steadily he grew worse. Reporters mounted a twenty-four-hour deathwatch over the house, with their eyes fixed on the sickroom in the second story. The newspapers readied special editions, filled with tributes from the nation's leaders, to be released the moment Grant's death was announced. One paper, dwelling on the General's suffering, ran the headline "General Grant Is Anxious To Die."

One night the General suffered a hemorrhage in the throat. The doctors rushed to his bedside and worked over him for a quarter of an hour to bring him back to consciousness. From then on, afraid of choking to death, Grant tried to sleep half sitting up in a chair. A few weeks later he had another hemorrhage. The doctors found him sitting in his chair with his head on his chest. He tried to speak but was interrupted by convulsive gaspings for air. Dr. Shrady administered shots of brandy by hypodermic needle. A minister stood by, uttering prayers. Once again, the General was revived to endure more suffering.

Then one evening he allowed himself to be carried upstairs to bed. It was a sign that his work was done. Grant was grateful that he had been spared so long. He scribbled to his family, "I first wanted so many days to work on my book so that its authorship would be clearly mine. It was graciously granted to me. . . . There is nothing more I should do now. . . . [Therefore] I should prefer going to enduring my present suffering for a single day without hope of recovery."

It was over now, the concatenation of events that led from the collapse of a Wall Street brokerage house to the writing of one of the world's distinguished military memoirs. Under conditions of suffering that have rarely been equaled, Grant in eleven months wrote two volumes amounting to over a quarter of a million words. He completely revised and edited the first volume but died before he was able to edit the second. Others had to complete it.

But he had accomplished his aim. He had put his family financially on its feet again. And he died knowing this. A few days before the end, he had received a report from his publishers indicating that a subscription campaign had already brought in advance orders for 50,000 sets, assuring a royalty check of over $200,000 even before the book was published. The final royalties reached almost $500,000. For the public, moved by the General's last illness, eagerly bought the book.

Long after the collapse of the brokerage house, after the money panic had broken out, and Ferdinand Ward had been sent to prison for larceny, the offspring of an ill-starred partnership on Wall Street exists as a treasure for historians, teachers and students. Grant's *Memoirs* are the Street's unwitting contribution to literature.

**EX-PRESIDENT GRANT AT WORK ON HIS MEMOIRS
SHORTLY BEFORE HIS DEATH.**
COURTESY OF THE NEW-YORK HISTORICAL SOCIETY, NEW YORK CITY

4
THE BULLS AND THE BEARS*

HARRIMAN'S SECRET FOR MAKING A QUICK FORTUNE—THE TRICK THAT LAUNCHED U.S. STEEL

As America progressed deeper into the nineteenth century, the stock market continued to serve as a barometer of its social and economic turbulence. Wall Street acted as a catalyst for successive waves of industrial expansion and was in turn influenced by the forces it had helped to unleash. First, as noted, there had been the great explosion of canal building, and the first high-flying stocks to be boomed on the Street were the canal companies,

*The bull is an investor or trader who bases his operations on the expectation that the price of stocks will rise and that he will make his profit from this rise. The bear is the short seller who bases his trading on the anticipation that the price of stocks will fall and who expects to make his profits out of this fall. Since a fall in stock prices frequently cleans out large numbers of investors and traders who are on the bullish side and has often been followed by business recessions, the professional bear who speculates on hard times has usually been castigated as an antisocial individual.

pioneered by the Morris Canal, which was the initial one to go public. When the Erie Canal was built, linking the Great Lakes area with New York and the Atlantic Seaboard, a brisk trade grew up in the livestock, grain and lumber that were shipped eastward from the Middle West and out through the port of New York to overseas markets. This mushrooming business touched off lively speculation on the exchanges.

As early as the 1830s, stock in railroads began moving into the forefront of market trading. The first road to be listed on the Exchange was the Mohawk and Hudson, in 1830. It ran from Schenectady to Albany, a distance of 17 miles and carried over 300 passengers a day. The discovery of gold in California in 1848 touched off a wave of speculation in mining stocks. And in the 1850s, when oil was struck in the first commercially usable amounts near Titusville, Pennsylvania, speculation in a new dazzling growth industry was begun.

As the pace of America's industrial expansion accelerated, the New York Stock Exchange doffed its breeches and put on long pants. Until the Civil War it had conducted its business in complete privacy. The public was not allowed to examine its operations. Indeed, business was so comparatively scarce that trading, as previously noted, was engaged in only at intervals during the day. The brokers made their trades quickly and departed. The constitution of the Exchange incorporated specific rules for attendance at these call periods. Any member leaving the room while a call was in progress was fined 25 cents, unless he had to go to the toilet. If he failed to show up for a call, unless he was ill or away on out-of-town business, he was fined 6 cents.

The practice of continuous trading was not inaugurated until after the Civil War. The membership of the Exchange swelled to over 1,000 after the war. In 1881 forty additional seats were sold to underwrite the expenses of moving to new quarters; and the membership remained unchanged at 1,100 until 1928, when, under the impact of exploding trading volume, it expanded to 1,375.

As trading accelerated, the price of a seat on the Exchange kept pace. Before the Civil War, the Board of Governors had decided that a member could keep the right to his seat during his life. In 1861, James Bleeker, the treasurer, died and his seat was put up at an auction for charity. It went for $460. By 1928 the price of a seat, as noted, had skyrocketed to over $600,000.

In the meantime, as new industries were launched and the opportunities for speculative profits mounted, astute Wall Street traders honed the techniques of their market operations to an increasingly fine point.

The mainspring of the stock market has historically been speculation and the successful Wall Street plungers have been masters of psychology. The price of a stock frequently consists not of the intrinsic worth of the company it represents but in what people *think* it is worth. There is nothing either good or bad, as Shakespeare put it, but thinking makes it so. To unload at a decent price a stock one feels is no longer worthwhile to hold, one must convince someone else that it is *eminently* worthwhile buying. This requires some bit of doing. Highly skilled manipulators are born, not made. It is a most difficult trick to manipulate a stock in such a way that it does not seem to be manipulated. Anybody can buy or sell a security. But only the most highly talented operator can unload a stock while conveying the impression that he is buying it and that the price of the security is bound to climb higher.

The methods Wall Street's pioneer speculators engineered for striking it rich were highly effective for the times. Businesses in those days were thinly capitalized, and only a small amount of stock was outstanding, so that speculators could induce volatile moves up and down virtually at will. Various devices were used to make a stock look active in order to whet the appetite of other traders and manipulate it upward. One was the "washed sale." The manipulator had one of his brokers sell, let us say, 2,000 shares of a stock to another broker, who shortly afterward "sold" the same 2,000 shares to a third, all this by prior arrangement. This transaction would show up in the records as a 4,000-share turnover and give the impression that the stock was in highly active demand. Although "washed sales" were officially outlawed by the Stock Exchange before the Civil War, the practice continued under various disguises for generations.

Another favorite technique used effectively by the early plungers was to corner a stock. A "corner" was achieved when a manipulator was able to trick a number of holders into selling short on a stock—selling more in fact than was actually available for buying back. A short sale is the reverse of the normal long sale. Instead of buying stock and then hoping it will go up in price before selling it, the short seller first sells a security and then hopes it will go down in price so that he can buy it back later at a lower price and make a profit on the difference between the sale and purchase prices. To sell stock which he does not legally own, the seller borrows it usually from a broker. Eventually the short seller must "cover" his line—that is, buy back the stock and deliver it to the broker from whom he has borrowed it. If in the meantime the price of the stock has gone down, he makes his profit. If the price has gone up, he suffers a loss. The manipulator of a corner would trick a number of traders into going short in the expectation they could buy the stock back at a lower price. In the meantime he quietly bought up all the available stock afloat until there was none left for anybody to acquire. In the inimitable words of Daniel Drew, an astute plunger in Wall Street's early years: "He who sells what isn't h'sn, must buy it back or go to prison." With the stock cornered and unavailable for buying back, the manipulator could then name the price at which he would release the stock to let the panicky shorts settle up.

A wide arsenal of other devices was employed to drive a stock up or down, depending on the aims of the manipulators. To buy a stock cheaply, the plunger would drive down its price by unloading blocks of it to the professional floor traders at a price substantially lower than the public was willing to pay for it. This had the effect of terrifying timid holders of the stock into selling it and thereby driving the price down still further. When enough of a panic had been whipped up, the operator would snap up the stock at a bargain level and begin to push it up to a more legitimate value at a substantial profit.

Similarly, tricks were devised for driving up the price of even the most worthless stock to the highest possible level, thus stirring up a flurry of simulated trading to whet the public's appetite. To attract the attention of other traders, an individual or syndicate of manipulators would initiate buying and selling operations, with the buying outweighing the selling, so that the stock would move upward a few points. Then, when the fish nibbled, the operators withdrew their support and let the stock drop a few points before moving in to push it up again. This pattern would be repeated. Each time the stock stopped advancing, the manipulator moved in to give it a little more buying support. When enough trading action had been generated to lure in other professional traders, these would, in turn, bring in the general public. In this way, sluggish, even worthless, stocks were made to look attractive. As the stock climbed higher and higher the trading activity registered on the tape was the best possible advertising. The public became wildly enthusiastic about a stock that no one had looked at a few weeks before. People who would not touch it at $15 a share now scrambled desperately to snap it up at $50. The company behind the stock hadn't changed one iota. Its prospects were no better than before. It may not have paid a penny in dividends. No matter. In this fairyland of market evaluation, the chimney sweep had overnight become a prince.

Once a stock had been pushed up to the highest possible level, the manipulators were then faced with the problem of how to turn their paper into profits—in other words, how to unload their holdings without depressing the market to a level at which it couldn't absorb their stock at a decent profit to them. To accomplish this, manipulators have had to deceive the public into believing that the very moment *they* were ready to abandon ship and pull out from under a stock was the most desirable time to buy it. In short, they had to convince John Q. Citizen to continue to buy on declining prices. Manipulators have been able to achieve this feat of legerdemain time after time throughout the history of stock market operations because of the invincible optimism of the public. Due to a surprising quirk in human psychology, the public has been led to deduce that if a stock has gone from $15 to $50 and then tumbled to $40, it must be an alluring bargain at $40. (After all, hadn't it previously been at $50?) And so, the public moves in to take the stock off the manipulators' hands. The master plungers—Gould, Keene, Harriman—frequently made their financial killings *not on the way up, but on the way down, unloading their holdings on declining prices*. This has been their cardinal strategy.

In the final analysis, it takes two to make a bargain, and the history of stock market trading graphically underscores this. Very few people have been fleeced who didn't have a touch of larceny in their own hearts. Most "lambs" have been as innocent as the "Johns" who on their prowl for a fling with a streetwalker have been blackjacked and rolled by the pimps—and then have come in to register a complaint with the police. Moreover, in the frame work of life's larger irony many master manipulators themselves ended up tragically. In the process of trying to outwit their opponents they frequently overextended themselves and got ambushed.

In any event, as time went on and the laws became a little more stringent, and the public a little less gullible, skillful speculators refined their techniques to keep pace with increasingly sophisticated conditions. And this growth in trading subtlety was greatly spurred by advances in technology. As early as the 1840s the invention of the telegraph had made possible the linking up of Wall Street with buyers and sellers

PANIC ON WALL STREET
WOODCUT IN HARPER'S WEEKLY, 1884
COURTESY OF THE NEW-YORK HISTORICAL SOCIETY, NEW YORK CITY

all over the nation. And the telegraph was put to novel uses by pioneer operators of advisory investment services who scrambled to come up with information on "hot stocks." One resourceful Bostonian, D. H. Craig, hit on the notion of using carrier pigeons to get financial news more quickly from Europe. Whenever a steamer bound for the United States hove into view off Halifax, Nova Scotia, Craig boarded it with a covey of pigeons and remained aboard for its run to Boston. En route he read the latest European newspapers, wrote a digest of the major financial happenings on tissue paper which he rolled into pellets, tied to his pigeons and then released them from the deck to fly to his associates on shore, who relayed the news by telegraph to subscribers of Craig's service all over America.

In 1866 the first cable was successfully laid across the Atlantic, tying Wall Street directly in to London and other European financial centers. And a thriving business was opened up in arbitrage—the making of a profit on the difference in the quotations of the same stock on the European and the New York exchanges by taking advantage of the time differences that existed between them. In 1878 technology took another stride forward. Telephones were put onto the floor of the Big Board, ultimately hooking in Wall Street with brokers across the land. These were the days when electric cables were not yet required by law to be placed underground in New York City, and the Stock Exchange building took on the appearance of a huge spider sprawling at the center of a web of wires that fanned out to all corners of America. So dense did this network become that even a sparrow couldn't have wriggled its way through.

In the meantime, technology added other refinements. Traditionally, brokers conducting trading wrote down their quotations on pads and transmitted them to one another through messenger boys called "pad shovers." But in 1867, E. A. Calahan, a former telegraph operator, conceived the idea of a ticker tape—that is, telegraphic equipment that would print out the names of stocks and the quotes for each as they were traded on the floor. He developed a recording instrument together with a transmitter that sent the data from a central keyboard to a network of broker offices, and he obtained from the Governors of the Exchange permission to put his agents on the floor to report the stock transactions.

Just before Christmas, 1867, Calahan placed Wall Street's first ticker in the broker office of David Groesback and Company, where Daniel Drew had his headquarters. A crowd six deep gathered around the ticker waiting to see whether it would work. Sure enough, as soon as the Exchange opened for trading, the quotes began to pop up on the tape. One trader standing at the machine called out the first prices and the gathering let out a rousing cheer. But some diehards held out, preferring to keep the "pad shovers" rather than trust the newfangled mechanism. Chief among them was Bill Heath, a hyperactive broker dubbed the "American deer" because he had been running from office to office bawling out prices for years; he stubbornly continued to make his appointed rounds, barking out his quotations above the clicking of the tickers.

Indeed, embarrassing bugs cropped up in the ticker equipment, threatening for a time to end its usefulness. It seemed to possess a malevolent itch to get out of alignment and print its figures in a jumble. Henry Van Hoeven ironed out this difficulty by developing an adjustment that, attached to the Calahan ticker, kept it in honest alignment. But another hindrance became increasingly annoying. Each broker who installed a ticker had to generate his own electricity to run it, using a battery consisting of four glass jars filled with sulphuric acid, zinc and carbon. The jars had to be refilled twice a week with the chemicals, and be lugged to each broker's office early in the morning before the market opened, causing all sorts of accidents. The acid frequently spilled, ruining carpets, damaging clothing and furniture. For a time it seemed that these cumbersome batteries would cut short the career of the ticker. But the astute Mr. Calahan saved the day by hitting upon a scheme for operating his ticker with larger chemical batteries placed in a central building, relieving the individual broker of the upkeep of individual jars.

The ticker became an extremely powerful instrument in the hands of shrewd traders. For the tape booming out its story of stock prices provided the most impressive news medium yet for advertising the drives and counterdrives launched by pool manipulators, which they deliberately desired to publicize. The action of actual stock prices spoke more eloquently than a thousand tips.

Edward Harriman, the mousy, droopy-moustached little financier who rose from stock clerk to become the king of the American railroads, once made a significant observation about the impact of publicity and described a whimsical facet of human psychology. Asked by a business associate whether he would be able to unload for him at 80 a line of stock of Southern Pacific, one of the roads he controlled, which was at the time priced at 70, Harriman replied that he didn't believe he could. But, he added, he could boost the stock from 70 to 150 and then sell it down to 100 without any trouble at all. The reason for this, he explained, was that with the stock selling at 70, a mere 10-point rise would not excite the imagination of the public, but an 80-point advance would whet the appetite of a huge number of people and would create such a broad market that it would be easy to unload virtually any amount of the stock on a fall of 50 points.

Harriman's strategy of operations, like that of other talented manipulators, had an incisive imprint and stamped him as a highly individual trading personality. To get a stock at a bargain price before he began a large-scale accumulation of it, he didn't resort to heavy selling to drive it down precipitously. On the contrary, he so manipulated the stock as to create a sluggish market. He realized that nothing so tired out and discouraged the public as an inactive market. Many more investors can be coaxed out of their holdings in a sluggish market than a declining one, since on a sharp break traders tend to cling to their stocks, waiting, even if deludedly, for a rally on which they can sell and minimize their losses. With this in mind, Harriman would begin a campaign to accumulate a heavy position by pushing the price of a stock down to as low a point as he considered feasible. If some of the stock he wished to obtain was still being held by stubborn investors, he would shake them out by launching further downward flurries, weeding out traders who had placed stop orders and who got frightened at a sign of weakness. Then Harriman would keep his stock inactive for weeks at a time, within a narrow trading range of a few points, so that no one could make any profits in the stock, and flushing out the last intractable holders, who would despairingly move into more active stocks. On the ticker tape, the activity in the stock would slow down to a virtual standstill, just before the big move upward began.

The recognition by Harriman that sluggish markets were the most discouraging ones to the rank and file trader was put to effective use by other sophisticated manipulators. Almost invariably during the nineteenth century, a bear market was followed by a period of convalescence in which any inclination for a stock to advance was promptly nipped in the bud by the insiders, whose strategy it was to keep prices as quiet as possible while they were in the process of accumulation. The public's reaction to this inactivity was a very bearish one. In those days (as now) it became a truism to observe that just before the beginning of a major bull market the feelings of the public were at the most depressed level. The night was blackest before the dawn—which is exactly the way the insiders wanted it to be.

The development of the ticker tape, besides putting into the hands of sophisticated insiders a powerful instrument of propaganda, also gave birth to a new breed of trader—the man who specialized in reading the tape and planned his operations not on the strength of financial news about a company or the economy but on the price action of the stocks themselves.

The first of the great tape readers, and the man considered by some market historians to be the greatest of all, was James R. Keene, an Englishman who came to New York in the 1870s during the height of railroad speculation and who won the nickname "Silver Fox." Keene accumulated and lost several fortunes. He was heavily committed to the bull side of operations and made the observation "You don't see any Fifth Avenue mansions built by bears"—a remark that was more picturesque than accurate, in view of the highly successful careers of Jesse Livermore and other short sellers, as we shall see.

Keene loved fast horses as well as fast stocks and he owned a number of prize racers. When his favorite, Sysonby, died, he gave the animal's skeleton to the Museum of Natural History, and whenever he was seized by a mood of nostalgia he would go to the Museum and stand in front of Sysonby's remains for hours, reminiscing to friends about the nag's exploits. All life was a sporting proposition to Keene, and the race went to the swiftest and surest. Once, when he was asked why, after making all the money he needed, he persisted in risking it in the market, he replied, "Why does a horse chase his thousandth rabbit? All life is speculation. The spirit of speculation is born with men."

Keene devoted every waking hour to his job as a speculator. Only a fool believed that making money in the market was an easy way of life. Actually, successful speculation required as much skill and concentration as any job on earth. The master trader worked as hard at his discipline as a highly skilled surgeon or lawyer. He kept to as rigorous a work schedule as an athlete preparing for the Olympics. Like all virtuoso speculators, Keene learned by hard experience that the only way to make money was not to place piker bets on what the next few quotations were going to be, but to anticipate what was going to happen in a real big way. The sucker trader loved to buy on declines, waiting greedily for them, measuring his bargains by the number of points he had managed to buy from the top. The astute plunger would have none of that. He learned to play as the crack billiard player operated. Instead of considering merely the particular shot before him, he looked much further ahead. He developed a knack of playing for position.

To Keene the ticker tape was a microscope for putting the battlefield of the trading floor under the most minute analysis. It showed him at any moment how his own forces were deployed and progressing and how the enemy was meeting his offensive. Keene's moods were mercurial. When the market was going his way, he paced the room like an imprisoned animal, muttering imprecations. When the market turned against him, he became strangely calm and gentle. When something unexpected turned up on the tape, he stood immobile beside the ticker, tense as a lion toward whose lair an unknown beast was stalking. Keene considered himself highly successful when he was able to guess right on 50 percent of his trades.

He not only studied the tape, but used it actively as a weapon of publicity in his own operations. To bull up the worth of his holdings he would boost the price with artful little flurries and cadenzas of trading activity. These rapid movements made exciting reading on the tape, providing tempting bait for the outsiders. For himself, he would enter into a heavy stock position slowly and only after much thorough testing, using the market as a research laboratory. He would put in a small test bid for a stock and raise it in stages to see how the market reacted to his offering. If he got his bid accepted at a steadily rising price, this indicated to him that the market was strong and warranted a heavier commitment. He didn't mind the cost generated by these rising prices. Like all astute traders he had learned that it was useless to try to buy as cheaply as possible. He was willing to pay the price for getting into a sound strategic position from which he could then cash in on the big swing that followed. His credo was that of all big money winners: Get into a strategic position, spending as much money as necessary on the testing needed to accomplish this; then cash in on the big swing to follow—whether it be on the up or the down side.

Keene was a proud man. In 1904, William Rockefeller, the son of John D., and several associates launched Amalgamated Copper Trust as a public company, overloading it with a heavily inflated capitalization. Desiring to coax the public into footing the bill, they called in Keene to handle the delicate job of unloading their stock. With consummate skill he whipped up activity and managed to get rid of the insiders' line for over $20 million in profits. One of them, H. H. Rogers, sent him a check for $200,000 "in gratitude for his service." This was a little like the society dowager who gave a janitor 75 cents for finding her $50,000 diamond brooch. Keene returned the check, replying crisply that he was not a customers' man looking for a commission and that he was glad he had been of some little service.

Keene's masterpiece was floating the capitalization of the U.S. Steel Corporation, which in 1901 was the largest corporation launched up to that time in America. The Morgan group sponsoring the offering had to find a public ready to absorb $1 billion worth of securities, half in common and half in preferred—a capitalization that was inflated heavily beyond U.S. Steel's actual worth. Keene was called in by Morgan to handle the job. Without depressing the price of the stock, he managed to unload so much of it onto the public that the Morgan group had to put up only $25 million of its own money. Indeed, under Keene's talented handling the stock rose from its offering price of 24 to 55. Three years later, after Keene, like the proverbial Arab, had quietly folded his tent and stolen away, the common stock slithered to a mere 8⅞.

In short Keene and his fellow speculators progressively sharpened their tools and stepped up the sophistication of their sleight-of-hand dealings.

Keene represented Morgan in another venture shortly after the U. S. Steel capitalization. One of America's major enterprises at the turn of the century was the operation of its railroads, and Wall Street was involved in the very thick of this. Two groups in particular were engaged in a no-holds-barred warfare for control of the nation's transportation system. One, financed by Morgan money, was headed by James Hill, a railroad builder who had lost an eye, which added a sinister quality to his dealings. Opposing the Morgan-Hill group was a syndicate backed by Rockefeller money and led by Edward Harriman. These adversaries were embroiled, among other things, in a titanic struggle for the freight and passenger traffic from the Great Lakes to the Pacific Northwest.

The Chicago, Burlington & Quincy Railroad became a strategic pawn. The Morgan-Hill people desired to own the railroad because it not only served as a gateway into Chicago but also as the basis for a system stretching to the Pacific Coast, challenging Harriman's Union Pacific Railroad, which lay to the South. In March 1901 the Morgan-Hill group attacked secretly and grabbed control of the Chicago, Burlington & Quincy stock, catching Harriman asleep at the switch. Following this coup, Morgan, who had just completed his herculean labors to bring the U. S. Steel Corporation public, sailed for a vacation in Aix-les-Bains, France, where he soaked himself in the hot mineral baths, making the social rounds with a French noblewoman amidst lively gossip.

While the banker was sunning himself miles from Wall Street, Harriman was seized with a brilliant inspiration. Blocked by Morgan from acquiring control of the Chicago, Burlington & Quincy frontally, he decided to sneak in through a rear entrance by capturing the stock of the Northern Pacific Railroad, which was owned by the Morgan people and which controlled half the stock of the Chicago, Burlington. Harriman calculated through his network of intelligence-gathering that he would need almost $80 million to conduct his back-door raid successfully, but the prize was worth it. By adding the C, B & Q to his properties he would end up controlling a large part of the freight and passenger traffic from the Southwest to the Pacific Northwest and south into California.

The Morgan group was taken completely by surprise. Normally one could capture control of a railroad by acquiring as little as ten percent of the capital stock. But in the case of the Northern Pacific the Morgan people owned almost thirty percent of the preferred stock, which had the voting rights, and it controlled the bulk of the common. It had never occurred to Morgan in his wildest imaginings that anybody would be daring or reckless enough to try to wrest control from him by buying in the open market a majority of the $155 million worth of C, B & Q preferred and common stock. Accordingly, when Morgan sailed for Europe he was convinced he had matters completely in hand.

Harriman bided his time until Morgan's ship was out of sight. Then he moved with a series of lightning thrusts. Cleverly masking his forays, he seized over $40 million of Northern Pacific preferred, constituting the majority of the issue, and captured almost $40 million of the common stock, which missed control by only 40,000 shares.

The sudden rise of Northern Pacific stock, triggered by this behind-the-scenes maneuver, caught the attention of Wall Street brokers and traders. Jim Hill, the boss of Northern Pacific and Morgan's confederate, scanning the ticker tape in his Seattle office, became uneasy. To his astonishment the stock of his railroad was rising sturdily, propelled by heavy buying, and he couldn't understand why. To add to his worry, his ally Morgan was absent in Europe, leaving his operations to be carried on by his underlings.

Hill's anxiety reached such a peak he decided to rush to Wall Street to find out exactly what was going on. He commandeered a special train to carry him as quickly as possible across the continent. Exercising unlimited right of way as head of his railroad and shunting other trains onto sidings to let him roar through, Hill made the fastest run from the Pacific Coast to the Mississippi achieved to that time. Changing trains in St. Paul, Minnesota, he continued eastward, reaching Manhattan on May 3.

Discovering to his horror that Harriman, through Jacob Schiff, his banker, had been secretly grabbing up the stock to take the Northern Pacific away from him, Hill hurried over to the Morgan offices and ordered Robert Bacon, a Morgan associate, to cable his boss, asking for immediate authorization to buy 150,000 shares of Northern Pacific common and fend off the Harriman onslaught. An astonished Morgan received the cable at his Grand Hotel quarters and promptly gave his permission, but his wire didn't reach his Wall Street office until Sunday, May 5.

In the meantime, Harriman was becoming worried on his own. He had majority control of the preferred but not yet of the common stock. And the preferred could legally be retired by a vote of the board of directors at any time. To safeguard his position, Harriman figured he needed 40,000 more shares of the common. But to complicate matters, he had taken ill and was confined to bed. As he lay fighting the fever, he tossed and turned, with mounting anxiety.

Finally he picked up the phone and called his banker, Jacob Schiff, at Kuhn, Loeb and Company, to ask him to buy 40,000 shares of Northern Pacific common. The day was Saturday, May 4. Schiff, a religious man, had gone to the synagogue to pray and couldn't be reached by phone. An aide who was dispatched to the synagogue tiptoed up to Schiff and whispered Harriman's urgent request. Schiff replied he would conduct no business on the Sabbath.

The delay proved to be critical. Had Harriman's order been executed on Saturday, it would have been too late for the Morgan group to retaliate, since the banker's cable giving his authorization didn't reach his associates until the next day, Sunday, May 5. Accordingly, the Morgan group was provided the breathing time it needed. On Monday morning, May 6, Jim Keene, representing the Morgan interests, began buying every share of Northern Pacific common he could lay his hands on.

The sensational rise in the stock stunned everybody. None of the onlookers, the brokers, traders or investors on Wall Street, had the slightest inkling of what was taking place behind the scenes. They had no hint of the gigantic struggle occurring between the two financial groups but saw only that the stock was skyrocketing, and they rushed in to take advantage of this.

Meanwhile, a group of short sellers watching the price soar for no reason they could fathom and convinced it was too high and would have to tumble, moved in to sell Northern Pacific short. Certain they would be able to cover their lines at a much lower price, they accumulated a massive short interest. Nobody, least of all these bears, realized that every single share of Northern Pacific stock snatched up by the warring parties was being taken out of the market and going into safety-deposit vaults in a desperate battle for control. There would be virtually nothing left for the short sellers to buy back. Yet under the rules of short selling they were compelled to do so or face ruin.

On May 8, the short sellers were seized with hysteria as they finally realized the stock had been cornered and taken out of the market. As they bid frantically for shares, the price continued to climb, from 149 to 500 to 700. On May 9, in a frightening further leap upward, it reached $1,000 a share. While Northern Pacific soared into the stratosphere, virtually all other stocks on Wall Street collapsed as holders got rid of them in a frenzied attempt to raise cash, which was in critically short supply. Not only did the short sellers face imminent ruin but also the broker houses they did business with, representing half of the firms on the Street, were on the brink of going down with them. Panic engulfed not only Wall

Street but also spread to major financial centers all over the world.

With America in the throes of an economic crisis, heavy pressure was brought on the Morgan and Harriman groups to settle up with short sellers, not on extortionist terms but at a reasonable price. And the warring parties, sobered by the financial catastrophe they had triggered, agreed to settle with the short sellers at $150 a share, a far cry from the $1,000 the stock had soared to. Moreover, an armistice was signed whereby the combatants formed Northern Securities, a holding company, into which they placed their stock and over which they exercised joint control.

The Northern Pacific corner was a prime example of the workings of an unregulated stock market. Six years later Morgan was to rise above his normal role of partisanship to provide statesmanlike leadership that helped resolve another major financial crisis.

In the meantime, the character of Wall Street was gradually changing from the time when Morgan, Harriman and Keene first landed there and began their operations. In addition to railroad stocks that were being heavily touted, a whole complex of industrial securities was mushrooming up as America plunged into the systematic exploitation of her mineral resources, capital equipment, and consumer-goods industries to satisfy the needs of her exploding population. This had a significant impact on the physical as well as the economic structure of the Exchange.

For one thing, as the tempo of industrial expansion accelerated, and as more and more capital offerings were brought to the Street, the Board of Governors of the Stock Exchange had to face up to the need for greatly enlarged quarters. The building they had moved into after the Civil War, though it extended an entire block from Broad Street to New Street, became inadequate for its needs. And by the turn of the century ground had been acquired on either side and construction begun on a larger home. Eight leading architects were invited to submit plans for a new building and one was finally selected.

On April 22, 1903, the new home was ready and the Board of Governors moved in amidst flamboyant ritual. Flags were displayed from broker offices and the financial center was thronged with onlookers. A musical medley was played by the 7th Regiment Band. The Reverend Dr. Morgan Dix of Trinity Church offered a prayer that concluded with this pointed observation, "The silver is thine and the gold is thine, O Lord of Hosts."

The building, bounded by Broad, New and Wall streets, was a lavish one, erected, at a cost of $4 million, in white Georgian marble, styled in Roman Renaissance with a façade of six Corinthian fluted columns. The board room was done in white and gold décor. A dining room for the members was furnished in mahogany. On the third floor were baths where a member could soak himself in Sybaritic splendor.

But the most striking feature of the building was located at the entrance to the Stock Exchange's luncheon club. It was a statue done in bronze of a bull locked in a death struggle with a bear. Neither adversary appears to have the upper hand. But each has his opponent completely at his mercy. The bull has a horn poised on the verge of goring the bear. The bear's hind legs are braced tightly against the bull's belly, threatening at any instant to rip out his intestines. To many observers, this sermon in bronze summed up perfectly the formidable enigma of a struggle that would never be resolved this side of heaven.

5

THE GREAT SOCIETY— YESTERDAY

WALL STREET'S FIRST LADY BROKERS, FROM A BROTHEL TO HIGH SOCIETY—J. P. MORGAN, THE JEKYLL AND HYDE OF THE STREET

Balzac, who wrote *The Human Comedy*, that great nineteenth century epic on the sounds and smells and the jangled nerves of the rising world of money, would have found Wall Street perhaps an even more tempting canvas than Paris for his literary brushwork. Indeed, the age which launched the American millionaire in the flower of his manhood required a Balzac to probe it with the most certain justice.

Wall Street, after the Civil War, became the financial headquarters of America, and its money and power transformed New York into the social capital as well. Manhattan was populated not only by home-grown Wall Streeters but also by traders who had made money elsewhere—in the California gold fields, in the cattle ranges of the Far West, the wheat pits of Chicago—and who had moved east to settle down in seignorial splendor surrounded by the plunder of the Old World. While they haggled and plotted to send the price of their stocks up on the Exchange, their wives gave champagne suppers and cotillion balls and made the rounds of Newport, Saratoga, and Palm Beach. The wealth that was concentrated in New York would have been envied by the doges of Venice. It was a wealth that put into pale the world's legendary fortunes—possessed by Solomon, Croesus, Kublai Khan.

Actually, the aristocracy of wealth did not reach its apogee until after the Civil War. When Henry Breevort, New York's merchant prince, was disclosed after his death in 1848 to have accumulated over a million dollars, his fellow citizens looked upon this achievement with a respect bordering on awe. The term "millionaire" had not been coined until Pierre Lorillard, the cigar and snuff maker, died in 1843. At the time, an obituary writer sweating out a deadline minted the phrase, and it passed into the language. Subsequently there would be fortunes amassed that would make Lorillard look like a penurious gypsy.

With their winnings from the market, Wall Street's plungers put up residences styled in Italian Baroque and French Renaissance, turning Fifth Avenue into a bazaar of parvenu opulence. With the profits of a plunge into Union Pacific or American Tobacco, they ransacked the Old World for Tudor furniture, Italian terrazzo flooring and medieval armor from castles on the Rhine. They tore out whole staircases and walls of French chateaux for shipment to New York, uprooted Japanese gardens and Grecian grottoes, wrested marble from the quarries Michelangelo had mined. All this was transported into the young nation at which, not so many years previously, the snobs of the Old World had turned up their noses as a gauche frontier. Truly, as Lord Canning had remarked in another context, the New World had been called into being to redress the Old.

The foundations of America's great art collections were laid by the virtuosos of the put and call. Many of the rare illuminated manuscripts, medieval tapestries and collections of ancient China that grace American museums found their way into America on the blessings of money made in Wall Street. And before these *objets d'art* were bequeathed to museums they were bought and sold like stocks and bonds for the private gratification of speculators. Indeed, fine art and the fruits of manipulation became inextricably commingled, like Siamese twins, and came to be thought of interchangeably as symbols of value. Henry Frick, the steel magnate, during an outburst of enthusiasm for the iron rails that were mushrooming up over the continent, was moved to exclaim: "Railroads are the Rembrandts of investment."

This money that came so easily with the formation of a pool, the flotation of a heavily inflated stock on the unwary, brought with it the problem of how it was to be spent. This required a resourcefulness that Wall Streeters, for all their ingenuity, were hard-pressed to provide. But they made a valiant attempt. These American-style maharajas and maharanis gave dinners, costume balls and cotillion dances whose extravagances beggared the exhibitionism of Old World royalty. Parties costing $10,000 and up were commonplace. Frederick Townsend Martin, a leading chronicler of society's doings, recalls one party he attended at which the host passed out cigarettes that were rolled in $100 bills and engraved with his initials in gold letters. At another party, the guests were served oysters which, upon being bitten, disgorged huge black pearls.

Lavish ingenuity was displayed in décor, costume and lighting effects. At one social function, dancers were imported from the ballet who, garbed like heavenly angels, drove translucent tennis balls back and forth across a net that glittered like a rainbow under iridescent lights. At another fete, the dance room was changed into a mammoth cavern of ice which, melting under the electric lights, dissolved into a waterfall of shimmering colors, providing a spectacular effect. Frederick Martin wrote how at one dinner given in a New York restaurant by one Wall Street plunger, the floor was carpeted with flowers, foliage and grass. In the center, an artificial lake had been constructed "suspended from the ceiling by a gold wire network. Four white swans swam about during . . . the banquet. From various rings in the ceiling hung golden cages containing rare songbirds that twittered incessantly, and the guests ate fruit bread from the branches of dwarf trees."

Fancy costume parties were the vogue. The wives of lard and copper kings turned up as Queen Elizabeth, Marie Antoinette and Helen of Troy. One plunger's spouse made headlines on the social page when she appeared as "Music," wearing in her hair a harp fashioned in France, which was illuminated with a diadem of fancy little gas jets spurting out blue flame. Not until she launched into the cotillion, did the lady deign to remove her fiery crown.

When the appetite for giving parties on a flamboyant scale for humans became jaded, Wall Street wives turned to giving dinners for their dogs, sitting them at the head of the table as guests of honor and presenting them with $10,000 collars. One Wall Street nabob, seeking assiduously for thrills, had holes drilled in his molars into which a dentist inserted rows of little diamonds. When he smiled, he positively coruscated. In the hunt for the unusual, "poverty parties" became the mode. At one such social, the guests arrived in tatters. Scraps of food were dished up on wooden platters; the diners sat on broken soapboxes. They drank beer out of shabby tin cans. The newspapers gave a big play to this latest wrinkle in reverse snobbery.

Apropos of this histrionic concern for the poor, the Bradley Martins—he was a wealthy Wall Street plunger and brother of Frederick, the chronicler—gave a ball that was a climactic illustration of American Bourbonism. One morning during the winter of 1896–7 in the midst of a business recession, Mrs. Martin, reading in the newspapers about unemployment, conceived the idea of holding a party that would give local tradesmen a shot in the arm. Before she was through, her dutiful husband had forked up $370,000 for the cause. A corps of dressmakers were put to work to sew costumes in which the guests would appear.

For weeks, the international press brimmed with news about the event. Miss Anne Morgan, the daughter of the Wall Street banker, it was reported, was preparing to come as Pocahontas in an authentic costume sewed by American Indians. August Belmont planned to turn up encased in medieval armor which would set him back some $7,000. All over America family heirlooms were dusted off to be worn at the festivities. Headlines informed readers how the Oglethorpe gems from Georgia and the Fairfax diamonds from Virginia had just arrived in Manhattan under heavy guard. The ballroom of the Waldorf-Astoria, which had been rented for the occasion, was being turned, readers were told, into a replica of a hall in Versailles. Biographies appeared on the lucky guests who had been invited and the even luckier ones who had been chosen to dance the cotillion. One paper broke the bleak news that "James Van Alen Cannot Go," reporting how after a soul-searching debate, this socialite had arrived at the decision that he would not be able to dance in the *quadrille d'honneur* because of the sudden death of a relative. It was a heart-rending decision to make, it seems, since Van Alen had been rehearsing the dance for weeks at Mrs. Astor's house under the supervision of Professor Karl Marwig, a specialist in such choreography.

As the great day approached, ominous reports poured in. Several anarchists, it was rumored, had been seized planting dynamite under the Martin mansion, and plans were said to be afoot to throw explosives through the windows of the Waldorf while the quadrille was at its height. Pinkerton detectives were placed around the hotel and stood guard outside the Martin home. When the gala night arrived, hordes of newsmen descended on the Waldorf to report on the members of the golden circle as they stepped from their carriages. Every last ounce of human interest was extracted from the proceedings. One reporter divulged how "a little man with a gray beard stood for a moment beside the awning, watching the passage of the guests." He was told to get going. " 'Bradley Martin and I were schoolboys together,' " he murmured. But the detectives heartlessly shooed him off.

The ball had a rather less entertaining aftermath. The opulent activities reported so widely in the press touched off a rising tide of resentment across the nation. America was in the midst of a depression. New York was swarming with unemployed people. The city authorities moved in and sharply raised Bradley Martin's property taxes, and the Martins sold their home in anger and moved to London, where the feeling against royal goings-on was not nearly as intense. Frederick Martin, Bradley's brother, wrote that he simply couldn't understand "why this entertainment should have been condemned. . . . We Americans are so accustomed to display that I should have thought the ball would not have been regarded as anything very unusual."

However, idle play wasn't Wall Street's only contribution to American mores. The Street served as the storm center for ideas that were to reverberate through every level of American thought. As far back as the 1870's, when most women in the middle and upper classes were confined like pet parakeets, Wall Street gave a brisk thrust forward to the emancipation of woman. In at least one curious instance, it embraced the concept of occupational equality by permitting two females to become the first women, as far as the records denote, to carry on a brokerage business on the Street.

These lady brokers who stormed the bastion of the male—the Claflin sisters—were, as might be expected, unusual personalities, not only for their day but any day. Their origin and background were definitely unconventional. They came from the backwoods of America (western Ohio), from a family of migrants. Their father, Buckman Claflin, was a ne'er-do-well, just a hop and a step ahead of the policeman. The mother, Roxy, who bore Buck ten children, was a mystic who doctored her kids with faith healing and held séances at which she transmitted "messages" from the Great Beyond. The young Claflins, too, went into trances and told one another of the wondrous world they had "visited" while out of the material one.

The family led a nomadic existence, staying just long enough in a community to stir up controversy with its neighbors, and move on. It formed a peripatetic medicine show, peddling quack nostrums for every conceivable ailment. Brother Hebern billed himself as a cancer healer; Mother Roxy stirred up in a cauldron vaporous potions whose formula, she assured her audience, had been whispered to her by heavenly spirits. The family swooped down on town after town, showering it with handbills and scooping in the money with quack medicines for the gullible. They took in enough cash in Toronto to rent the leading hotel, fit it out as a medical dispensary, peddling "cures" for cancer, and free love on the side. A spate of gamey gossip hovered about the Claflins. Tongues wagged that the girls, Victoria and Tennessee, had been caught running a bordello. In one town, Tennessee was named in an adultery suit and the family had to leave precipitously.

About this time a new individual joined the cast to further spice up the family's affairs. He was Colonel James H. Blood, Commander of the Sixth Missouri Regiment, a philosopher and an anarchist with strong overtones of the mystic. Blood was a leader in spiritualist circles; and reports had reached him through the grapevine of the talents of the Claflin family—Victoria and Tennessee in particular—who summoned up spirits from the other world.

Blood visited Victoria to witness her achievements firsthand. The girl chatted with the handsome young officer. Then she sat herself in a chair, turned chalk-white and passed into a trance. Speaking rapidly and unnaturally, as if a supernatural being were forming the words through her, she told Blood that it was his destiny to be married. What was more, his bride was to be none other than Victoria Claflin herself. Then, as Blood later told the story to friends, the two ardent spiritualists were married on the spot in as unusual a ceremony as ever took place between a man and woman—betrothed "by the supernatural powers who hovered over them." It happened that Victoria already had a husband. Eight years previously, at sixteen, she had turned the head of a man thirty years older, a physician who married her and ever since followed her around like a devoted puppy. But this was no obstacle whatever to the irrepressible medium.

Victoria, Blood and Dr. Woodhull (the first husband) constituted a curious *ménage à trois*. While Victoria remained, according to the letter of the law, married to Dr. Woodhull, she plunged into her duties as a "spirit" wife with inordinate gusto and the two men got along famously. They made the rounds of the towns in a covered wagon. Vicky called herself Madam Harvey and read the palms of the rustics. Blood was the barker who suckered in the crowds. His fierce whiskers and booming basso belied the gentle mystic who moved in a world of philosophical introspection behind all the huzzahs.

The following few years are shrouded in obscurity. The next history records of the Claflins they turned up in New York, in 1869, gravitating, as always, to where the money was. The wealthiest man in the city happened to be Commodore Vanderbilt. And the sisters turned their blandishments on him.

The possessor of the greatest fortune wrested by an American up to his time, Vanderbilt was an uneducated, hard-drinking, hard-swearing old coot who had started out as a ferryboat operator and moved into the burgeoning new railroad industry, putting together a complex of roads that linked the Eastern Seaboard with the Middle West, adding a classic chapter to the annals of finance with his stock manipulations and his business brawls. His pugnacity and cynicism spilled over into his private life. He ruled his family with an iron hand. When his wife refused to move to a new residence, he had her clapped into an insane asylum. He cheated his sons in order to teach them lessons in conducting business. Once when associates went back on a deal Vanderbilt wrote to them: "Gentlemen, you have undertaken to cheat me. I will not sue you, for law takes too long. I will ruin you." He turned his son, Cornelius, into a hopeless neurotic who ran away from home at twenty and became a compulsive gambler, spending hours at the gaming table until he fell to the floor in an epileptic fit.

Such was the man the Claflin girls attempted to cultivate upon arriving in New York.

It was a case of lightning being attracted to a magnetic rod. A superstitious old galoot in his seventies, with a streak of mysticism underlying his pragmatic approach to affairs, Vanderbilt was impatient with doctors who were unable to alleviate his physical aches, and he patronized any quack who promised to restore him his youthful vigor. With one shrewd eye on the Beyond, he was mightily impressed with mediums who could communicate with the dead and find out how things were really going up there. Under the circumstances it was not difficult for Tennessee Claflin, whose reputation as a medium had preceded her, to arrange an appointment with Vanderbilt. He had heard that Tennessee was especially successful in generating enough electricity to prolong life for years simply by touching the favored one's fingers with her own. She was a highly charged battery, she explained to her clients. Her right hand transmitted positive electricity; her left hand, the negative current; and when she joined hands with a customer she completed a circuit that stirred up the juices of youth in even the wheeziest old body.

Tennie visited the Commodore and promptly wove her enchantments around him. She was a comely young thing in her twenties. Vanderbilt was a widower with gamey physical fantasies. The Commodore was soon inviting the medium to hold hands with him in daily séances. And word got out that their tête-à-têtes were not all business. According to gossip, he asked Tennie to marry him and only the most emphatic objections by other members of the Vanderbilt clan stopped him from carrying out his plans. He quieted the hornet's nest by settling for a wealthy young aristocrat with the intriguing name of Frankie Crawford.

But while Tennie failed to become Mrs. Vanderbilt, she was consoled with a lush outpouring of gifts from the Commodore. And he capped these extravagances by setting up Tennie and her sister Vicky in a brokerage business on Wall Street.

In January, 1870, the New York *Herald* ran a story announcing the debut of two elegantly garbed female brokers. The report caused quite a stir. The most venerable resident of the Street could not recall a woman's having operated a broker office before. When rumors spread that Vanderbilt was behind the sisters, giving them lucrative stock tips, reporters swooped down for interviews. The girls put on a striking show. Victoria was a woman of thirty-three with dark, expressive eyes and a highly articulate tongue. She wore diamonds on her fingers and a red carnation in her hair. Tennessee was seven years younger and equally enticing. While the austere old bankers were suspicious and resentful of these "Queens of Finance," as the newspapers dubbed them, the patronage of Vanderbilt made it impossible for the girls to be ignored, and every financial institution of note sent an emissary on a courtesy call to their office.

The piquancy of two exotic women invading a bastion of the male, flouncing about in Empress Eugénie finery with pencils tucked roguishly behind their ears, added gusto to the picture. Whenever the sisters emerged from their office to promenade along Wall Street, crowds snowballed behind them. So many people pressed for entrance to their office that the girls were forced to put up a notice: "All gentlemen will state their business and then retire at once." Women, too, besieged the 44 Broad Street broker house. The acquisitive, the curious and the gullible drove up in their carriages and deposited their cash with these women who had the ear of Vanderbilt. The sisters held court regally, sitting behind lavish walnut desks and dipping into a bowl of sweets as they dispensed their investment advice.

As for Commodore Vanderbilt, he was hugely delighted by the furor his protégés were causing. The elderly gent wallowed in adulation. Victoria bellowed with the most unladylike laughter whenever the Commodore cracked his little jokes—for example, when he boasted that the sisters had bought stock in his New York Central Railroad just to get his picture, which was engraved on the certificates. Tennie slapped him on the back and called him "My Old Boy." The sisters held séances for him, obligingly summoning up from the dead whomever he wished to speak with. Shortly after Jim Fisk, the financier, was shot to death over a love affair, the Commodore was seized with the desire to receive some hot stock tips from the old pro, figuring that a man dwelling in the Beyond had a pretty good idea of what was going to happen tomorrow. The sisters rapped on the table, went through the prescribed incantations, and shortly a voice purporting to belong to Fisk's ghost passed on celestial advice regarding Erie Railroad stock. It was all good clean fun, and the Commodore was only too happy to foot the bill. It was a whopping bill, indeed; the entire Claflin clan—the sisters, Vicky's ménage of husbands, the raffish father, the fanatic mother—were ensconced in a mansion that was fitted out like the Petit Trianon in the palmiest days of the Bourbons. It was a far cry from the days when the Claflins were moving from town to town peddling snake oil.

Underneath the shabby adventuresses, there lurked in the sisters—especially in Victoria, the older and more prestigious-minded—a fierce desire for intellectual respectability. Vicky craved to be admired not only for her beauty but as a spokeswoman of ideas. She told Commodore Vanderbilt that she would like to publish a magazine in which she could air her views on social events and he docilely put up the money. In so doing, the senile financier was unwittingly to become responsible for ideas that would turn his sensibilities crimson.

Victoria was curiously susceptible to men of cerebral pyrotechnics, and recently an individual had entered her life who was to exploit this to the utmost. He was Stephen Pearl Andrews, a minister's son, an ardent follower of Swedenborg and a dabbler in mysticism. He had an obsession to reform, to innovate, to shock. He experimented with the use of a universal world language (before the days of Esperanto), attempting to develop a vocabulary based entirely on sounds that had different meanings for different ideas. He became a student of Chinese, learning it well enough to write a textbook on it. He talked of establishing a world government to take the place of national states, to be administered by a supreme council of philosophers (shades of Plato's *Republic*).

He carried his odd notions into his daily life. For several years he lived in a "free love" community in New York State called "Modern Times," whose inhabitants swapped goods and wives without inhibitions. America in the mid-seventies had broken out in a rash of social experiments in which disciples of free love mingled with spiritualists and other exotic cultists to raise sexual promiscuity to the level of a religion. According to the free-lovers, the state had no right to enforce marriages; conjugal ties should be entered into and dissolved at will, whenever the individuals desired. Some aficionados went so far as to proclaim that a man could be admitted into heaven after death only if he sought entrance with his natural love-mate and not with the spouse to whom he had been legally but lovelessly knotted. Since this crusade to unshackle the libido was tied in with a desire to destroy the state in general as an instrument of control over the individual, it attracted many political anarchists and other far-out souls for whom sexual licentiousness was made respectable by being packaged into an ideological creed. And one of the most zestful converts was Stephen Andrews.

His outlook was very similar to Colonel Blood's, Victoria's lover, and Vicky lent a willing ear to him. True, there seemed to be an obstacle to the consummation of this intellectual affiliation. Vicky was uneducated and only semiliterate. She wasn't able to write a sentence clearly. But this didn't bother Andrews one bit. With the debut of *Woodhull & Claflin's Weekly*, published from the office of the Broad Street broker house, there poured forth under the name of Victoria Claflin a flood of articles representing the sophisticated meanderings of Andrews and Blood. Articles appeared analyzing the governments of the ancient world and of contemporary primitive peoples. The societies of Athens and Rome, early Egypt and Mesopotamia were dissected on a sociological and economic level. The doctrines of Mill, Hegel and Locke were criticized and expatiated upon. An editorial crusade was launched for the practice of eugenics to produce healthier and wiser children. Women must become intellectually emancipated, argued the *Weekly*, so that they would insist on reproducing only superior children and, to this end, cohabit only with superior men, whether or not they happened to be their husbands.

As week after week these provocative articles were launched from Wall Street, they engendered a lively reaction. All over America, radicals, dissenters, and bohemians, alienated from the Establishment, found a rallying point in these stinging, iconoclastic essays; Victoria became "must" reading in salons from Boston to San Francisco.

No group was more impressed with Vicky's writings than America's suffragette leaders, who were campaigning to lift women from their status as second-class citizens and give them the right to vote. Elizabeth Cady Stanton and Susan Anthony were aggressive, hard-driving females who were thoroughly convinced that the mother of men would be the savior of the human race once she was enfranchised, her shackles removed. A typical proponent of this notion was Mrs. August Belmont, the New York society matron who when a fellow suffragette confessed she was beginning to feel discouraged by the long struggle for rights, slapped her on the back and chirped, "Don't be disheartened, sister. Tell your troubles to God. *She* won't let you down."

The suffragette leaders took Vicky to their hearts. And she moved to the forefront of the movement, delivering fighting talks from platforms all over America. Whenever she appeared to lecture, crowds jammed the streets in front of the hall, snarling up traffic for blocks.

Then it finally happened. Several hundred of Vicky's most committed disciples met to organize a "People's Party" in Apollo Hall, New York, and to offer her the top place on the ticket for the coming national elections. And so the expeddler of quack medicines became the only woman ever to be nominated for the Presidency of the United States.

She ran on one of the most extraordinary platforms ever to be presented an electorate—free love. She campaigned for the abolition of marriage, which as an institution, she declared, doomed women to remain enslaved to men they detested. A woman had the right to live with any man to whom she was attracted, she averred, and the right to leave her husband at any moment in the pursuit of love. She insisted that it was morally and eugenically better for a woman to have a dozen healthy children by a dozen different, superior men than to have twelve children by one fellow who was a mental or physical weakling, just because he happened to be her legal spouse.

These lectures, when they were reported in the press, caused an uproar. Women all over America were scandalized—and titillated. For their part, their husbands were infuriated by this frontal assault on their happy homesteads. Haunted by the specter of being turned wholesale into cuckolds, they forbade their spouses to attend Victoria's exhor-

VICTORIA CLAFLIN WOODHULL RUNS FOR THE U.S.
PRESIDENCY ON A PLATFORM OF FREE LOVE.
CARTOON IN HARPER'S WEEKLY, 1872
COURTESY OF THE NEW-YORK HISTORICAL SOCIETY, NEW YORK CITY

tations on love. But they themselves sneaked off to listen, fascinated by the beautiful woman who dared to translate into ideological utterances their own salacious yearnings. However, no respectable man dared associate with her openly. The great and the dignified of the world—those who had once sat on the platform with her—drew off as if she were a leper.

More significantly—so far as Victoria's financial security was concerned—the Wall Street community, which had given her unwitting sustenance, bristled with anger. For some time the antics of the lady broker had been burning the ears of the impeccable investment bankers, most of whom from the beginning had looked with suspicion on her. They had shaken their heads over Vanderbilt's endorsement and wondered how quickly his chickens would come home to roost.

The Commodore, when he realized that he was responsible for financing a crusade that was threatening to undermine the pillars of American respectability, did a quick double take. He informed Victoria curtly that he was withdrawing all financial support from *Claflin's Weekly* and the brokerage business.

Now at this low point in her fortunes, with the need for funds to keep her magazine afloat growing desperate, rumors spread that Victoria had begun resorting to tactics that would not have been smiled upon on the playing fields of Eton. She was privy to the racy secrets of a number of bankers, brokers and assorted playboys on the Street, and it was gossiped that she had launched a campaign of blackmail, threatening to expose the actual or imagined peccadilloes of prominent Wall Streeters, sending proofs of the articles she proposed to publish about them and demanding money to keep them out of print.

Then Victoria took an extreme step. Going quite far afield from Wall Street, and its peccadilloes, she published an article alleging that Henry Ward Beecher one of America's most celebrated preachers, and the brother of Harriet Beecher Stowe, who had written *Uncle Tom's Cabin*, was having an affair with a young married woman, the mother of several children and a parishioner at his church in Brooklyn.

Victoria reported every salacious detail with clinical zest. The Beecher story appeared in the November 2, 1872, issue of *Claflin's Weekly* and it created a furor. When the issue hit the Wall Street area, people mobbed the newsboys for copies and by evening the few that were left were selling for $40 apiece.

Beecher's friends retaliated vigorously. They charged that the story was untrue and libelous, and they put pressure on the authorities to take action. A warrant was sworn out for the arrest of Vicky (and Tennessee, who was listed as co-publisher of *Claflin's*). The girls were picked up while they were promenading along Broad Street passing out the *Weekly*, and they were hauled before a Federal magistrate on the charge of distributing obscene literature.

Plunging into an urgent hunt for an attorney, the sisters approached the firm of Hummel and Howe, a celebrated team of lawyers who had established an extraordinary legend of successful litigation. Abe Hummel and William Howe were extremely versatile. They represented the cream of Wall Street bankers, the headliners of show business—Lily Langtry, Edwin Booth, P. T. Barnum—and they had a monopoly on the town's criminal practice. Indeed, some irreverent people went so far as to hint that whenever criminal clients became scarce, the indefatigable pair stirred up their own business by planning robberies, counterfeiting and other "jobs," and collecting fees for defending the actual perpetrators when they were picked up by the police.

The physical appearance of the pair was as freakish as their minds. Little Abe Hummel was a humpty-dumpty figure of a man, five feet two, with a huge, bald head standing like an inverted egg over a belly perpetually distended with an excess of Bavarian beer. Howe was tall, lean and as hungry-looking as Cassius, with a funereal manner that was in striking counterpoint to Hummel's air of *gemütlichkeit*.

Through deft maneuvers, the pair played havoc with the rules of the legal game. On one occasion, discovering a technical flaw in the law, they succeeded in freeing a hundred criminals from the Tombs prison, sending the city into an uproar until the legislature rewrote the law. In another instance, a troupe of Egyptian belly dancers, performing at a New York music hall for the relaxation of tired businessmen, was arrested and hauled before a magistrate. The girls put in a hurried call for Hummel. Abe listened to the charge that the Middle East terpsichoreans had indulged in "lewd and lascivious contortions of the stomach." Then he whipped out a medical dictionary and insisted that the indictment should be thrown out for being inaccurate. It was impossible for the police to have observed the contortions of the stomach, he insisted, since the stomach was "nothing but a small sac in the abdominal region, whose contortions, if any, could not be observed unless one were watching from *inside* the body." The magistrate solemnly agreed and dismissed the indictment, such was the caliber of legal talent the Claflin girls hired to defend them.

The hearing was held on November 4 in the Federal Building. Word had passed quickly through the financial district, and the courtroom was jammed. Brokers deserted their offices, customers' men turned away from price boards, order clerks laid down their pads. The Stock Exchange was emptied of traders, who fought to get into the courtroom.

The spectacle lived up to its billing. The sisters entered the dock looking as demure as kewpie dolls in girlish bow ties. Howe, the partner who had undertaken to present the defense, added his own touch of the picturesque. Melancholy-looking, with a face that glowed from too much alcohol, he loved to impress courtroom audiences with his flamboyant haberdashery. He appeared on this occasion in a plum-colored waistcoat topped by a lavender scarf. His shirtfront and fingers blazed with diamonds. Only one item of sartorial elegance was missing. He wore no tie, since it was a superstition with him never to wear one except to a hanging or a funeral.

Howe tore into the obscenity charge. He made an impassioned plea for free speech, warning the jury against any infringement on the right to print the news guaranteed by the Constitution.

After legal wrangling lasting over a series of hearings, the sisters, through the efforts of their astute lawyers, were released. But their sojourn in jail had not sobered them one bit. As they were leaving prison, reporters swarmed around and asked if they had any fault to find with their treatment. Tennessee replied that the only thing that had really angered her was a newspaper article, which she had read in her cell, charging that she was smoking bad cigars. "If I had been out of jail where I could deny such statements, I wouldn't have minded them so much," she stormed. The cigars she smoked, she wanted it to be known, like the wine she patronized, were only of the best. As for Victoria, when asked how she had fared in her cell, she struck a histrionic pose in the spirit of Sarah Bernhardt. "As Madame Roland said, when the French Revolution broke out in the streets of Paris—'Oh liberty, what things are done in thy name!'"

The inimitable Victoria had no intention of quitting her crusade. She immediately plunged into a new lecture tour, preaching free love and spicing her speeches with further accounts of the Beecher scandal. With a surefire touch, she billed her lecture "The Naked Truth."

The Beecher article had wide ramifications. It led to a suit brought against Beecher and to his trial on charges of adultery. The jury was unable to agree whether or not Beecher was guilty, and the case was dismissed. But in the meantime it stirred up spirited discussions in parlors from coast to coast, causing Americans to reexamine their moral assumptions about extramarital sex and the double standard for men and women.

Wall Street, the stronghold of middle-class sanctity, by taking two queer sisters to its bosom and financing their piquant fantasies, had launched an intellectual time bomb whose fall-out caused significant mutations in America's social thinking.

As for Commodore Vanderbilt, who had been the unwitting catalyst of this explosion, he was nearing the end of his own odd career. He had, as noted, cut himself off completely from the Claflin sisters. He lived a little over a year after the Beecher trial. And to the end he remained his crusty, disputatious self. Even on his deathbed, surrounded by his wife, children and grandchildren, who dutifully sang hymns to facilitate the old soul's flight to its final reward, he displayed the pathological strain of penny-pinching from which, oddly, only the Claflin girls had at one time been exempt. When the doctor suggested a little champagne to bolster his spirits in his final hours and ease his way through the pearly gates, the possessor of $100 million was utterly shocked by such extravagance. "Doctor," he muttered weakly, "won't sody water do instead?"

Although the Commodore had continued to shun the Claflin sisters, the consequences of his association with them haunted him even after his death, which is perhaps only proper for a dyed-in-the-wool spiritualist who believed so devoutly in celestial spooks.

Vanderbilt left behind $100 million—the biggest fortune achieved in the nation up to then, as noted. The newspapers worshipfully reported this achievement. It was great front-page news. Editors pointed out for the enlightenment of their readers that the fortune was so huge that if the money were measured out into piles of silver, it would take all eight of the Vanderbilt children over thirty years to count it. When Chauncey Depew, the president of the New York and Hudson Railroad, visited England, he found that the news of the Vanderbilt fortune was the chief subject of gossip among the British nobility.

The newspapers in America and abroad were to be treated

to even more piquant news. For no sooner was the Commodore lowered into his grave, than a quarrel erupted among his descendants over his will. Impressed with the means used by the British aristocracy to transmit its wealth intact, Vanderbilt had decided to apply the principle of primogeniture to his own estate. Of the $100 million, he arranged to leave $95 million to his oldest son, William, whom, he felt, he had successfully educated into an astute businessman. He left a mere $500,000 to his wife and he allocated the remaining $4.5 million among his seven other children.

These heirs were enraged at the prospect of receiving such a pittance, and a suit to have the will voided was brought by Mrs. May Alice La Bau, one of the daughters, in which she was joined by Cornelius, Jr. They argued that their father had not been in his right mind at the time he drew up the will. As proof of his mental instability, they mentioned his susceptibility to spirit mediums and his constant attendance at séances.

During the hearings it became increasingly clear that the plaintiff's lawyers intended to build their case around Vanderbilt's association with the Claflin sisters. They introduced testimony about how the Commodore had believed illnesses could be cured by casting a spell over a picture in a locket or a lock of hair. They told how he attended séances to find out how his stocks would perform. When he had been asked if he wanted a message from his departed wife, he had grunted that he didn't give a damn whether she was in heaven or hell, but he'd jolly well like to know whether Northern Pacific was going up a few points tomorrow.

Vanderbilt's physician, Dr. Jared Linsly, was put on the stand and, under cross examination, admitted that he had seen the Claflin girls frequently at the Commodore's home behaving familiarly with him. Another witness testified that he saw Vanderbilt handing money over to the sisters to finance their *Weekly*. Even old Buck Claflin, the sisters' father, was hauled to the stand to testify that Vanderbilt had asked for Tennie's hand in marriage. It was evident that the plaintiffs were leading up to the climactic touch of putting the girls themselves on the stand. But William Vanderbilt and his lawyers were determined to have none of this. The prospect of the vinegar-tongued Vicky and Tennie speaking out in court regarding their relationship with the Commodore was more than William was willing to endure. The stakes were too high—$95 million. Accordingly, he paid the girls a hurried visit and offered them a sizable amount of money if they would leave the country and stay away indefinitely. The girls boarded the quickest available ship and sailed out of reach of the plaintiff's lawyers.

The sisters showed up in England and set themselves up in style on the Vanderbilt largesse. And even now they couldn't resist doing the unpredictable. Ensconced in the tight-laced little island, they proceeded to turn an intellectual somersault, completely disavowing their free-love teachings and denying they had ever been a part of the radical movement in America. To decisively lay the ghosts of the past, Victoria issued a geneological pamphlet, which she presented to the British people as her "family tree." She insisted that she was descended from the kings of Scotland and England. On her father's side, she maintained, she sprang from British and Scots royalty, and on her mother's side that she came from the Hummels and the Moyers, who were of royal German blood and connected by marriage to the family of George Washington. (Poor Buck Claflin didn't even rate a footnote.)

Before arriving in England, Victoria had gotten rid of her "spirit" husband, Colonel Blood, as well as her legal spouse, Dr. Woodhull. Still attractive in her early forties, she won the attention of John Biddulph Martin, the son of one of Britain's most distinguished bankers, and he proposed marriage. It was a splendid consolation prize for the ex-practitioner of free love who had failed to become President of the United States.

Tennessee also married a wealthy aristocrat, an elderly widower named Francis Cook, who held the title Visconde de Montserrate. Lady Cook lived with her husband at Doughty House, a splendid old mansion overlooking the Thames, which was renowned for its art gallery and for the Cook family's collection of antique rings.

Lady Martin and Lady Cook penetrated to the inner sanctum of the British Establishment. True, from time to time the American press cropped up with embarrassing disclosures about their past. A retired New York police inspector, invited by the Brooklyn *Eagle* to write his reminiscences of the most notorious adventurers he had known, handed in an article on the Claflin girls. An ex-member of the Cincinnati police force testified during a trial that he had arrested Tennessee Claflin for running a bordello. Other witnesses popped up in different parts of the country to recall how they had been victims of blackmail by the sisters. To all such accusations, the sisters huffed and puffed, threatening libel suits which never materialized.

Tennie died in her seventies, but Victoria lived into her nineties. When her husband passed on, the old lady retired to his baronial estate at Bredon's Norton, where she ruled as a grande dame. Bredon was a mosaic of rolling countryside, festooned with rose gardens and evergreen parks overlooking the Avon River. Victoria became famous for her rose shows, which drew the gentry from miles around. The vicars eulogized her as a benefactress of the poor. This was beyond the most extravagant dreams of Buckman Claflin's gypsy daughter when she scrounged for business in the American backwoods.

Now her name was a shining one in the registry of high society. The former peddler of quack medicines and spiritualist "cures" became the intimate friend of no less a person than the Earl of Coventry, Dean of the House of Lords. Vicky and the Earl were photographed sitting in front of her country manor.

Victoria died in her ninetieth year, the epitome of British upper-class respectability. If she ever got together with salty old Commodore Vanderbilt in that afterworld of celestial spooks in which they both professed belief, what a ribald laugh they must have had.

The marriage of the Claflin sisters into the British nobility was but the forerunner of a trend that took hold of Wall Street society after the Civil War. America's status-seekers were hard put to free themselves from an inferiority complex, since they lived in a country where the most venerable families belong to American Indians. The men who made money on kiting a stock or leading a bear raid on the bulls provided only the façade of status. It was their wives who struggled to achieve the substance.

There was little use in belonging to the world's wealthiest ruling class if one lacked the proper credentials of aristocracy. This the nobility of the Old World could supply in abundance. Europe's wealth had been exhausted through centuries of attrition. The Continent fairly teemed with impecunious noblemen. Marrying Wall Street heiresses and swapping a title for cash became one of Europe's major industries. Indeed, in the early 1900s, the outbreak of *quid pro quo* alliances reached epidemic proportions. The German press carried full-page advertisements offering to place impoverished Prussian junkers in touch with the daughters of Wall Street plungers. The King of Serbia (the last of the Obrenovich dynasty), in a desperate endeavor to save the finances of his family, which was on the verge of bankruptcy, sent his diplomats scurrying to find the daughter of a well-heeled lard or copper king who could be induced to marry his son.

In the early 1900s, *Life*, America's leading humor magazine, ran a cartoon of an American millionairess pursued on a ballroom floor by two British fortune hunters, one tall and skinny, the other short and portly. Two society dowagers ogle the goings-on through their lorgnettes. Exclaims the first, "Both those lords are after her and she doesn't know which to accept."

"Isn't one as good as the other?" inquires the second.

"Yes. But she can't tell in advance which is the cheaper."

The most highly publicized alliance of the times was that of the young Duke of Marlborough with the daughter of Mrs. William Vanderbilt. It was strictly a cash arrangement. The bridegroom, possessor of Britain's oldest dukedom, was urgently in need of money. Mrs. Vanderbilt was badly in need of a title to crown a lifetime of social climbing. As part of the arrangement, the Duke magnanimously agreed to take 50,000 shares of the Beech Creek Railway Co., a subsidiary of the Vanderbilt-owned New York Central, which, according to Wall Street estimates, amounted to almost $3 million. Blenheim Palace, the Duke's country seat, was in urgent need of repairs. The stockholders of the New York Central must have been quite astonished to learn that their railroad was going to be used as collateral for the upkeep of a rundown British castle and that thanks to this largesse, the Duke would be able to draw $100,000 a year for maintenance expenses. One irreverent artist drew in *Life* a cartoon of the groom as a Columbus clad in rags landing on the rocky New England coast and being greeted with heaps of Indian wampum by the Vanderbilt tribe. Consuelo Vanderbilt was dragged to the altar at St. Thomas, kicking and screaming, figuratively speaking, while the organ boomed out the wedding march from *Lohengrin* and the choir sang seraphically,

O! perfect love, all human thought transcending,
   That theirs may be the love that knows no ending,
Whom thou forevermore dost join in one.

The loveless alliance limped on for thirteen years until it was terminated by a separation and then a divorce that cost Vanderbilt $9 million. Even after the ties were severed, the Duke continued to receive under the terms of the marriage contract $100,000 annually for the upkeep of Blenheim Palace, to the chagrin of the long-suffering New York Central stockholders.

The prestigious Duke was only one of a swarm of locusts who descended on America. Count Boni Castellane, a French aristocrat who had drunk and wenched his way through a fortune, talked Jay Gould into letting him marry his daughter, Anna, and he proceeded to squander $6 million of her Wall Street inheritance. The Earl of Yarmouth, pressed to the wall with debts, tried his darndest to marry Byrd Thaw, a young Pittsburgh heiress, and when she turned him down, he transferred his affections to her wealthy aunt, who accepted him. Fleeing to the States, the Earl was tracked down in Pittsburgh by his creditors. They persuaded the police to arrest the Earl, but he informed the cops that he was on the verge of marrying an American millionairess and that the wedding contract would be signed that very day. He invited his creditors to accompany him to the nuptials. They agreed and waited outside in an anteroom while the groom and the bride's family bargained heatedly over the last-minute details of the dowry. The wedding guests waited patiently in the church for over an hour for the bride to appear, unaware that in a nearby room the path of true love had been blocked by a haggling over money. Finally, matters were straightened out, the groom put his signature on the contract, the creditors departed and the minister was able to give his blessing. The match was dissolved in five years.

This drive to achieve status, manifesting itself in marriages for titles, was part of a basic insecurity which cropped up in other ways among Wall Street families and other members of the nation's elite. The richer they were, the more pathological seemed their need for acceptance by others.

Indeed, America's nabobs of finance were frequently shy, insecure individuals, as sensitive to the opinions of the public as a skittish old maid with a gentleman caller; and they went to curious lengths to show their anxiety. The grandson of John Jacob Astor, William Waldorf Astor, who had inherited a large part of the $40 million amassed by his grandfather and had added millions on his own, left America in the fear that members of his family would be kidnapped and settled in England. Publicly he became a savage critic of his native land. Yet, although he had cut the umbilical cord, he was morbidly concerned about the esteem of his erstwhile countrymen. To find out what the rank and file American really thought about him, he had a report of his death planted in the U.S. newspapers and braced himself to read the obituaries. Unfortunately—or perhaps fortunately, for his ego—the hoax was discovered before the first notice appeared.

Another strangely tortured man of success was John Pierpont Morgan. The son of the founder of a banking fortune, Morgan became in his own right the mover and shaker of America's money marts from 1880 until his death in 1913. The most powerful man on Wall Street, imperious, terrifying, aloof, Morgan, like the fictional Cyrano de Bergerac, was haunted by an ugly joke nature had played on him—his nose. It was a hugely inflamed proboscis that marred his otherwise handsome features. Unlike Cyrano, who had only dreamed of reaching the moon, Morgan had actually got there, figuratively speaking. He had achieved all he had ever dreamed of in the way of financial and social position. Yet he spent hours in secret turmoil over that terrible misalliance inflicted on his face. When a news writer referred to him as the "ruby-visaged magnate," he never wholly recovered from the blow. Other scribes seized upon the phrase; the news columns were spiced with references to this blushing appurtenance, and cartoonists treated the nose with malicious exuberance. Morgan loathed the entire newspaper fraternity. This man who numbered among his friends the King of England and the Archbishop of Canterbury remained deeply insecure about his appearance. Yet, when an associate suggested that his nose could be helped by plastic surgery, he resisted with unexpected bravura. "Everybody knows my nose. It would be impossible for me to appear on the streets of New York with a changed version of it."

On one level Morgan was a superb pragmatist. As the

nation's leading banker there was nothing equivocal about his approach. Virtually singlehandedly he imposed a structured order upon American industry. His great genius was his skill at leveraging other people's money. He dominated both sides of a business operation, acting as the banker who controlled the money lent out to key corporations and serving at the same time, personally or through lieutenants, on the boards of directors of these corporations. Playing both sides of the street, he infiltrated one industry after another.

After the Civil War, the nation's railroads fell into the hands of cliques of American-style condottieri who warred as savagely with one another as the freebooting captains of the Middle Ages. Morgan moved in with his control of capital funds and forced the roads into integrated systems that set costs and prices all down the line. He entered the infant telephone industry, subdued the warring factions into a tight-knit communications system. He amalgamated five of the nation's top farm machinery concerns into an imperium regnum. He got control of General Electric, which made electrical equipment, bought up plants all over the nation and regrouped them into a supertrust that controlled the nation's power business. He found the steel industry split into bickering fragments. In 1901 he consolidated ten of them into the U.S. Steel Corporation, the largest combine organized up to that time.

Throughout his life, Morgan displayed the lese majesty of a Renaissance prince. When Theodore Roosevelt assumed the Presidency and began his trust-busting activities, ordering his Attorney General to proceed against the Northern Securities Company, in which Morgan had a controlling interest, for allegedly violating the anti-trust laws, Morgan approached the matter as if he and Roosevelt were the heads of two separate and equal principalities. He sent a message to the President, "If we have done something wrong, send your man to my man and they can fix it up."

And yet, on another level, Morgan was worlds removed

from the kingdom of finance and the Napoleonic posturing he assumed within it. His grandmother, on the maternal side, had been a Jacksonian reformer and had transmitted strange nuances of liberalism to her posterity. Morgan, the archetype of the conservative banker, ardently admired three of the world's most bohemian poets—Byron, Shelley and Keats. Indeed, he named his yacht the *Corsair* after one of Byron's early works. He snapped up for his collection the original manuscript of *Leaves of Grass* by Walt Whitman, who was considered an eccentric even by his fellow bards and whose panegyrics to sex scandalized conventional Americans. The attraction of the austere, Bible-reading banker to the homosexual spinner of free verse is a fascinating problem for the psychologist.

Like artists in other lines, the virtuoso financiers frequently possessed idiosyncrasies that were part and parcel of their intuitive genius, which in the business field translated itself into a deep, psychic feel for the tide and trends of money. Morgan shared with other outstanding financiers, a strong mystical bent. Toward the end of his life he visited Evangeline Adams, an astrologer, to consult with her on the changing confluence of the planets and their impact on his business fortunes.

He was a deep-rooted aesthete who, to compensate, some believe, for his own physical blemishes, gathered around him men and women who had the physiques of the Greek and Renaissance sculpture he so eagerly collected. Aloof, cold, frequently brutal to his business associates, he had outbursts of religious fervor during which he would halt a business conference and rush to church, where he would drop to his knees and pray for hours. He loved to sing hymns and shower bishops with his largesse. Although he was the leading lay figure of the Episcopalian Church, he was drawn compulsively to Rome. He worshipped its imperial splendors, the artifacts of the Caesars, who had mastered the technique of ruling an empire just as skillfully as he had. At the same time, he loved the grandeur of the more modern civilization that stood on the other bank of the Tiber, the magnificence of St. Peter's, the frescoed ceilings at the Vatican, the blazing galleries of art. These opulent offerings to God ignited deep feelings in Morgan. At times it seemed as though he had mastered the arduous discipline of corporate finance simply to amass enough money to possess the far grander world of art.

He bought whole eras of art. But there was one thing even his money could not purchase. Toward the end of his life he spent hours in the Sistine Chapel in the Vatican, regarding with longing and rapture Michelangelo's flaming paintings of the Last Judgment. Had these treasures not been beyond any man's capacity to own, Morgan would have seized the Sistine Chapel stone by stone and had it transported to his home. As it was, the world's great peddler of money spent his final hours in the Eternal City, dying just a few steps from where Peter, poorest of the poor, is said to have ended his career peddling for human souls.

Morgan's death in 1913 marked more than the end of an individual. It was the finish of an era. With the outbreak of the First World War, this age of elegance and leisurely living, of patrician instincts and Victorian inhibitions, of unbridled spending and somewhat repressed humanity was over.

6

BANK RUNS AND A MONEY PANIC

THE BIRTH OF THE DOW THEORY

So much for Wall Street's Great Society. Let us resume the story of the New York Stock Exchange as it entered the twentieth century. Now, as in the past, the stock market continued to project the tumult and the tensions of a fast-growing nation. As new industries arose and flowered, the market mirrored the fortunes of each with faithful detachment.

After the Civil War, as noted, the biggest rise in stock prices had been chalked up by the boom in railway building. The roads were launched in topsy-turvy fashion, and it was necessary for the bankers to move in to consolidate, amalgamate and streamline them.

Then, to bring new tidiness into other areas of the economy, the bankers developed a highly effective technique for eliminating competition and administering prices. They engineered the trust, under which they integrated entire industries vertically—from the supply of raw materials up to the final distribution of the finished product. And the stock market doted on this trend. As the steel, oil, tobacco, mining and agricultural equipment industries fell into line, they became big favorites for speculation on Wall Street; for the trusts provided powerful stock leverage, control was in the hands of a minority, and the price behavior of the stock was a simple matter of the wishes of the insiders. Prices were extremely volatile, subject to wide swings, which were the speculator's delight.

One theme that continued to dominate the economic and political scene, and influence the behavior of the stock market in particular, was the nation's currency situation. The advocates of cheap and hard money clashed incessantly, and their struggle had inevitable repercussions on the stock market. Over the years the gold question remained a highly inflammable issue, and when farmers and workingmen, together with Western Populists, who advocated cheap money, organized into a "free-silver movement," Wall Street, the leading advocate of hard money, shuddered. Stock prices fluctuated with the political fortunes of the free-silver people, who reached the climax of their crusade in the 1890s. In 1896, when William Jennings Bryan attacked hard money in his "Cross of Gold" speech at the Democratic National Convention, the stock market went into a tailspin. But the election of William McKinley later that year signaled a major victory for the gold forces, and a big bull market was launched that carried right through McKinley's second term.

Foreign events also had their counterpart in stock behavior. When war with Spain threatened in 1898, stock prices stumbled, and for six weeks after the blowing up of the battleship *Maine*, they went into a sharp decline. Then, as the news of American victories poured in, the market recovered. Admiral Dewey's triumph over the Spanish fleet at Manila gave a tremendous lift to the entire list.

This victory over Spain triggered one especially notable financial coup. Bernard Baruch, a legendary Wall Street plunger who in his later years served as an adviser to five Presidents, was spending the Fourth of July weekend with his parents and brother in Long Branch, New Jersey, when a business associate phoned and told him that he had just received a tip from a friendly news reporter that the U. S. Navy had won a major battle, sinking virtually the entire Spanish fleet. Baruch instantly recognized the portentousness of the moment. The victory meant that America's war with Spain was coming to an end. Baruch was in possession of a tip that could send the stock market skyrocketing. But he had a problem. It was Sunday evening. He was stranded on the New Jersey coast, and there were no trains running to New York that night.

The situation was incredibly tempting. The following day was the Fourth of July, and all business in America would be closed. But the London Stock Exchange would be open. Baruch knew that if he could figure out a way to get back to Wall Street that night he could cable orders to buy American stocks on the London Exchange at rock-bottom prices and make a financial killing when the New York Exchange opened twenty-four hours later and the stocks he had bought soared on publication of the battle news.

Baruch contacted some railroad people and talked them into renting him a special coach and locomotive. He, along with his brother, roared through the countryside past mile after mile of sleeping villages and farmhouses. Reaching the ferry on the New Jersey side of the Hudson River, he crossed over to Manhattan, arriving at his office at two in the morning. Fumbling in his pockets, he realized with a shock that he had forgotten to take his key along. But as luck would have it, the transom had been left open. Baruch's brother, Sailing, was blessed with narrow hips and shoulders and weighed only a hundred and fifty pounds. Baruch hoisted Sailing onto his shoulders. His brother managed to wriggle through the transom and landed on his feet inside, opening the door to a sigh of relief.

Toiling through the wee hours, Baruch sent cable after cable to London, scooping up choice American stocks for his clients and himself. Twenty-four hours later, when the New York Exchange opened, stocks exploded on the news of the U.S. naval victory, and Baruch cashed in to the hilt. He ended up a multimillionaire by bringing the talents of a meticulous researcher to the Wall Street game, scoring dazzling coups in copper, tobacco, and sulfur.

During this time when the stock market was being buffeted by economic and political events, astute students explored all aspects of stock behavior to sharpen their own trading success. In earlier days, when trading was a more primitive operation and the market was dominated by a few big plungers, most professional speculators operated chiefly on the theory that money was made on the basis of price fluctuations in individual stocks. But the more sophisticated plungers, as time went on, grasped a more realistic concept; that the really big killings were realized not on the fluctuations of individual stocks but on the basic trend of the market as a whole. The trick was to size up the main movements, to pass from price fluctuations to basic economic conditions.

And since it was the basic swing of the averages that was the key, it was not necessary, even if it were possible, to count on buying as cheaply and selling as dearly as possible, but to move into the soundest strategic position for the long range. Position was everything that counted. Many market technicians (at the turn of the century quite a cult of chartists mushroomed up who based their trading along technical lines) went on winning regularly on balance by pitching their forecasts on the intermediate ups and downs and using some highly shrewd averaging—only to be hit hard by the outbreak of a war or some other unexpected and overwhelming political or economic development that knocked their calculations into a cocked hat. But the man who saw the game as one of maintaining a proper position during both boom and panic was the man who came out in much better shape. Trying to snatch a few points here and there was a ruinous proposition. And the only way to keep a proper position was to estimate properly the economic trends that underlay the market as a whole.

One tool that was developed to enable traders to gauge more accurately basic trends was the development of market averages. The first such widely adopted averages were devised by Dow Jones & Company, the publisher of a daily financial letter which first appeared in the 1880s and which won an enthusiastic following on Wall Street. When Dow Jones decided to expand its financial letter into a newspaper—the *Wall Street Journal*—the paper made its debut in 1889— the averages were taken up by it.

The first averages to appear in the D-J market letters in 1884 were made up of eleven stocks that were considered to be the most active and representative of the list and indicative of the trend of the market as a whole. Since railroad stocks dominated trading, it is not surprising that nine out of the eleven stocks chosen for the averages were rail securities. With the expansion of American industry, spurred by the formation of the trusts—which became prime trading favorites—it was decided to construct a separate average for industrial stocks, and this appeared in 1896. Not until January, 1929, would an average for utilities be added.

The growing use of the averages since the 1880s was a clear indication that a rising number of Wall Street traders were learning to look for basic trends rather than individual price fluctuations in their market operations. But merely grasping this concept of trends was not enough. For, while it became widely assumed that the stock market acted as a barometer for forecasting future business conditions, it was mighty difficult to decide what trends in the averages were the really significant ones and which were the minor ripples. Time and again the ripples were mistaken for the tidal waves, with unhappy results for the trader.

The first systematic attempt to ferret out the significant

trends was made by Charles H. Dow, a newspaperman who started out as a reporter on the Springfield *Republican*, served for a while as a broker and floor trader on Wall Street and became co-founder of the Dow Jones & Company news service and subsequently of the *Wall Street Journal*.

In 1901 and 1902, Dow worked out a theory of trends which he discussed in an informal, undogmatic way in market letters and editorials. The theory was expatiated upon, broadened and refined by his successor, William P. Hamilton, who, as editor of the *Wall Street Journal* until 1929, wrote a series of articles on the Dow Theory for *Barron's* and a book called *The Stock Market Barometer*. Dow and Hamilton offered the theory not as a method for yielding investment tips, but for evaluating stock price averages in relation to developments in the economic cycle. It is rooted in the premise that the stock market is far more important than a place simply for making money for a trader; it serves as a barometer for major turns in the nation's economy, signaling periods of prosperity and depression.

According to Dow and Hamilton, stock prices represented the sum total of what everybody felt, knew, dreamed and feared, distilled into the "bloodless verdict" of the marketplace. And a careful study of the averages as a barometer enabled a student to anticipate how the public appraised American business even before it was consciously aware of its own analysis.

In the view of Dow and Hamilton, the stock market at any given moment reflects three movements—a major trend either upward or downward; an intermediate trend; and the day-to-day fluctuations of prices. The major trend has been compared by Dow analysts to the tide of the ocean; the intermediate trend, to the wave; the daily fluctuations to the ripple. The major trend is indicated as being a bullish one when the average of one high point exceeds that of previous high points, just as the tide of the ocean is established to be rising when the top of each wave that rolls in is higher than preceding ones, and the trough is higher than previous ones. If the tops and troughs of waves fail to exceed previous ones, then the tidal direction has turned.

After a major upward or downward trend in the market has been in operation for some time—from one to three years, according to Hamilton—secondary or intermediate movements will develop against the major trend. A downward reaction will carry a bull market temporarily lower; an intermediate rally will carry a bear market temporarily up. In contrast to the primary trend, the secondary reactions last from a few days to many weeks. These reactions carry in the opposite direction to about three-eighths of the primary movement.

To Dow's original theory Hamilton added the concept that both the rails and the industrial averages must corroborate each other before the signal for a basic change in the market has been given. In a major trend, while the two averages may vary in strength of movement, they will not vary materially in the direction they go.

Hamilton added still another concept—the phenomenon of "making a line." When stock prices fluctuated for a number of weeks within a narrow range, this indicated, he said, a period either of stock accumulation or distribution when the buying and selling were in equilibrium. When the two averages broke out of this line, rising above its high point, this was a strongly bullish indication, at least for the short term. When the two averages fell below the line, it was a strongly bearish symptom, since it was obvious that the market for stocks had reached a saturation point.

Applying his theory to the stock market from 1900 to 1921, Hamilton found that there had been six major bull and six bear markets. The bull markets had lasted almost twice as long as the bear markets; the average length of the bull was twenty-five months, compared with fifteen months for the bear.

The first bull market for the period studied began in the

WALL STREET IN THE 1890'S, LOOKING WEST FROM
SOUTH STREET.
COURTESY OF THE NEW-YORK HISTORICAL SOCIETY, NEW YORK CITY

summer of 1900, preceding the reelection of McKinley. A
temporary reaction occurred during 1901 when the Morgan-
Harriman forces engaged in a bitter struggle for control of
the Northern Pacific Railroad and cornered the stock, sending
the market tumbling. According to Hamilton, the Dow barometer projected the money panic of 1907 and the quiet,
sluggish market that prevailed in the years before World War
I. (Sluggish markets were the trickiest ones of all for the
trader, he pointed out, since they whipsawed many who tried
to predict the daily fluctuations.) The Dow barometer registered the bull market touched off by World War I that ended
in 1916 and forecast the bear market that set in during 1917,

when the outcome of the war hung in the balance and the business community took into account the grim possibility of a German victory. The barometer also projected the bear market from June to August, 1921, which occurred as the aftermath of war production.

In only one case, claimed Hamilton, did the rail and industrial averages fail to corroborate one another during a major trend—and this was the exception that proved the rule. From October, 1918, through November, 1919, the industrials moved into a major bull market and the rails went into a decline. The latter occurred, Hamilton was convinced, because the Government had taken over the railroads as a war measure and had reduced them to the status of bond holdings. With their speculative incentive eliminated, the railroads began to act like bonds and followed the same downward path as bond prices as the cost of living soared upward.

The original Dow theory, which has been given here in a simplified version, has since Hamilton's day been embroidered upon, refined, revamped and reinterpreted by an army of market traders and analysts.

Although over the years the Dow theory has been criticized, as well as defended, for its usefulness as an analytical tool for the trader, it was to prove its worth to the trader during one especially dramatic occasion—the market crash of 1929. On October 25, fifty-two days after the great bull market came to an end and the Dow-Jones averages dropped 80 points, the Dow analysts were flashed a warning signal. At the time when most observers were confident that business conditions were essentially sound and that the bottom of the market had been reached, William Hamilton, in an editorial in the *Wall Street Journal* called the "Turn of The Tide," warned of a continuing precipitous drop in prices and of a business recession ahead. The Dow signal was 80 points tardy, but it alerted its disciples to get out *before the market dropped another 150 points*—a by no means modest achievement.

Charles Dow was only one of a group of financial writers and editors who set up business near the end of the century. John Moody, a Wall Street securities analyst, hit on the idea of putting together information on corporations and industries and marketing it in bound volumes at a premium price. Clarence Barron, an editor from Boston, started a financial magazine and wound up writing his reminiscences as a reporter, providing a richly analytical insight into the big financial operators of his time. B. C. Forbes played the role of an ambitious Boswell to tycoons cast in the Johnsonian mold. Richard Wycoff started the *Magazine of Wall Street* and became a leading exponent of tape reading, running articles by leading speculators on how they had made millions through a technical analysis of market conditions.

In addition to traders who reported their exploits, there were a number of professionals who, unbeguiled by the narcissistic urge to get into print, honed their tools quietly. A classic weapon in their arsenal was short selling, which historically has been a catalyst for the most creative kind of speculation. To exercise full virtuosity in trading, the speculator has always needed freedom of movement, down as well as up the market, just as a virtuoso pianist needs it on the keyboard. For this reason, although the attitude of society has been critical of short selling, the technique has had tremendous powers of survival; indeed, thanks to its historic durability, it might not inaptly be called the third-oldest profession. As early as 1610 the Government of the Netherlands outlawed short selling on the Amsterdam Exchange after stock of the East India Company had been hammered to a frightfully low level by bear operations. In 1733, the British Parliament abolished short selling, but the law was rendered powerless by court rulings, and it was finally repealed in toto in 1860. Napoleon looked upon short sellers as traitors to the state. The German Government outlawed them in 1896. In America short sales have had a stormy legal history. In 1812 the New York State Legislature banned them, but the law was consistently violated, and in 1858, as a result of the pressure of big traders, the law was rescinded.

Professional short sellers usually have a zestfully unbiased attitude toward men and affairs. They are often men of biting humor. After all, their stock in trade is an ironic transubstantiation of values—a satiric commentary on the standards of men. One of the most successful of the tribe in the years following the Civil War, William R. Travers, was a rare wit who not only operated with surgical detachment but had a jaunty quip for every throat he cut.

One company in whose stock Travers traded was very public-relations conscious. It embarked on the practice of inviting its stockholders to look at its records and to come forward with any advice they had to offer. Travers, who was a stutterer, visited the firm's offices. "I-I-I'd like to s-s-see the b-books." The executive smiled benevolently. "Of course you have a legitimate interest in our company?" "By God, I-I sh-sh-should s-s-say so. I'm twenty thousand sh-sh-shares short of your s-stock."

Unlike many bear operators who were wiped out by an excess of dangerous living as traders, Travers managed to hold onto his money to the end. He died in Bermuda in 1887, and his humor did not desert him even at the end. A friend who visited him on his deathbed sought for something cheerful to say. "What a nice place Bermuda is for rest and a change." "Why, y-y-yes," Travers muttered. "The wai-waiters g-g-get the ch-ch-change and the ho-ho-hotel keeps the r-r-rest."

Some bear traders were merely adept at cashing in on economic adversity. Others were imaginative enough to create the conditions from which an ideal bear situation might arise. One such operator was John "Bet-a-Million" Gates, a compulsive gambler who would bet on anything at the drop of a hat. Watching two flies alight on a lump of sugar, he would offer to wager a wad of cash with dinner companions on which would be the first to fly away. He was president of the American Steel and Wire Company. One evening in the lobby of the Waldorf, which was crowded with Wall Street traders, he remarked loudly to a friend that he planned to shut down his steel mills the next day because business conditions were so poor. The following morning he closed his doors, dismissing a large number of employees. In the meantime he had gone short on his company's stock, which tumbled from the mid-60s to the 30s. Then, when he had covered his line and cleaned up, he calmly opened his mills with the announcement that business had improved unexpectedly; and for good measure, he took a further profit on the upside as the stock rebounded.

Some short sellers reaped hay especially by accurately anticipating business depressions, and during the nineteenth century these occurred with monotonous regularity. Between the end of the Civil War and the start of the First World War the nation suffered eight major business downturns. In some cases, market manipulations were a direct factor in touching off the panics. In other instances, the primary cause lay outside Wall Street, but the market aggravated the declines and was in turn affected by the momentum they generated. Richard Wycoff, a tape reading expert who made an intensive study of recessions and their influence on stock prices, found that during the nineteenth century, the market followed a remarkably consistent pattern of behavior after these panics. For about two years following a crash, prices would advance upward for a time from the low point reached during the crash, only to bounce down again to the low point before beginning a major prolonged swing upward.

One depression in particular, the panic of 1907, was notable in that it was responsible for the launching of the first comprehensive investigation by Congress into the nature of stock market trading. Since the turn of the century, Washington had become concerned about the increasing number of rank and file Americans risking their savings in the market.

The 1907 panic, which plunged the country into a depression after a decade of free-wheeling speculation, engendered in its wake a widespread feeling that stock manipulations had been a major factor in bringing on the crisis. The panic, one of the worst in Wall Street history, which forced J. P. Morgan, the banker, to play an uncharacteristically histrionic role, was essentially a monetary one.

In 1907 the world's leading financial centers were feeling the squeeze of tightening money. England was still experiencing a financial strain brought on by the Boer War. Interest rates were rising all over Europe. An earthquake had struck San Francisco, destroying millions of dollars' worth of property and causing widespread unemployment.

The crisis was touched off by a series of bank failures. These were the days before the Federal Reserve System. The nation's banking system was vulnerable since it was a helter-skelter assemblage of national banks, each autonomous of the others; true, some were confederated into local clearing house associations to provide temporary support for one another in times of crisis, but they had no means of mobilizing their resources on a nationwide basis to meet a sudden emergency wherever it arose. Moreover, while state banking laws usually prohibited banks from using their money in stock market speculation, many banks circumvented these by setting up affiliates, through which they speculated to their heart's content. This was the Achilles' heel of the system.

Matters were brought to a head in 1907 when Heinze's Mercantile National Bank, one of New York's leaders, became involved in a series of speculative stock manipulations, and when the money market grew tight, it found itself acutely short of cash. News got around town of its trouble, panicky depositors began a run on it to extricate their holdings, and it was forced to close its doors. Financial columns spread disquieting rumors about other banks. And every time a name cropped up, depositors swooped down on the bank in question; several more went under in this way.

And then one of the most prestigious of all crept into the news—the Knickerbocker Trust Company. Word spread through the grapevine that it was in difficulties. At first this seemed unbelievable. The bank was a pillar of the financial community. Its main branch was located just across from the Waldorf-Astoria; its marble halls and exquisite furnishings tabbed it as one of the showpieces of Fifth Avenue. It numbered among its depositors some of the wealthiest names in Gotham. And yet, the rumors were true. The bank was in deep trouble and needed money to pay off its obligations.

In its extremity the board of directors did a foolish thing. It scheduled a meeting to discuss how to extricate the bank from the mess in an upper room at Sherry's restaurant of all places. Sherry's was a gathering place for the most fashionable circles. It was a hotbed of rumor and malicious chitchat. No sooner had the directors assembled than word sped through the restaurant that they were upstairs discussing the Knickerbocker's financial plight. Diners by the score excused themselves from their tables and slipped up to the meeting place. The door of the room had been left open carelessly, and the eavesdroppers listened with amazement to the Knickerbocker directors as they argued about whether they should open their doors for business the next morning.

By daybreak word had swept from one corner of town to the other. Thousands of New Yorkers raced through their eggs, gulped down their coffee and hurried down to the Knickerbocker to get their money out. An hour before the bank opened, the lines wound for blocks down Fifth Avenue and the side streets. And when the tellers opened their cages for business, men and women poured into the great marble hall, rushing pell-mell for the pay counter. The tellers doled out cash, but the lines grew larger. Fifth Avenue became clogged with vehicles that rolled up, disgorging bejeweled ladies and elegant men in derbies who joined the lines of citizens waiting nervously for their cash. The spectacle drew huge crowds, who lined the sidewalks, while hotel patrons peered in fascination out of the windows of the Waldorf. The Knickerbocker catered to the cream of society, and the bank run looked like the gala opening of the New York Philharmonic's music season.

As the money grew shorter and the crowd grew larger, the tellers used every conceivable subterfuge to stall for time. They closed most of the cages, leaving only two open. They made an endless check of signatures and records, disappearing at the slightest excuse for a prolonged consultation of their files. They paid off in the smallest change, with a slow, deliberate count. Time after time a pile of coins would be knocked to the floor "accidentally" by a teller's elbow and the tedious process of counting the coins would have to begin again.

But all these dodges were fruitless. As fast as one depositor was paid off, ten more appeared, to ask for their money. Interspersed throughout the lines were youngsters who had grabbed places with the idea of selling them to depositors at fancy prices. The business was briskly competitive. One kid called out that he had a choice place for $10. Another chirped up that he would sell his for $5. A third kid, standing farther to the rear, offered his for $2. And still people came.

Within two and a half hours after the Knickerbocker had opened—in addition to the branch on Fifth Avenue it had branches in Harlem and the Bronx that were also experiencing a run—the bank had paid out over $8 million and had reached the end of its resources. At half past twelve a vice-president strode into the vestibule and announced that there would be no more payments. For a moment the crowd was stunned. Then women burst into sobbing; men shook their canes. The collapse of the Knickerbocker traumatized the city. After this, no bank was safe. The slightest chance remark was liable to touch off a run. Within four days, eight city banks and trust companies folded.

Amidst the general gloom, piquant incidents lightened the hearts of the more sardonic-minded. The collapse of the

Knickerbocker had dealt a blow to the city's leading book-makers, who had been heavy depositors with the bank. Indeed, several had made their headquarters only a few blocks from it in order to accommodate their fashionable clientele. The news of the bank's collapse reached them while they were at their favorite watering place, the Jamaica Race Track. One bookie, regaining his presence of mind quickly, offered to sell his bank balance at a 30 percent discount. A speculative-minded colleague bought it and then went around offering to buy up other accounts for 70 cents on the dollar. He was accommodated to the extent of $20,000.

Now, in its extremity, the financial community turned to its acknowledged leader—John Pierpont Morgan, who had virtually single-handedly organized the nation's banking system. The crisis was a banking one. Wall Street was faced with the collapse of a system Morgan had spent a lifetime presiding over. He was now seventy—a tired old man. And he was suffering from a severe cold. But the Government in Washington was not equipped either with the experience or the inclination to step in without help from private quarters. It had to be Morgan, and the old man assumed command.

He summoned the leading bankers and other financial kingpins of Wall Street to his palatial home on Fifth Avenue to discuss what had to be done. The others did the talking while he sat in a corner playing his favorite game, solitaire. As they debated and haggled, the old man hunched over his silver box with the two packs of cards, analyzing the financial problem in depth as he smoked one cigar after another. It was a curious setting in which to be dealing with a financial crisis—this lavish library that looked like a room out of the Medici Palace in Florence, with its red brocade walls, its gilded ceiling, its Fra Filippo Lippi saints smiling down benignly from exquisitely carved altar pieces. For hours these bankers argued over how to support the tottering banks. The air grew thick with smoke. Morgan's cold was growing worse. Exhausted by fever, he continued to play solitaire until his head dropped onto his chest and he drifted into sleep. But even now, unconscious though he was, the power of his presence was felt.

No statements were given out by Morgan or other participants in the library conferences. But the press was hungry for information. News reporters took up a twenty-four hour vigil outside the main entrance, ready to pounce on anyone entering or leaving. The pickings were lean. The news hawks were under the impression that there was only one entrance to the library. They didn't realize that there was a hidden entrance through which a stream of visitors was able to enter and depart without being seen. Time and again, a cab would stop at the house next door, which was owned by Morgan's son-in-law, Herbert Satterlee; callers would dash inside and then be escorted through an inner garden connecting the two houses and into the library by a side door. And upon leaving, they exited by an alley and were able to slip into a cab unobserved.

The crisis continued to spread, passing from the banks to the brokerage houses. With the arteries of money drying up, traders began unloading their securities to get urgently needed cash.

The morning after one of the market's worst days, Morgan became seriously ill. Ordinarily he was an early riser so that he could get down to his office to put in a long day. But this morning no one could wake him. Satterlee rushed up to his bedroom, called him, shook him. But the old man remained in a stupor. Satterlee worked over him until he opened his eyes. They were glassy, uncomprehending. Satterlee asked a few questions to determine whether he knew where he was. Morgan replied in a hoarse whisper. A doctor was summoned. Morgan was given a gargle for his throat. It was sprayed with medicines. He insisted on being helped out of bed and dressed. He sipped several cups of black coffee, picked up a cigar and the color came slowly into his face.

The old man ordered his carriage to be brought to the

front door. An hour later, at ten in the morning, a cheer rose from the crowd that had gathered in front of Morgan & Company at the corner of Wall Street and Broad as the carriage, drawn by a dark brown horse, was sighted coming down Nassau Street. It drew up to the entrance and applause rang out as Morgan, his cigar clutched between his lips, descended and made his way inside. Hopes rose. Morgan was up and about. Everything would be all right now.

When Morgan entered his office he discovered that an emergency demanded his attention. A run was under way at the Trust Company of America. The Trust was located on Wall Street, and if it went under, that could have an even more serious impact psychologically than the folding of the Knickerbocker. Oakley Thorne, the chairman of the bank, pleaded for help. Morgan had his associates go carefully over the bank's securities to determine whether they were sufficiently sound to warrant a loan. And, when his men reported favorably; he decided, "Then this is the place to stop the trouble!"

Time was growing short, the line of depositors at the Trust was growing. By one in the afternoon, Oakley Thorne reported that the bank's balance was down to $1.2 million. By half past one it had dwindled to $480,000. Thorne reported that he could not hold out until three, which was the bank's closing time.

Morgan asked Thorne to bring over his top-grade securities as collateral for a loan. Thorne scoured his vaults, stuffed his securities into bags and cartons and marched down to the Morgan office at the head of a line of assistants who carried the luggage in single file behind him. They entered Morgan's office and passed the table where the banker sat with a pencil and paper. As each security was dumped on the table, a Morgan associate read out its name on the certificate and its face worth. Morgan jotted it down. The securities were transferred to his vaults.

Morgan got several fellow bankers on the phone and asked

them to contribute to the pool of funds he was organizing. Shortly afterward, messengers emerged from his office. The first two carried a large tin box and they were followed by four others lugging suitcases crammed with money. They pushed their way through the crowds, heading for the Trust Company of America. The first installment of cash reached the tellers when the bank's balance had slipped below $200,000. As a result, the Trust was able to keep going until closing time.

This was only temporary help. The next morning the run continued in heavier strength. Twelve hundred people converged on the doors of the Trust. Inside the entrance to the building, the depositors were formed four abreast, and as they entered the inner circular rotunda, they were thinned into two lines. As each depositor was paid, he made his way across the vestibule through the double lines and was let out into the hallway through the rear door. At one time when the crowd was at its peak, several hundred people were admitted through the cellar so that the street in front of the building could be cleared.

The crowd was calm and orderly. One newsman, watching from a balcony across the street, reported that the progress of the line was best marked by observing the women. This was particularly true of one lady with red roses in her hat, "the one really bright spot in the scene." She entered the doors of the bank from the outer hall at eleven-thirty in the morning. She waited on line, moving to the other end of the hall and then winding back all the way to the teller's window. She drew her money at three in the afternoon, having waited a little over four hours.

A variety of tricks were attempted to circumvent the line. One woman unwittingly hit upon an effective approach. She appeared at the bank apparently oblivious to the news that a run was on and made known that she wanted to make a deposit. The bank guards took her by the arm as if she were a duchess and escorted her into the bank and over to the teller's cage. After making her deposit the sweet young thing decided that she had miscalculated and had put in too much cash. When she told the guard she wished to draw money, he motioned her to go to the end of the line. She looked at him in amazement and protested, "But I just made a deposit without waiting a minute!" A depositor observing the incident had an inspiration. He announced that he wanted to make a deposit too, and received permission to go into the bank. He made out a deposit slip for $10 and then quietly slipped down the line and over to the paying teller's window before anybody noticed what he was doing, and drew $9,800. Shortly afterward another man tried to work the trick but was caught and sent back.

There were other incidents to enliven proceedings. One woman stood by the teller's counter after she drew her money and, determined to keep it safe at all hazards, lifted her skirt. "It's going into her stockings," murmured several male bystanders, gallantly averting their eyes. The lady, however, pinned the yellow and green bills to her petticoat, smiled and walked out.

The crowd had other chances to chuckle. One fellow who had managed to extricate his money from the Knickerbocker just before it folded by getting into line early and standing for hours had transferred his cash to the Trust Company of America. This morning he was standing in line for a second run, highly agitated. He managed to get his money out again and he vowed to a friend he would stuff it under the mattress.

In some instances, the Trust tellers paid depositors in gold, and when some received unexpectedly heavy loads of metal, instead of compact yellowbacks, they were surprised. One elderly man made a large withdrawal; he got it in gold, which made a sizable stack. Not having time to count it, he swept it into his hat and started across to one of the writing desks. On the way, one of the coins dropped to the floor. The aged man put his hat on the desk and stood looking after the shining gold piece. The hat was heavy. He couldn't make up his mind whether to leave it unprotected and go after the gold piece or to stay with it. Fortunately, a policeman resolved the conflict by picking up the piece and bringing it to the old man.

Not all people were as fortunate in getting out their money. One middle-aged lady appeared late with a younger woman, evidently her daughter, and took a place at the end of the line. At three in the afternoon they had reached within a hundred feet of the entrance to the building when the announcement was made that the bank was closing for the day but would be open tomorrow for business. The next day the woman and her daughter showed up at four in the morning. They brought along a campstool, which they shared. The mother sat holding her bankbook in her lap while the daughter carried a package of lunch. At three in the afternoon, reporters observed the daughter still sitting on the campstool about ten feet away from the teller's window. The mother stood anxiously, fourth in line from the window. Then suddenly came the announcement: "Closing. We'll open ten o'clock tomorrow morning, gentlemen." As the line broke up, the mother stood still. The daughter picked up the campstool and took hold of her hand. "I don't believe I could stand it another day," the older woman whispered as she moved away in a daze.

The next day the Trust Company opened for business again; huge crowds converged on it, and the Morgan syndicate continued to pour in money. This bank and the Lincoln Trust had been selected for the major support effort.

But the banks were not the only ones affected. The crisis was worsening on other fronts. With money being transferred by the public into safety vaults, the stock market was reeling from the squeeze. Stocks, led by the coppers, were plummeting, and the ability of brokers to pay their obligations became increasingly doubtful. Many gilt-edged securities that had been locked up in strongboxes for years were now being dumped by their owners on the market. There was a deluge of odd-lot selling, indicating that large numbers of small traders were being hard hit.

Matters reached a crisis on October 24. That afternoon, from one until two-thirty, there was virtually no call money at all available at the loan post on the floor. At one o'clock the president of the Exchange, Ransom H. Thomas (an apt first name under the circumstances,) paid Morgan a visit, informing him that cash for transactions was no longer available. Normally, accounts for the day's trading would be settled within an hour, by two-thirty. Unless more money was forthcoming, Thomas told Morgan, the Exchange would be forced to close.

This was bad news. The closing of the market, occurring on the heels of the bank failures, would be psychologically disastrous. Morgan summoned the leading bankers of the Street to his office. He told them they would have to raise a minimum of $25 million in the next fifteen minutes to meet the needs of the Exchange, or fifty broker houses would be pushed to the wall. He pounded the table, waved his cigar. The bankers scurried off and came back with $27 million, not in fifteen minutes but in five. When the word arrived on the floor of the Exchange, a roar went up.

The breach had not been decisively plugged, however. Again, Thomas came to Morgan for money, and the syndicate drummed up another $10 million. All told, $40 million would be sent over to the Exchange before the crisis was over. Morgan was concerned about rumors that professional bears, taking advantage of the situation, were hammering stocks down with heavy short selling. The copper stocks especially were taking a terrible pounding.

His suspicions were further aroused when he received word that James Keene, the celebrated operator of pools, wanted to talk to him. He suspected that Keene, hearing about the meetings that were taking place in the library and curious to know what Morgan's chances of stabilizing the situation were, was trying to pick up information to use as a basis for his own speculation. Morgan asked his son-in-law, Satterlee, to receive Keene and stall him.

To prevent Keene's being seen going into the Morgan home by reporters who might draw misleading conclusions, Satterlee called on the trader at his hotel and took him for a leisurely walk, engaging him in chitchat. He steered Keene over to his own residence, away from the picket line of reporters. Putting a phone call through to the library, he turned to Keene and regretfully told him that Morgan had left the house without leaving word where he had gone. Satterlee sat for three hours with Keene, regaling him with stories and listening sympathetically to Keene's reminiscences about his career. Then, when he thought he heard the sound of Morgan returning home next door, he dutifully put in another phone call. Again he informed Keene apologetically that the banker had once again slipped out and no one knew when he would be back. Keene was successfully stalled off by Satterlee and never did get a clue to Morgan's plans.

In the meantime, the runs continued at the Lincoln Trust and the Trust Company of America. Ministers, priests and rabbis spoke from the pulpit to try to calm the people. A depositor brought before a city magistrate for creating a disturbance was told that if he promised to keep his money in the bank, the charges of disturbing the peace would be dismissed.

To help allay the panic, Oscar Hammerstein, the Broadway impresario, who had $100,000 on deposit with Lincoln Trust, phoned the directors and said he was willing to send over $50,000 more if it were needed. He was told to send it immediately. Thomas F. McAvoy, the leader of Tammany Hall, made a brief brave show of confidence but then he buckled up. He appeared at the doors of the Trust Company of America and loudly assured friends in the crowd that he had every faith in the bank and wouldn't dream of withdrawing his money from it. As the day wore on he was seized with cold feet and got into line.

The Trust Company of America and the Lincoln continued to keep their doors open; the public showed up in droves;

and messengers from the House of Morgan kept arriving with bags and wooden boxes crammed with gold, silver and paper money.

When the banks closed their doors that first weekend of the crisis—on Saturday noon, October 26—people refused to go home. Many of them prepared to spend the weekend in front of the entrance rather than give up their places in line. The weather was miserable, and depositors shivered as the rain drove down. By Sunday night there were 118 people in front of the Lincoln Trust. Although most carried umbrellas, this didn't prevent them from being soaked to the skin.

Reporters interviewed a man who was first in line at the Trust Company of America. He told them he was Burnett Milburn, an agent for a building contractor. He was a man in his fifties and had a withdrawal check for $500 pinned in his inside coat pocket. He had been waiting in line since Friday. He had orders to stay there until he got his money. For three nights he had slept curled up in a corner of the vestibule, rolled in a red and black blanket. The money was needed to pay off immigrant laborers, he told reporters. His boss didn't dare to go home until he had the money. "He is afraid they will kill him because they do not understand this," Milburn said. A late arrival came up to Milburn and asked whether he would take $100 for his place in the line. "I would not take $495 for it," replied Milburn. "I have waited so long now that a few hours more don't matter much. I used to be a night watchman, anyhow, and can sleep comfortably in my blanket."

The rain kept driving down. Some in the line slept in chairs they had brought along. One man dozed off wrapped in a big storm coat with his felt hat pulled low over his face. He had slept this way Saturday night also—in his chair, behind one of the stone pillars to the right of the entrance. Before he drifted off, he told a friend, "I have smoked so much I am getting nervous and can't sleep as well as I should."

The panic lasted three weeks before it was decisively halted. Before he was through, Morgan had to save not only the trusts but one key broker, Schley and Company, from going under, by undertaking a complex bit of financing that involved the purchase of the financially overextended Tennessee Coal & Iron Corporation, in which Schley was heavily committed, by the U.S. Steel Corporation. While the Morgan syndicate succeeded in shoring up the trusts and the stock market, the Secretary of the Treasury, George Cortelyou, poured over $250 million of Government loans into the banking system to keep houses the nation over from being threatened with runs.

It was a massive joint effort. And yet there was no question that only Morgan could have successfully led the fight on behalf of the private sector. He alone was able to rally strong-minded people with such divergent interests as Harriman, Rockefeller and Stillman into a team to see the trusts through.

During these weeks of crisis, Morgan was an awesome landmark as he walked to and from his office on his errands to shore up the economy. People instinctively made way for the old man when they saw him barreling down on them, a half-smoked cigar between his teeth, his head lowered and his gaze fixed obsessively ahead. Those who were too absorbed in their own business to move aside for him, he elbowed away without looking up or breaking his stride. Morgan rumbled along the Street as though he were the one person in the world intent upon carrying out history's sole mission.

Nights, when the day's work was done, Morgan retired to his library for sessions lasting into the early morning. As others heatedly debated matters he sat playing solitaire, turning over one solution after another in his mind as he placed his cards into orderly piles before him. When he glanced up he could look into the door of his vault, where his rare manuscripts and his illuminated editions on vellum and precious bindings were stored, or his eye could linger affectionately on a ruby China vase nearby, dating from the K'ang Hsi period, an Etruscan bronze from pre-Roman days, or the Hans Memling paintings that were permeated with the spirit of medieval life.

There he sat, an autocrat, tough, unyielding. On one occasion when some banker friends raised objections to putting up any more money to stem the runs on the trusts, Morgan locked the front door of his library and put the key in his pocket to make certain none of them would leave until they had signed the agreement. Then, while they bickered among themselves, he retired to a cubbyhole and sat playing cards, periodically summoning a particularly recalcitrant banker to prod him into a more receptive attitude. At a quarter to five in the morning, the resistance of the bankers was broken and they queued up to sign. Morgan waved them out the front door. To one of his associates who had played a stellar role in the negotiations he offered congratulations and added, "You look tired. Go home and get a good night's rest—but be back here at nine o'clock sharp!"

With the panic finally stemmed, Morgan emerged more than ever the lion of the Street. However, the crisis had lasting repercussions that led to fundamental changes in the nation's economic structure, eventually putting an end to the kind of one-man rule Morgan exemplified.

For all his masterfulness Morgan would have failed but for the support given him by Secretary of the Treasury Cortelyou, who supplemented the Morgan pool's support of the trusts with Government loans to the banks. It was obvious that the nation's banks needed a continuing substructure of Federal support—in short, an organized Federal reserve system that would be geared to supply funds when any individual bank became overstrained. And in 1913, the year of Morgan's death, the Wilson Administration finally established this Federal Reserve System.

Moreover, the 1907 panic touched off two Government investigations of the stock market. In recent years, the public had become increasingly critical of a stock exchange unreg-

JOHN PIERPONT MORGAN, SR., WHO HALTED THE PANIC
OF 1907.
PHOTOGRAPH BY PACH
COURTESY OF THE NEW-YORK HISTORICAL SOCIETY, NEW YORK CITY

ulated by the Government, manipulated at the whim of insiders and capable of causing business depressions and mass unemployment.

President Theodore Roosevelt had been expressing the discontent of a growing number of Americans with his attacks on the business trusts and this tack was taken by a group of polemical-minded journalists—Ida Tarbell, Lincoln Steffens, Ray Stannard Baker—who explored with acid pens the financial, political and moral fabric of American society. So critical was their approach, they earned the label "Muckrakers" (referring to a character in Bunyan's *Pilgrim's Progress*). They dissected the history of great fortunes and corporations; delved into railroad and insurance scandals; analyzed political bossism, the relationship of big city police with the underworld and the links of corporations with judges and legislators. They spiced their revelations with a wealth of colorful anecdotes that exuded an atmosphere of behind-the-scenes authoritativeness, continually hammering away at the allegedly corrupt influence of American finance. As Vernon Parrington, the social historian, put it, theirs was "a dramatic discovery . . . when the corruption of American politics was laid on the threshold of business—like a bastard on the doorstep of the father—a tremendous disturbance resulted. There was a great fluttering and clamor amongst the bats and the owls. . . ."

The Muckrakers wrote their articles originally for *McClure's Magazine*, which, thanks to its role as a kind of Peeping Tom gazette for the American intelligentsia, skyrocketed in circulation in six years to 750,000—the largest readership garnered by an American magazine up to that time.

In short, Wall Street was becoming a bête noire in many quarters. The time was ripe for a political move against it. In 1909, New York's Governor Charles Evans Hughes named a commission to look into the abuses of the nation's investment banking system. But no regulatory laws came from it. Then, in the winter of 1912–13 a Congressional Committee headed by Arséne Pujo of Louisiana got even bigger headlines by embarking on an investigation of its own.

Inevitably, J. P. Morgan was summoned to appear as the number one witness to tell what he knew about the inside workings of investment banking. Morgan hated the idea of running the gauntlet of newsmen and photographers, going through what he considered to be a public relations folderol concocted by Senators gunning for headlines. He came to Washington flanked by seven lawyers. The night before the hearing, filled with gloom, he shut himself up in his hotel room, scowling over a game of cards.

The next morning he entered a committee room that was packed to the rafters. The crowds waiting to snatch a glimpse of the Old Man extended down the street and around the corner. The committee counsel sat surrounded with formidable piles of records.

Morgan took his seat and the grilling began. He was taken through a complex of questions designed to indicate that the power of Morgan and his associates rested primarily upon the fact that they were the providers of the nation's lifeline of credit and that they extended this credit only to a favored few—men who already had great wealth behind them.

Morgan retorted that he extended credit solely on the basis of his belief in a man, not on his financial assets. He insisted that a man once came into his office and received a check for a million dollars although Morgan knew that he had virtually nothing in the bank.

The committee counsel, Samuel Untermyer, raised his eyebrow. Wasn't bank credit always based upon property and financial assets?

"No, sir," insisted Morgan, "the first thing is character."

"Before money or property?"

"Before money or anything else. Money cannot buy it."

The committee counsel was annoyed. He wasn't prepared for a defense along the lines of "character." He was ready for any kind of legal sophistry, but not the answer given out by this Bible-reading banker who stoutly insisted that a money changer could be one hundred percent Christian. Time and again, Samuel Untermyer tried to lure Morgan into conceding that money was lent solely on financial connections. But Morgan insisted that a man he did not trust, even if he had "all the bonds in Christendom," could not get a loan from him.

Counsel snapped back, "That is not the way money is loaned on the Stock Exchange."

"This is the way *I* loan it," retorted the old man.

The next day the press, both in America and abroad, headlined, not the sensational disclosures of shabby dealings that had been expected to come out of the hearings, but Morgan's statement. "Morgan says character is the basis of credit."

Once again, the Old Man, who shuddered at the thought of phrase-making for journalists, had turned the tables with an expression that made the headlines. Nevertheless, despite Morgan's belief in the virtue of his calling, it seemed obvious to many that there were imperfections in the system that needed serious cleaning up. And the Pujo Committee came up with several recommendations. It suggested that the stock exchanges be incorporated and that the issuance of securities to the public be supervised by the Federal Government; that margin requirements be made more stringent; that all forms of stock manipulation be more effectively prohibited; and that companies coming to the public for funds be required to make a complete public disclosure of their financial situation.

Financial circles debated these proposals; the membership of the NYSE was split in sentiment. The older members stoutly resisted the attempt to change their trading procedures. But a group of younger men came out for the Pujo recommendations. These insurgents gained a victory over the Old Guard in 1913 when they succeeded in electing as president of the Exchange one of their group, James Mabon.

However, before any steps could be taken to reform trading practices, the First World War broke out. It was unexpected. The summer of 1914 had begun like many another summer. The weather was unusually hot and Americans flocked to the beaches, gobbled up more than their usual quota of Eskimo pies and sat sweating in their shirtsleeves on their porches, catching a few whiffs of cool air from electric fans. In thousands of parlors families cranked up Victrolas and listened to Enrico Caruso singing "Vesti la giubba." The tango was sweeping the country, replacing the dancing of Irene and Vernon Castle in the affections of youth. On the screens of the nation, Pearl White was titillating movie-goers in the *Perils of Pauline*, and Mary Pickford was emoting as "America's Sweetheart."

That July, the newspapers reported that the divorce rate in New York County was increasing alarmingly and that the per capita consumption of alcoholic drinks had jumped by nearly three gallons in the last ten years. (The bill for drinking had climbed $100 million in the last year alone.) On the other hand, Americans learned that a determined nationwide campaign to turn the Fourth of July into a safe, sane weekend was finally bearing fruit; only fifteen people had died in this year's celebration compared with forty-one six years ago. Thanks to the cooperation of most manufacturers in restricting the sale of giant firecrackers, and promoting "harmless contrivances that exploded paper by force of air," the Fourth of July was rapidly "losing its teeth" as the terror of parents and fire insurance companies. That July also Paris dressmakers issued a report to the press blasting American women who "insist on having freakish clothes that will attract attention and sacrifice beauty." A court action was started over whether a Broadway play called *Apartment 12-K* was or was not plagiarized from another play called *Twin Beds*. And sports fans learned that in Baltimore Babe Ruth, a kid pitcher who had been raised in an orphan asylum, was racking up new records with the Orioles.

The war came as a surprise not only to the man in the street but caught some of the top officials of the New York Stock Exchange off guard. Just a few days before the outbreak, the president of the Big Board divulged in a speech that his chief concern was with the growing scantiness of women's undergarments, which was cutting the yearly consumption of cotton fabrics by at least six yards of finished goods for each adult female.

However, there were some alert observers who for weeks had been glimpsing an ominous pattern of events. Overseas commerce had slowed down, and bankers were refusing to accept bills of lading as collateral. Heavy liquidation by Europeans of their holdings, coupled with an absence of buying support, was sending prices sliding on the European exchanges. By the final week of July the selling had become so serious that Vienna, Brussels and Budapest closed their markets. Before the end of the month every exchange on the Continent had been shut down. And with overseas investors turning their securities into gold at an accelerating rate, stocks on the New York Exchange joined the tumble. On the last day of July, a report was flashed announcing that the London Exchange had closed down for the first time in its history— it had remained open even during the Napoleonic Wars. On this news New York prices slid 20 points.

At the close of trading, an emergency meeting was held in the offices of J. P. Morgan & Company, where Big Board officials and bankers argued for hours whether to keep the Exchange open. The decision was at first affirmative. But several brokers with heavy overseas connections showed the Board of Governors a huge batch of selling orders that had just arrived from abroad. These brokers estimated that over two and one half billion dollars' worth of American stocks were held overseas, and that a massive unloading of these securities would cause havoc.

The Exchange officials took another vote and decided to close down indefinitely. The ticker flashed the announcement that for the first time since 1873 the gong would not be sounded the next day to open trading on the floor. (In 1873, the failure of Jay Cooke & Company, the fund-raisers for the

Civil War bond drives had brought on a temporary collapse of the nation's banking system.) Other exchanges followed the Big Board's lead, and trading came to a virtual standstill throughout the country.

But the urge to speculate is indestructible. Gradually, brokers not under the supervision of the Big Board commenced exchanging quotations among themselves and a so-called "gutter market" sprang up in August on New Street. But prices quoted there were far below the closing prices on the final day of the Big Board, and they continued to decline as other gutter markets mushroomed up.

Finally, in September, Big Board officials decided to open again to discourage these spurious transactions, and trading recommenced under severe restrictions. Prices for all actively traded stocks were fixed by the Board of Governors at a little below the prices that had prevailed on closing day, and no opening trades were permitted below these figures. The scheme to trade under such restrictions did not work out very well. The market stagnated until trading was resumed in April, 1915, on a completely normal basis. By this time attrition was setting in on war equipment. The Western allies had started placing huge orders for U.S. supplies. Steel, chemical and shipping stocks—the so-called "war brides"—took off for unprecedented heights.

The war was to change profoundly the economy of the United States and its financial role in the world, and along with this, the role of Wall Street. From its origins up to the time the conflict broke out, America was a debtor nation. In 1895, when U.S. gold reserves under President Cleveland fell to seriously low levels, one of the dangers aggravating the situation was that American gold was being drained off by European markets, which were paying a more attractive interest rate. A Morgan-Belmont syndicate offered to provide gold to help the Government through the crisis, and also undertook through its extensive European contacts to keep the gold Uncle Sam had from leaving the country. During the money panic of 1907 an important measure of help was a $30 million gold importation from London, which Morgan again wangled through his British connections.

However, the World War was to end decisively America's dependence on Europe's financial centers. Faced with huge expenditures for armaments, the Western Allies turned to Washington for loans. Not only were they compelled to sell most of the securities they held here to get money to buy American goods, but the Allies deposited much of their gold in America for safety's sake. By 1916 almost two billion dollars' worth of European gold had found its way into American vaults. With this as security Uncle Sam made heavy shipments of war equipment to the Allies. The House of Morgan, which had close connections with British bankers, was designated by the British Government to be its purchasing agent in the United States and the French followed suit.

By war's end, America had changed from debtor into the world's leading creditor nation, and Wall Street had replaced London as the leading financial center. Not only had Uncle Sam become banker to the world, but the nature of the American investment market was changing significantly. In 1917, to broaden the means of financing its allies and its own war effort, the Government launched a series of Liberty Loan drives, promoted from coast to coast by celebrities of the sports, entertainment and business worlds. Over twenty million Americans bought the bonds and for the first time were introduced to the heady business of investing. Until this time, market investors, while steadily increasing in numbers, had been confined on the whole to a relatively small segment of the population, those who were well off and who had money left over from their daily needs to invest. But the war bond drives conditioned a market of millions to enter Wall Street and play the game of stocks when the war was over.

These bond drives—there were five in all—had another important effect. They enormously increased America's national debt. In the short space of time during which America participated in the war, the debt climbed from a little over $1 billion to over $26 billion—the hugest rate of debt expansion this nation had ever undergone.

In short, when the war ended, the structure of America's economy had been transformed, with significant implications. The U.S. had turned into the world's banker. It had raised the ceiling of national debt to unprecedented proportions. And it had indoctrinated millions of grass-roots citizens into the habit of buying securities.

At the same time, the public's attitude toward Wall Street, which had reached a peak of hostility during the 1907 crisis, was undergoing an about-face. In the American folk mythology, the ogres of the Street were becoming heroes again.

When America entered the war, Bernard Baruch, one of the most publicized speculators, who had made over $400,000 selling short on hints that peace might break out and end the boom in war stocks, was given the accolade of respectability by being appointed by President Wilson to head the nation's industrial mobilization program.

The winnings of Baruch and other big traders whetted the appetite of the public to try its luck in the market. In their search for free expression, Americans put a typical twist on the Bill of Rights; they flamboyantly exercised their right to strike it rich.

This growing zeal for buying stocks induced the Big Board into undertaking a major enlargening of its physical quarters. The building it had moved into and occupied since 1903 was extensively remodeled, and it has remained essentially unchanged to the present.

Increased business on the nation's second-largest exchange also brought about changes. The American Stock Exchange had homely origins. It had started up in the nineteenth century on the curbstone on Wall Street—hence its nickname, the Curb. Its business was conducted with helter-skelter informality. At one period the gong was sounded by banging on swill buckets. The younger, frolicsome delivery boys and runners played leapfrog, jumped into manholes, and raised hell when the mood seized them. The important traders had assistants perched on the windowsills of high buildings next to telephones. Upon receiving a customer's order, the clerk transmitted it to the trader below with an ear-splitting shout. Or, if the noise in the street were too great, he would send it through a system of hand signals as elaborate as those concocted by pitchers and catchers on the baseball field. To make themselves stand out clearly, the clerks wore highly colorful clothes. They lived dangerously, frequently tumbling into the gutter in their zeal to transmit an order. The traders plied their business on the cobblestones in all kinds of weather. During the most severe snowstorms they were open for business, rubbing their freezing hands as the snow piled high, taking swigs of whiskey to keep their spirits hearty. Fistfights broke out regularly. Members whipped up by liquor picked quarrels with passersby, turning over merchandise carted by delivery carriages through the street.

However, with the war at an end and America ensconced as banker to the world, the Curb became more respectable in its habits. In 1921, over the vigorous opposition of some of its more rambunctious members, it moved into a building off Broadway behind Trinity Church. The move into unfamiliarly warm quarters caught many of the "open air" boys short, and caused an outbreak of colds among men who had never so much as coughed in the freezing cold. For the next thirty years the Exchange continued to refer to itself as the Curb, as if it were still conducting its business on the cobblestones. Not until 1953 did it change its name to the American Stock Exchange.

In short, the old order had changed. The America that the House of Morgan had dominated was gone. For better or for worse, the nation was to be faced with new problems, new dangers and opportunities and was to assume responsibilities of serious new proportions.

7

THE BULLS SEE RED

THE BOMBING OF WALL STREET, A MYSTERY AND MADNESS

To understand the stock market of the 1920s, the runaway boom and the crash that followed, it is necessary to understand the times in which it existed and the psychology of the people who played in the financial sweepstakes.

The Twenties was an era of affluence—not quite the equal of its big brother of the Fifties and the Sixties, but no less smug and carnal. It was the era of the jazz baby, the raccoon coat and bathtub gin; an age when Hollywood turned out celluloid fantasies, as one movie advertised itself, of "Brilliant men, beautiful jazz babies, champagne buffs, midnight revels, petting parties in the purple dawn, all ending in one terrific smashing climax that makes you gasp."

America had entered the age of the flapper; up and up went ladies' skirts, in spite of the wailing of textile manufacturers. The boyish body became the beau ideal of American womanhood. Milady's dresses became so shockingly scant that some business pundits warned that the textile industry was threatened with a serious depression. New empires arose on the ashes of the old. Making women beautiful became a big-time industry. Beauty shops mushroomed up in every American town, and the lusty new science of plastic surgery was enlisted in the battle against old age. It was an era of high rouge, flat breasts and chain smoking of cigarettes by women. Warner Fabian wrote a novel called *Flaming Youth*, and the phrase entered the national lingo.

It was an age when over thirty million thirsty citizens thumbed their noses at the Prohibition laws, and the underworld entered the lucrative trade of providing ample supplies of "red eye" to "wet the whistle." Private yachts, modified into rum-runners, carried the whiskey in from the Bahamas, dueling with hijackers and running the blockade of revenue cutters with the free-wheeling audacity of old-time buccaneers along the Spanish Main. It was an age when women left their jobs as seamstresses or hostesses of coffee shops and entered the bootleg racket as "whisper sisters," renting respectable quarters as a façade for speakeasies, driving sporty convertibles loaded with smuggled moonshine across the border from Canada and taking their kids along as a cover-up to deceive the prying.

In this age of dyed-in-the-wool materialism, even speculative excursions into the mystical had a curiously physical tinge. A striking example was the belief in spiritualism that mushroomed up in the 1920s. The conviction that the dead continued to exist in another world and were trying to communicate with their loved ones caught on like wildfire. The emotional climate was ripe for it. Many Americans, grieving over the loss of sons in World War I, wanted desperately to believe in an afterlife. And mediums who claimed to possess the psychic ability to communicate with the spirits of dear departed ones reaped fortunes holding séances. Mina Crandon, one leading psychic from Boston, who conjured up the prints of "spirit fingers," caused tables to be lifted by invisible hands and messages to be written when everyone present

had his arms bound behind him, developed such a rabid following that a group of Harvard psychologists was persuaded
to undertake a lengthy investigation to determine whether
there was any basis for her insistence that she was in touch
with the dead. In June, 1923, William H. Burr, the president
of the New York State Assembly of Spiritualists, delivered an
address in which he called for the abolition of capital punishment, declaring that he had been in communication with
the ghosts of executed murderers who had reported to him
that they had endured so much physical suffering in the electric chair he was compelled in all good conscience to bring
their experience to the attention of the public.

The craze for Ouija boards, which reportedly could be
used to "receive" spirit messages, reached such proportions
among high-strung Americans that in the little village of Car-
rito, across San Francisco Bay, five people were driven insane.
The New York *Times* reported in April, 1922, that John Cor-
nym of San Francisco shot and killed two of his sons, one
seven and one eight, because he had been in communication,
he said, with his dead wife, who asked him to send their
children to her. A Barnard College student fell in love with
a spirit and committed suicide to join him in the other world.
And, when a law was introduced into the New York State
Assembly to ban spiritualistic séances, it couldn't muster enough
votes to pass.

A favorite service of quack mediums was to have the deceased wife or husband "materialize" in front of the surviving
partner. During one séance, a friend of Houdini, the magician,
was told by the medium that his wife was about to appear.
He asked permission to kiss her. "She must have forgotten to
shave," he recalled later to friends, for he had felt the stubble
of a beard.

By the mid-Twenties, America was going through a hon-
eymoon of burgeoning prosperity. Industry had produced
two technical miracles that permeated every facet of life, the
radio and the automobile. During the 1920s the buying power

of the workingman increased at a rate of almost 3 percent annually. Millions had the necessary $250 in cash to buy America's first mass-produced auto—the Model-T Ford. But even Henry Ford did not understand the insatiability of American ambition. He built his cars in a single price range. General Motors, which started out as a poor relation to Ford in sales, took over the leadership of the industry before the decade was over by recognizing that inherent in the American ego-drive was the need to trade up in the quest for higher and higher status. Millions of American workers, once they had bought their Model-T, were not content with trading it in for another one, but yearned for the higher-priced Chevrolet. When the American got more affluent, he traded this in for a still higher-priced Pontiac and so on. General Motors, by merchandising its popular car at a price a little higher than the Ford and providing a hierarchy of models for subsequent trade-ups, took away the thunder from poor old Henry Ford, who labored under the illusion that all the consumer really wanted was a car to take him somewhere. But, then, Ford was a mechanic; he knew nothing about Freud.

The success of General Motors was a litmus for the psychology of Americans in the 1920s. A man who was not content with keeping a Model-T all his life was a man who moved into the stock market in the hope of making more money than he could possibly earn from wages. Many felt that the market was a place where one could make millions for nothing.

Americans have been called a nation of cynics by some unkind social critics. But this is a patent libel. There were millions of ardent believers in America; millions who believed with an evangelical fervor that the purchase of Lux toilet soap would transform a homely woman into one with a charismatic personality; that paying $4.98 for a mail-order book would turn an amiable mediocrity into a masterful executive adept at winning friends and influencing people; that it was possible to achieve wisdom and worldly success by mailing a 15-cent coupon to Box XYZ. It was not at all difficult to persuade a man who believed there wasn't "a cough in a carload" of cigarettes, as a celebrated tobacco firm advertised, that a stock that had paid no dividends and hadn't increased its earnings in ten years was a much more attractive buy at 100 than it had been at 50.

As a result of this attitude, the efforts of Big Board reformers to abolish illegal manipulations left wide room for the trader who was astute enough to tickle the greed of the susceptible. Stock analysts and market-letter writers kept telling Americans that the market was bound to go up indefinitely. And who could doubt this? There were many free thinkers, particularly among the intelligentsia, who scoffed at the traditional worship of God but very few doubted the religion of bull stocks.

Indeed, the American business boom became a most convincing theology not only for laymen but for many of the frocked. So imbued were some theologians with the glory of American salesmanship that they nearly burst their gaiters with ardent advocacy. In New York City, the Swedish Immanuel Congregational Church launched a fund-raising drive by promising everyone who contributed that God would certainly not forget him; He would lay aside for each in His kingdom "an engraved certificate of investment in preferred capital stock." Business success had been raised to a national mystique. Pep talks for salesmen began with spiritual services conducted by bishops, priests and rabbis before the canvassers stormed forth to sell their vacuum cleaners and encyclopedias. Bruce Barton, an advertising executive, wrote a book, *The Man Nobody Knows*, arguing that Christianity was nothing more than successfully applied business techniques. And it hit the top of the best-seller lists. Insurance salesmen were told to study the Bible and use the methods employed by Saint Paul in converting the heathen to Christianity to convert their prospects to a policy.

An indication of the desire of Americans to play the capitalist game for all its worth was the rise in volume of trading on the New York Stock Exchange. Americans turned en masse to Wall Street, pored over stock price tables, learned the nomenclature of trading operations. By 1925 the volume of daily trading had broken the record of three million shares which had been set at the turn of the century.

But there were some in this age of affluence who were in open or furtive rebellion against the blessings of capitalist largesse. Some of the alienated belonged to extremist groups—the I.W.W., the Anarchist party, the followers of Emma Goldman and the Bolshevik party line. To them, the American profit system was a tool for exploitation, and Wall Street was the epitome of all that was evil.

In October, 1917, the Bolsheviks had stormed the Winter Palace and taken over power in Russia. Shots fired in the revolution were heard around the world. Everywhere, militant Marxists manned the ramparts or mounted the soapbox to warn of the approaching day when the worldwide proletariat would destroy the capitalist system. When the Red flag was run up on the Winter Palace, the radical labor movements around the world reacted sharply to this shot of political adrenalin.

The Bolsheviks and I.W.W. fringe Reds in America were no less busy than their foreign brethren preparing for the new order. In April, 1919, the mayor of Seattle, who had made vigorous stump appearances around the nation, warning of the Communist danger, was sent a bomb through the mails as a reminder that Big Brother was watching. Luckily, the infernal machine, tiny enough to be wrapped in a box but powerful enough to blow out the side of the State Capitol, was discovered and defused before it reduced His Honor to fragments. But the Comrades were by no means discouraged. The following day they mailed a bomb to Senator Thomas Hardwick, a Southerner and chairman of the Senate Immigration Committee, who had been vociferous in urging that Russian Bolsheviks be kept out of the United States. When the Senator's maid opened the package, the bomb exploded and tore off her hands.

The next morning, Charles Caplan, a clerk in the New York Post Office, was riding home in the subway when he unfolded his newspaper and saw the headlines about the bomb that had been mailed to Senator Hardwick. As he read how the midget bomb had been wrapped in a package of coarse brown paper six inches long, something triggered his memory. He had seen packages exactly like that—*indeed that very day*. He rushed out of the train at the next stop and took another downtown to the Post Office. When he arrived, he rushed over to a shelf where he had placed sixteen brown packages. Each was marked with the return address of Gimbels, the New York department store. One was addressed to Justice Holmes of the Supreme Court; another to A. Mitchell Palmer, the Attorney General; a third to the Secretary of Labor; a fourth to the Commissioner of Immigration; a fifth to the Postmaster General. The remainder were addressed to J. P. Morgan, John D. Rockefeller and other top figures in the financial community.

Caplan had not mailed the packages but had put them away on the shelf because of an irregularity he had discovered. Each package had been sealed with red wafers, indicating that it was to be mailed first class, but the postage on them was sufficient only for parcel post delivery. Detectives were summoned; they took the packages into a nearby firehouse and began the dangerous job of disassembling them. They found inside each wrapping a tiny wooden cylinder with a little glass vial set with mercury percussion caps. The sixteen packages were defused harmlessly.

But the jaunty Comrades refused to abandon their efforts. Thwarted by the mails, they adopted other means of delivery. Several weeks later bombs exploded in eight major cities. The most celebrated target was Attorney General Palmer. He lived in a house in Washington, on R Street, Northwest, just across the street from the stylish young Assistant Secretary of the Navy Franklin D. Roosevelt. A little after eleven o'clock on the evening of June 2, the Attorney General, who had taken home a pile of work for afterdinner study, put away his papers, turned off the lights in his library and climbed upstairs to bed. Suddenly the house shook from the impact of an explosion; the whole front was blown away. Two passersby were reduced to fragments. The Attorney General and his family were extremely fortunate to have escaped unharmed. And Franklin D. Roosevelt, who had just returned from a party and stepped out of his car across the street, was also lucky to have escaped being hit by flying fragments.

The bombing scandalized an already anxious nation. But the most gruesome episode was yet to come. As much as the radical fringe detested Washington officialdom, it reserved its maximum efforts for Wall Street, the epitome of capitalist finance. It was inevitable that the Street would receive a love letter from the Comrades.

Wall Street is always a busy place during working hours, and the numerous clerks, errand boys and messengers speeding about their tasks are usually too absorbed to notice what is going on around them.

It was this way just before noon on September 16, 1920. No one paid any attention to a rusty brown wagon, pulled by a dark horse, which plodded into Wall Street and came to a halt in front of the doors of J. P. Morgan & Company, just across from the Subtreasury Building. The driver stepped out of the wagon and slipped into the crowd. The lunch hour had just begun and the normal traffic was swelled by stenographers and clerks pouring out of offices to grab an early bite.

Suddenly there was a shattering sound. The wagon exploded with a blinding flash, sending forth waves of eerie green lights. The foundations of buildings for several blocks around rattled and shuddered as a rainfall of shrapnel poured down, streaked with sulfurous smoke. Thirty-three people were killed and over two hundred injured. The interiors of the Morgan offices were wrecked. The boss himself was abroad, but the chief clerk was killed and seventeen other workers had to be rushed to the hospital. Fragments of iron blasted through the windows of the Bankers Club in the Equitable Building, narrowly missing the occupants. The explosion shook the New York Stock Exchange, smashing its windows. Occupants on the east, or Broad Street, side luckily escaped injury, since the windows were shielded with heavy brocaded curtains, which, since they were drawn together, softened the impact. However, the trading floor was thrown into panic. The largest crowd had been gathered around the Reading Railroad post and it fled, fearful that the dome would fall. The president rang the gong and suspended trading for the day.

Outside on the street the scene was grim. A messenger boy for one of the broker offices lay with his head severed from his shoulders; and a packet of stocks was burned to cinders in his fist. A stenographer had been hurled against a water hydrant and she lay as limp and lifeless as a rag doll, her face expressing stunned wonder. A few yards away a man tried to raise himself but he fell back on his knees, moaning as he crept a few feet, the blood pouring from his mouth like a spigot. But oddly enough, in the midst of this carnage, the statue of George Washington that stood on the stairs leading to the Subtreasury Building, just a few yards from where the bomb had exploded, remained untouched.

Detectives moved in and searched for clues to the bombing. They began with the remains of what once had been the horse that had pulled the brown wagon. The carcass had been blown to pieces; nothing was left but bits of its harness, together with fragments of steel and wood and canvas from the wagon. It seemed obvious that the bomb had been delivered in the wagon and that it had gone off from the interior shortly after the driver jumped from it. Laboratory technologists of the police department, calling in expert veterinarians and wagon makers, managed to reconstruct what the horse and wagon had looked like.

A manhunt for the driver was launched. The horse's iron shoes had been found in the wreckage and three hundred blacksmith stables were checked, all the way from Boston to Chicago, in an effort to find the smithy who had made them. He was tracked down; he turned out to be Dominick De Gracia, who ran a smithy in Manhattan and who informed detectives that a man driving a horse and wagon had called on him to make a pair of shoes for his horse. These matched the shoes found in Wall Street. De Gracia reported that his customer was an Italian, probably a Sicilian, judging from his accent. He was in his twenties, smallish in build, weighed about 160 pounds, had raven black hair and a bristling little moustache.

In the meantime other evidence was uncovered. A Manhattan street cleaner came forward, revealing that he had been sweeping a street several blocks away when the explosion occurred and had been knocked to the ground by an iron ball. He had kept it and he showed it to the police, who concluded it was the knob from a portable safe that had apparently been standing in the wagon when the explosion took place. A number was engraved on the knob, identifying its manufacturer. Detectives traced the sales records from the original purchaser through various secondhand buyers. It had been used in an Army barracks before World War I and had been taken by a regiment to France, where it had been shipped to headquarters on various battlefronts and after the war returned to Hoboken, New Jersey. At this point the trail was lost and further search turned up nothing.

Leads were checked on other fronts. A mail carrier reported that at almost the moment the bomb went off he found, pinned to a mailbox just a few blocks from Wall Street, sheets of paper on which a message was printed: "Remember we will not tolerate any longer—free the political prisoners or it will be sure death to all of you—American Anarchist Fighters." For weeks the search went on.

At one stage in the investigation, a tennis player well

known to readers of the sports pages, Edwin P. Fisher, became involved. It was learned that several days before the explosion Fisher had mailed postcards from Toronto to several friends, prophesying that a catastrophe would take place on Wall Street at noon on September 16 (which turned out to be the date of the explosion) and warning his friends to stay away from the place. Fisher was arrested and during rigorous questioning claimed that he had received a warning of the tragedy from "visions in the air" and that the spirits had ordered him to send out his postcards. Fisher was sent to the psychopathic ward of Bellevue Hospital and dropped from the case as a crank. That was the last lead of any sort. Nothing more has been turned up to this day. It remains a matter of speculation whether the explosion was planned by one man or a group of men.

Coming on the heels of the other bombings, this latest episode thoroughly aroused the nation. Politicians and newspaper editors cried out for vengeance. Fumed the Minneapolis *Tribune*, "Right or wrong, the first feeling of most people is that it represents the work of radicals." Exploded the Indianapolis *News*, "Those who have any respect for the human race will prefer to believe as long as they can that the explosion was accidental.... Yet we know that there are men in this country—and all countries—who are prepared to commit wholesale murder, if by so doing they can dispose of a few 'enemies' or as they think further their cause. There is therefore nothing improbable in the theory that the ... murders were the work of the Reds." Declared the Denver *Rocky Mountain News*, "A nationwide, a world-wide, dynamiting conspiracy exists to wreck government and society and the Wall Street horror was part of this conspiracy." The *Literary Digest*, however, found a bright spot amidst the gloom. The fact that the statue of George Washington, father of his country, was left unharmed by a bomb that exploded only a few feet away from the Subtreasury Building was a strong indication, reported the *Digest*, that a benevolent destiny had intervened. Other papers also looked upon this as an excellent omen. The New York *Evening Sun* was certain that in former times this would have been regarded by the people as a miracle, a sign of intervention by Heaven itself. The Indianapolis *Star* drew a further moral from the tragedy: "It used to be that even New Yorkers looked to the wild west for danger and adventure but with daily holdups and robberies, automobile slaughter of the innocent and now dynamite explosions, the perils of life in the Metropolis far outdo anything the west ever knew."

The rash of bombings, culminating in the Wall Street crime, was a major factor in unleashing a vigorous reaction against left-wing circles in America. Attorney General Palmer launched a Red hunt, rounding up hundreds of known Communists, sympathizers, union leaders and anyone else labeled "un-American." Scores were thrown into jail; Russian-born suspects were deported. The net was flung far and wide to haul in the merely suspicious as well as the guilty. Right-wing groups all over the nation followed Palmer's lead. Movies and books by suspected writers were banned by neighborhood watchdog committees. Schoolteachers were investigated for their political leanings. A handful of Socialist members of the New York State Assembly were expelled on the charge they were part of a "disloyal organization composed exclusively of perpetual traitors." The next day the New York *Times* announced that the Assembly's action was "an American vote altogether, a patriotic and conservative vote."

Attorney General Palmer's methods had spectacular results. Old-fashioned liberals fell over one another in their zeal to be accepted as one-hundred-percent Americans. Teachers, editors and preachers dropped their subscriptions to left-wing magazines, afraid of being seen with them by prying neighbors. Top officials of the American labor movement strove assiduously to appear as capitalistic as John D. Rockefeller.

But eventually the Red scare subsided. It became apparent that the Communists were unable to manage their affairs in

Russia competently, let alone take over the rest of the world. Moreover, as incomes grew and prosperity spread over the United States, many old-time Socialists became more interested in getting a slice of the capitalist pie than in throwing it into the garbage can. Bohemian writers and folk singers moved from Greenwich Village to Hollywood to sun themselves beside swimming pools and spout Marxist theories between cocktails. And everyone turned to the stock market to indulge in the number one sport of speculation.

8
THE BIG SWINGERS

THE FABULOUS RISE OF GENERAL MOTORS— HOW TO MAKE MILLIONS SELLING AMERICA SHORT

Wall Street has been a rich laboratory for the study of that most whimsical creature on earth—man—in his most vulnerable mood—the search for quick, easy money. Historically, bull after bull has plunged into the market on the assumption that it would somehow defy the laws of gravity and go up and up with only minor reactions, simply because the mass of bull traders wanted it to. People forget that the market throughout its history has been a two-way street. It has been subject, like everything else on this planet, to the pull of gravity. It has steadfastly followed the law that everything that goes up must come down; and the further up it goes, the harder is the fall.

And so it was in the 1920s. True, in an effort to protect the grass-roots trader, the Big Board in the early 1920s instituted new measures of surveillance. It established a policing committee to halt stock-rigging practices by its members.

It formulated stricter requirements for stock listing; and in 1922 it adopted a resolution demanding the right to examine the books of member firms. Finally, it amended the rules which had allowed brokers to bid for round-lot stocks without having to accept less if they were offered less. The power of a trader to select what he wanted to purchase and reject other offers at the same price had greatly facilitated stock market riggings in the days of Keene and Harriman and Vanderbilt.

But the efforts of reformers to curb the more extreme practices of manipulators still left plenty of room for sharp stock operators to thrive in.

While the Eastern banking fraternity played an important role in pool operations that stoked the stock market boom of the 1920s, leading to the crash, a great deal of the momentum was generated by people not traditionally identified with Wall Street. Indeed, since World War I the nation's investment power had become diffused, spreading from the banking houses of the East to business centers in the Middle and Far West.

After the death of Pierpont Morgan no single man was ever again to dominate the nation's investment affairs and keep them so tightly in his grip. That business fell into the hands of a number of contesting parties, none of whom possessed Morgan's ability to maintain an iron rule of stability. For one thing, the financing needs of American corporations in the 1920s were vastly heavier than before the war, and this meant that investment bankers could no longer supply the needs or assume the risks single-handedly. The financing had to be done by a network of syndicates acting together; and many of these operated outside Wall Street. True, the House of Morgan, headed by Pierpont's son, Jack, still led the field in the volume of underwritings, but Jack, while competent, had none of his father's genius. He was a leader among his peers, not a prophet towering above his disciples.

A great deal of the impetus for the market of the 1920s

was generated by an entirely new breed fresh from the Midwest—from the lustily growing auto industry in Detroit, the wheat pits of Chicago—who took over much of the action from the Eastern investment bankers, who had historically dominated the market. The men who called the power plays—Billy Durant, the seven Fisher brothers, John Jacob Raskob—had all been involved in the ruthless business of promoting a dramatic offspring of America's miraculous technology—the automobile. In the rough-and-tumble competitive atmosphere spawned by the rapidly growing giant, they had developed an aggressiveness, combined with a flair for public relations, an excess of ambition and the guts to gamble for heavy stakes. And they were to put on a display of trading fireworks that would never be surpassed.

Their market operations were huge. Billy Durant, the prime mover of the group from 1924 through the spring of 1929, headed a syndicate of over twenty multimillionaires who plunged an estimated $3 to $4 billion into stocks of their choice, bulling them up to inordinate heights and luring in millions of Americans in their wake. This $4 billion investment fund may well have been until then the largest block of money to be devoted to stock manipulations by a single syndicate or interrelated group of traders.

To understand the power of these financiers and the influence they were able to exert on the trading of millions of Americans in the Nineteen Twenties, it is necessary to turn aside and delve into an exploration of their careers before they came to Wall Street.

Billy Durant, the leader of the bull consortium, was a man who was larger than life. Physically a bantam-sized individual who bounced along when he walked, with a mass of white hair that sprouted up from his head like a faintly disreputable halo, William Crapo Durant was drunk with the gamble of America, obsessed with its highest article of faith—that the man who played for the steepest stakes deserved the biggest winnings. He was an individual with no formal education but blessed with a poet's imagination and a persuasive tongue. He was a genius of a merchandiser, and this talent for selling sparked the pyrotechnics of his career. The grandson of H. H. Crapo, the Civil War Governor of Michigan, Durant was born in Boston and spent his boyhood in Flint, Michigan. He was a laborer, a grocery boy, a drugstore salesman, a traveling medicine man, an insurance promoter and the manager of a tobacco shop—all before he was thirty. Like Ibsen's Peer Gynt, he was a liar in the largesse of his fantasies, but he had one blessed gift—unquenchable hope.

In 1886, chafing at the drabness of selling cigars for a living, Durant scraped together $2,000 from friends and bought into a carriage factory. The horse and buggy was the basic form of transportation in those days, and within four years Durant built his business into one of the world's largest carriage makers, with over a dozen plants, strung across the United States and Canada, producing more than 150,000 vehicles a year. One day he was told about an odd-ball inventor who was tinkering around with a new kind of carriage—a horseless one—and Durant rushed over to meet him. The "screwball," David Buick, was experimenting with a piston engine. He had not yet developed the body to encase it. But Durant's imagination was ignited.

He was convinced that the automobile was bound to replace the horse and carriage and that this was the business for him to get into.

By 1903 the time seemed ripe for entry. Durant bought control of a shabby old firm, the Flint Wagonworks, which was on the verge of bankruptcy, and he renamed it the Buick Motor Company. There were by now over a hundred small firms tinkering with versions of automobiles to supply a select market of luxury buyers. Durant planned to take over as many companies as would be necessary to win control of the infant industry. He had notions of becoming the world's biggest auto maker. He had studied the success of the industrial trusts—sugar, steel, oil and rubber—and he envisaged a giant auto trust patterned along the same lines. Using Buick as the king piece of his projected empire, Durant snapped up Cadillac, Oakland, and Olds; then he added a slew of body-making facilities and parts-making plants. And he incorporated all of this into a single organization which he called General Motors. One important auto maker remained outside the fold—Henry Ford, a mechanic who had gone into the building of his own cars and was the last remaining obstacle to Durant's ambitions.

One morning in 1909, while Durant was sitting at his desk going through his mail, an assistant came in and reported that a Mr. Couzens was outside and wanted to see him. James Couzens, later to become a Senator from Michigan, was the minority partner in the Ford Motor Company. Durant was curious to discover what had brought him to his office.

"Show Mr. Couzens in."

The tall, lean Couzens entered and without any preliminaries declared:

"Mr. Ford would like to offer you the Ford Motor Company."

Durant was astonished. He had heard that Ford was struggling with debts. The money market was tight and loans were hard to get. Still, Durant had no idea that matters had reached this point.

"How much does Ford want?"

"Eight million dollars."

"Where's Henry? Why didn't he come over himself?"

"Henry is suffering from stomach pains. He's in terrible agony, unable to get any relief in bed. I left him lying on the floor on a pillow."

Since Ford's chronic gastritis was as well known to the trade as his Model-T, the picture of the eminent mechanic stretched out on the floor of his hotel did not unduly surprise Durant. Scarcely believing his good fortune, he plunged into negotiations with Ford and Couzens. A series of conferences were held at the Belmont Hotel, where they were staying. Initially, Ford demanded that the $8 million be paid in cash immediately, but Durant persuaded him to take $2 million as a cash down payment and the rest to be paid over a couple of years.

Durant was prematurely optimistic. Imbued with enthusiasm over the potential of the automobile, he was elated at the chance to buy out Ford for a paltry $8 million. But he failed to reckon with the unimaginativeness of his bankers. They told him they were not at all sure that the auto industry was here to stay and that $8 million was too much to gamble on Ford. So Durant failed in 1909 to get his hands on the Ford Motor Company. Twenty years later nobody could have bought Ford for a hundred times that price. The banking brotherhood had pulled an historic boner.

No sooner had Durant shrugged off this rebuff than he was handed a second one. The banks that had been extending credit for a General Motors' expansion program suddenly pulled in their horns. This was 1910. Money was dangerously tight. Durant had borne the burden of expansion of the fledgling company by carrying the credit in his own name, signing personal notes to obtain working capital. He needed over $10 million to continue in business, but his resources were exhausted. The banks agreed to make the loan but in return they took an absolute voting trust of the common stock. With this lever, they pried Durant out of the control of General Motors.

But Durant's buoyancy was unimpaired. Thrown out of the company he had founded and built into a thriving adolescent, he looked around for other ventures to develop from scratch. Previously he had come across an inventor, Louis Chevrolet, who had designed a low-priced lightweight car. Seizing upon this as the ideal vehicle to compete with the Ford Model-T, Durant now scraped together $100,000, and, within a year of stepping out of General Motors, organized the Chevrolet Company. Launched on a shoestring, the auto maker made a million dollars in profits within the first twenty-four months of production, and Durant now launched one of the most astounding coups on record.

General Motors had recently been listed on the Big Board as a publicly owned company. Out of the booming earnings of Chevrolet, Durant quietly began buying up General Motors' voting trust certificates in the open market. Chevrolet had become a lusty baby, and Durant aimed for nothing less than to have the baby swallow up the father. On September 13, 1915, he recapitalized his Chevrolet Company at $20 million and increased this within several months to $80 million. Then, suddenly, he made a tender offer to General Motors' stockholders to exchange five shares of the Chevrolet Company for one of GM. Durant had developed so widespread a reputation as a shrewd moneymaker that a large number of GM shareholders decided to cast their lot with him, snapping up his offer. When the General Motors board of directors—the banking group that had driven him out—met in September, 1915, Durant walked into the room and calmly announced that he held enough GM stock to take over control, and he demanded that a special meeting be called immediately. Actually he was premature. A count disclosed that he and the banking group were stalemated in their holdings; each held 80,000 shares. The balance of power was in the hands of another group. Ironically, several years previously, Durant, while head of General Motors, had induced his friend John Jacob Raskob, the financial adviser of Pierre DuPont, to invest in GM stock, persuading him that GM's future was extremely bright. Raskob, in turn, convinced his boss to go in with him, and these were the shares, held by his friends and now voted in his behalf, that tipped the scales for Durant and enabled him to walk back into the control of General Motors.

Durant's enthusiasm for the auto industry had not been dimmed one whit by his heartaches with GM. He continued to bubble over with plans for the future. Fewer than 400,000 automobiles were being sold annually to the American public. They were crudely built cars designed for wealthy hobbyists. They were strictly a sporting toy. No autoist knew when he started out whether the engine would conk out before the trip was over. However, Durant was convinced the auto would become the number one means of mass transportation. As early as 1912 he was present at a gathering of auto makers who exchanged guesses on what the next year's production would be. Each man dropped a slip of paper with his forecast into a derby hat. That year output had risen to an eye-popping 378,000 cars. Durant estimated that in 1913 a half million cars would be made. The others were skeptical. People wouldn't buy that many cars, they insisted. And even if they wanted to, the industry didn't have the facilities to produce that many. But Durant warned his colleagues not to sell the purchasing power of the American people short.

"Gentlemen, I look forward to the time we'll make and sell one million cars a year," he declared.

Durant remained incurably visionary. He had put money into David Buick's invention when it had been nothing more than an engine perched in an improvised body. He just couldn't resist calling on inventors. Once, two friends asked him to save their father from a business venture that was costing him more money than he could afford. The father had a firm called the Guardian Frigerator Company, which was backing a fellow who was trying to make electric refrigerators in small units for household use. At this time the only known way of keeping food fresh at home was in an icebox.

Durant's imagination took fire. He rushed to Detroit, where the inventor, Van Russell, was working, scampered up two flights to a loft which had been converted into a factory. One look at the paraphernalia Van Russell was struggling with convinced Durant that he was witnessing the birth of the greatest thing, next to the automobile, that could be put on the market. He moved the inventor and his equipment to a small brick factory run by his Cadillac Company in Detroit. "Produce for me the best electric icebox you can make," he told Van Russell. Then he launched a prize contest to find a name for the product. The moment he received the suggestion "Frigidaire" he knew he had a winner. The other GM

WILLIAM C. DURANT, AUTO MOGUL AND WALL STREET
PLUNGER, ENTERING HIS CAR.
COURTESY OF THE BETTMANN ARCHIVE, INC.

executives were skeptical; they felt that Durant was going off
half-cocked in his enthusiasm. Durant told them that the day
would come when the "Frigidaire" division alone would earn
enough to make them all wealthy.

In 1920, five years after regaining control of General Motors, Durant was tripped up once more by trouble. At the
conclusion of World War I, GM had launched a major program
of expansion. But the timing was disastrous. The country had
tumbled into a postwar recession. Money had become tight.
The auto industry found itself short of capital. The Ford Motor
Company narrowly missed going under, as Henry Ford fran-

tically went from bank to bank, pleading for $38 million in order to meet his debts.

Caught in the middle of the heavy expansion program, and rebuffed by the banks for loans, Durant turned to the stock market for help. He decided to offer $64 million of common stock for underwriting. GM stock was selling in the market for $38.50. An English-Canadian banking group volunteered to pick up $36 million of the issue at $20 a share. But this left $28 million still to be disposed of. A serious complication developed when several of the major shareholders of GM, disgusted with the firm's badly timed expansion program, now threatened to unload their holdings. Prices of GM stock had already fallen, together with other stocks, in a steadily declining market. Durant was afraid that large selling by these shareholders might collapse the stock. He personally owned $105 million worth of stock. He was convinced that, recession or not, the company would continue to grow; that the future for automobiles was virtually limitless. Moreover, he was a speculator who had played the market heavily for years. He was as anxious to protect the value of his personal holdings as he was concerned with the fortunes of General Motors.

He now decided, without consulting the other members of the board of directors, or his bankers, to take the risk of trying to hold up GM stock (and his own equity in it) by engaging in personal market operations. As large blocks of GM stock were offered for sale, Durant, together with friends who rallied to his support, purchased them privately. To raise money for the maneuvers, Durant offered his own personally endorsed notes. Despite this, GM stock continued to drop, from its original $38.50 to $32.30 and down to $28. To raise the $64 million for GM's working capital, Durant, as noted, had agreed to let an English-Canadian banking group buy $36 million worth of stock at 20. This still left $28 million to be disposed of. Wall Street investment houses offered to underwrite this block—but under severe conditions. They insisted on having as a bonus the right to purchase 200,000 additional shares at $10 a share. The market price at the time was just under 30.

Durant objected bitterly but, faced with the refusal of the Wall Streeters to underwrite the block, he gave in. News that a syndicate was being offered GM stock at 10 leaked out to the financial community, and on July 27, 1920, 100,000 shares of GM were suddenly dumped on the market. The price broke to 20½. To salvage something for his friends who had put in their money to support him so loyally, Durant moved in to buy everything that was unloaded, even as the price continued to tumble. Stock came into the market below 20½; he bought it; then when it was dumped at a still lower price, he picked that up too. Alone, unsupported, groggy from the beating he was taking, he bought the stock as it slid down to 12¾ a share. Finally, the odds became too steep even for him. His cash resources were wiped out. In a few months he had changed from a man worth some $100 million to one owing over $20 million.

In the meantime the tumble of GM stock became top news in Wall Street. Until the very last moment, Durant's associates at General Motors had no inkling of the scope of his personal involvement in the stock maneuverings. But he was now compelled to disclose the facts. He had been operating heavily on margin and he was in debt to 21 broker houses and three banks for over $20 million. The situation was critical. If he went into bankruptcy, the brokers and the banks might well go under with him. Moreover, the future of General Motors itself was at issue.

The other big GM stockholders, notably the DuPont-Raskob group, decided Durant must go. They could not very well allow the destiny of the corporation to be tied to the troubles of a single individual, even if he happened to be the founder of the firm. The DuPonts arranged with the House of Morgan to step in and assume Durant's personal debts with his banks and brokers, in return for which Durant would hand over the control of the company to the DuPont group. Durant had no alternative but to accept the terms. DuPont personally loaned him $500,000 to clean up his private affairs. It was estimated that Durant, with the GM shares he was allowed to keep, would emerge from the debacle with about $3 million of his original $100 million. However, Durant later disclosed, "There were many things I had forgotten and so when I really cleaned up and protected everybody else, I had nothing left."

He resigned from the presidency of the company he had organized on November 30, 1920. He had surrendered the control of a firm that within his lifetime would be worth over $1 billion. A few months previously he himself had been worth $100 million in paper profits. Now he was heavily in debt. He was sixty and calmly philosophical about the vagaries of fortune. Once he had said, "Money is only loaned to a man; he comes into the world with nothing and he leaves with nothing."

Now Durant returned to an old obsessive passion—the stock market—determined to make a comeback on Wall Street. When he was eased out of GM, there were rumors he had been given an option on a large block of stock. He probably knew more about GM stock than any other man in America. And he was determined to put his knowledge to good use. He was determined to devote his ingenuity to bringing the market price of the stock to a level at which his option price to buy would be a rank bargain.

So this supersalesman turned to a new career as a manipulator of the great bull market between 1924 and 1929. His headquarters was an office in mid-Manhattan whose windows remained sealed in all kinds of weather, for one of Durant's idiosyncracies was a fear of open spaces. None of his employees dared to open a window in his presence. He had his lunch wheeled into him, for he refused to interrupt his market trading to go out to a restaurant. When the trading day was over, he'd relax for a bit over a game of checkers. But his mind would be far ahead of the next move on the board; it would be submerged in tactical preparations for the next day's trading session.

So much for Durant. Several other key speculators were to play a big role in influencing the psychology of the American investment public. Important members of the consortium were the seven Fisher brothers, who, like Durant, had cut their eyeteeth in the bruising auto industry. The children of a blacksmith, each had begun work at a laborer's bench. Fred, the oldest, graduated to a draftsman's chair in a Detroit carriage factory, toiling in the same plant where the young mechanic Henry Ford had been given space to play around with an idea for an auto.

Like Ford and Durant, Fred Fisher foresaw the day when factories turning out horse-driven vehicles would be obsolete. In 1908, five years after he had entered the carriage business, Fred, his brother Charles, and an uncle raised money and launched their own firm in the infant automobile field— the Fisher Body Company, capitalized at $50,000. As each of Fred's other brothers came of age he took them into the business.

At the time Fred Fisher went into the field, autos were being turned out only in open models; motorists perched themselves on seats that rose like the hump of a camel and wore goggles to keep out the dust. Fisher decided to turn out closed car bodies, but the other auto makers scoffed. No sane motorist would ever risk his life riding in cars that were closed up and paneled with glass, they declared. In case of an accident, people would be trapped as if in a tomb—and with all that glass flying! Motoring was a risky business. Only a few years previously, President Theodore Roosevelt had taken his first ride in an auto, and an awed newspaper editor had remarked that this venturing into an auto exhibited a "display of courage . . . typical" of the old soldier of San Juan Hill.

But Fred Fisher insisted on making a closed auto. And he

found a way not only of engineering a workable body, but of mass-producing it cheaply from interchangeable parts. In so doing, he took the future by the horns. The closed car caught on like wildfire, and the Fisher Body Company burgeoned into one of America's biggest corporations. By the end of the First World War, it had over forty plants in a dozen cities, employing almost fifty thousand workers. It owned forests and timber mills; the National Plate Glass Co., its subsidiary, turned out twenty million square feet of glass annually. By 1922, Fisher was producing nearly 500,000 auto bodies a year.

In the meantime, General Motors, bent on a program of integrating its operations and already buying its bodies from Fisher, approached the brothers with an offer to buy them out. (In 1919 it had acquired a majority interest in the firm. In 1926 it acquired the remainder. The total buy-out offer reportedly amounted to about $200 million.) The price was one of the largest ever tendered by a company for its supplier. At such a price, the seven grandsons of an Ohio blacksmith couldn't afford to quibble. They sold out. From then on their major problem was what to do with their money.

Inevitably, as a calf turns to milk, the brothers turned to Wall Street. They organized an investment company and looked around for profitable situations. The news reached the press and excited much comment. Seven country boys had moved into Wall Street with $200 million in their jeans to teach their city cousins, the Eastern investment bankers, a lesson. The Fishers modestly referred to themselves as amateurs in investment matters, but with that kind of cash they were bound to make their weight felt. The situation positively intrigued Americans. Everyone knew of the fabulous success of the Fisher Body Company. The newspapers had been filled to overflowing with the details of the sale to General Motors.

And sure enough, the impact of their market plunging soon began to be felt. The Fishers purchased Texas Corporation, and the stock climbed 25 points. They moved into Richfield Oil and it shot up 30 points. They began accumulating IT&T and it soared over 200 points on a split in shares. They popped up on the boards of directors of one company after another; and their well-publicized market coups kept the financial press in an uproar.

Americans followed the news avidly and plunged into stocks favored by the brothers, hoping that the Fisher luck would rub off on them. Any boys who could squeeze $200 million out of General Motors couldn't be wrong in anything they did, people figured, and it was smart to follow them.

So the Fisher boys came to Wall Street and joined forces with Billy Durant and his consortium to play a major role in the big bull market that was launched in 1924.

And there was still another trader we must consider— one who also came out of the Midwest to join the Durant syndicate in its market operations. He was Arthur W. Cutten, a mild man with rimless glasses who looked like a high school teacher of biology and who had taken millions out of the Chicago grain pits. In one bold maneuver Cutten had reportedly made $10 million cornering the market for wheat, in the course of which he succeeded in purchasing more of the grain than, probably, any other human being had garnered since the legendary holdings of Joseph in Egypt.

Cutten brought to Wall Street the reputation of being the most successful commodities trader since the American grain pits first began keeping records, and, along with this, a cunning and single-minded audacity that impressed even the other virtuoso plungers in Billy Durant's stable. The swings in the commodity market were quicker and sharper than in the stock market; the trader had less margin to work on; he had to make his decisions more quickly and he stood in much greater danger of being wiped out by a single blunder. But if the punishment for a wrong guess was greater than in stock trading, so too was the chance for a bigger killing.

Cutten had started after his first million from the humblest beginnings. A Canadian, he arrived as a youth in Chicago in 1890, on a bicycle, with $90 in his pockets, and he took a position with A. S. White, grain traders, after a stint as a salesclerk. His job was to make out foreign invoices, translating American dollars into sums in sterling and other world currencies. Each day when trading commenced, he had to be on the floor to get the opening prices and cable them to European branches of his firm. Through White and Company he became exposed to the intricacies of pit trading. And the way the big speculators carried on their business enthralled him.

Grain prices inched up and down an eighth of a cent at a time, and on each fractional move millions of dollars could be made or lost. The shrewdest brains were pitted against one another in a gigantic game compounded of skill, experience and bluff. The very hand signals the traders employed to motion to one another on the floor were extraordinarily picturesque. Traders didn't bother to repeat the full price of the commodity when they wished to buy or sell. That would have been a waste of time, and speed was essential. When a trader wanted to buy, he placed the palms of his hands in front of his face. If he desired to sell, he put his palms out. To show the price of wheat or corn at any instant, he signaled the fraction that revealed on which side of the price he stood—three-fourths, or seven-eighths of a cent, and so on. There were other quaint gestures. When a trader gave a sell signal and then flexed his arm and slapped his biceps, this meant the selling was being done by Armour and Company, the nation's largest commodity dealer. A signal for buying, together with a finger pressed to the eye, would refer to the operations of a well-known Asian trader. A finger pressed to the mouth would refer to a trader who was a celebrated tobacco chewer.

All deals were closed without the scratch of a pen. Millions of dollars were committed without anything more than the informal signaling of a buyer and a seller. And there was no welching on a commitment even if the market crashed—or went through the sky.

Armour was the powerhouse among traders. Its dealings in commodities were so huge that they seriously affected the price of the market, and whenever Armour representatives appeared on the floor, other traders watched closely, trying to forecast whether the giant company was going to go long or short on a grain. To get a tip on Armour's intentions could mean a fortune for a smaller trader following its lead. When an Armour man stepped into the pit and whispered to an associate, astute traders standing fifty feet away read his lips. If an Armour agent wrote out instructions, there were brokers standing across the floor who watched the movement of the pencil across the pad and could tell exactly what he was writing. The smaller traders had other tricks for carrying out their operations. In his visits to the pit, Arthur Cutten observed a fellow named Arthur Binks, who used to sit in the gallery and was extremely fidgety. It wasn't until after several years of watching Binks that Cutten tumbled to the truth that each time he fidgeted about in his chair it was a signal for a confederate broker standing in the pit to buy 200,000 bushels of wheat.

It was a rough-and-tumble school young Arthur Cutten was exposed to, and he learned fast. While still in his twenties, he had become a broker and he not only bought and sold for his firm but "scalped"—that is, traded on his own behalf. Within five years he had made so much money on his own that he was able to quit the firm and trade entirely for himself.

The most successful commodity plungers were severe taskmasters in matters of research. It would have been suicidal to play by the pit of one's stomach. One had to study the size of crops, worldwide planting figures, the condition of shipping routes, the supply of vessels one could count on to successfully ship his grain, and so forth.

Cutten became a most thorough student. On the floor of the Exchange several traders kept bottles containing green-colored bugs and blades of wheat. Cutten learned to watch the behavior of the bugs carefully. Whenever they sucked the sap of the blades of the young and tender wheat in the bottle, he would rush into the pit to buy more wheat. The bug was a plant louse called the grain aphis. In years of normal weather this louse was held effectively in check from destroying the wheat in the bottle—and in the fields—by a tiny black wasp-shaped insect which deposited its eggs in the bodies of the green bugs, where they hatched out to feed on the bugs and destroy them. It was a pretty slender margin of the universe in which human beings live, but for other creatures—the plant louse, for instance—Cutten observed, the margin was even narrower. The wasplike insects which were so vital for the protection of the wheat crop, thanks to their living off the destructive lice, were active in their role of savior only when the weather was above 56 degrees Fahrenheit (at least 10 degrees warmer than the climate in which the green bugs breeded freely). Below this temperature they were ineffective; the plant louse bred and spread and was able to do its damage with impunity; and the wheat crop was doomed. In this life-and-death struggle, entomologists had discovered, lay the key to the sudden disastrous outbreaks of destruction in the wheat fields. Cutten studied the bottles with fascination. They were his talisman, the means to vast opportunities. Whenever he observed the green bugs destroying the green plant in the bottle, he knew that there would be a shortage of wheat in the fields and that this was the moment to buy.

In the summer of 1924, Cutten made a spectacular killing that landed his name prominently in the newspapers. Each night he was in the habit of going home with a copy of the weather map that had been issued that morning by the Chicago Weather Bureau of the Department of Agriculture. It was in these maps, during the growing months from April to September, that he usually glimpsed the first hint of developments that led him to take a position long or short in the market. In the spring of 1924, analyzing his maps, he arrived at the conclusion that there would be a corn shortage. He had learned to look on corn as behaving like a tropical plant, and he was convinced that heavy rainfall and frost were in the offing which would keep the corn from maturing on schedule. He commenced buying May corn contracts when corn was 40 cents a bushel. As the price climbed, he sold and exchanged them for July contracts. By the middle of July his corn had reached $1.10, and he took $1.5 million out of the pit.

The way ahead was not always strewn with roses. On one occasion, Cutten bulled up the price of wheat, accumulating three million bushels for May delivery. In so doing he caught in a squeeze J. Ogden Armour, head of the Chicago packing house, who had gone heavily short. A short situation in commodities is analogous to one in stocks. Cutten's title to three million bushels held for delivery was a virtual corner. All the grain elevators which could lawfully be used for delivery hadn't half that amount to ship to Cutten. However, Armour was a man with vast political connections and he brought pressure on the Chicago Board of Trade to spring him from the trap. While only the wheat deposited in public elevators was considered valid for delivery, Armour prevailed upon the Board to change the rule so that wheat held in freight cars and private graneries would be considered legal as well. Cutten opposed the change in rules vigorously but fruitlessly. Armour rushed in wheat by the carload at the final moment, delivering it to Cutten and covering himself. Under this flood of deliveries, the price of wheat broke 30 cents a bushel, and Cutten took a drubbing. But he did not turn a hair. A man who dealt in millions was as likely to spring back as quickly as he had been kicked down. In 1925, he cornered the wheat market again, buying grain at $1.32 and selling it at $2.00. Once more he had foreseen a shortage when everyone else judged there would be a surplus. The transaction netted him over $10 million.

It was a hazardous game and it required a rare breed of man to survive in it. Many people had brains and experience and were possessed of a vast knowledge of agricultural crops.

Those with lesser ambition went to work as clerks in the offices of commodity brokers or got into Government service or into the agricultural departments of universities. But to become a successful speculator required more than knowledge or experience or even ordinary courage. It required the stomach to stake everything on one's judgment, not through a desire merely for financial gain, but because of an all-consuming passion for the risk itself.

To the end of his career, Cutten remained a lone wolf trader. He had no employees. He took no one into his confidence. Until 1913, when Congress passed the first Federal income tax law, he kept no books on his transactions. His only records were the ledger sheets bearing his name in the various brokerage houses where he cleared his trades. For, as the volume of his trading accelerated, he no longer felt safe trading in only one brokerage house, since this would mean completely revealing his position to a single institution. There were too many small-salaried clerks who were prone to gossip, he felt, and this could constitute a serious risk to a speculator who might happen to be in an overextended position.

In the early Twenties the Federal Government, under a new Agricultural Act, began a systematic supervision of grain trading. Until then Uncle Sam had not scrutinized trading accounts, but now that he insisted on eyeing the records, Cutten lost his enthusiasm for trading. No one could do anything when the Government was looking over his shoulder, he grumbled. Information that he had never allowed anyone to share with him—the size of his market position, for instance—would now be the common knowledge of Government clerks. Cutten was convinced that the risks of speculating under such conditions no longer made the game worthwhile. And so he left the pits. That same year, 1925, was the last that Federal income tax lists were open for public inspection. They disclosed that Cutten was the largest taxpayer in the Chicago area, paying over $400,000 in taxes on his 1924 profits alone. That was the last time the public was permitted to look into his financial affairs.

When he left the pits, the Chicago Board of Trade, in gratitude for the years of excitement Cutten had provided with his spectacular dealing, made him a present of two stained glass windows that had looked down for decades upon the trading floor.

So Cutten left the pits and turned, like Durant and the Fisher Brothers, to the one place left to make a big speculative killing—Wall Street. He joined the Durant consortium and used his talents to lure masses of Americans into stocks he favored. Whenever he got high on a stock, word would quickly spread through the grapevine. Indeed, a whole host of securities came to be known as "Cutten" stocks, to which the public flocked like lemmings.

And there were other traders who joined the Durant clique—Jesse Livermore, for instance, a blond, taciturn, chain-smoking New Englander who could have written a library of books—and indeed did write one provocative volume on his experiences as a fantastically successful short seller. Earning a reputation as King of the Bears, fulminated at by the press, a man who almost single-handedly succeeded in having the Government ban short selling because of the animosity he aroused, Jesse L. Livermore had begun life humbly enough.

He was born on a farm in Shrewsbury, Massachusetts, and as soon as he got out of school, he obtained his first job marking the quotation prices for a display board in the Boston branch of the broker firm of Paine, Webber & Co. He was fast at figuring; he could add numbers, multiply and divide in his head without having to calculate on paper, and he would remember, down to the last fraction of a point, what such and such a stock had sold for in the previous trade. In watching the fluctuations of prices on the board day after day he came to develop a feel for price behavior. He became aware that the tape was a most powerful tool for analyzing the struggle taking place in the market. Instead of leaving the broker office when his work was done, he would stay for hours, jotting down the prices left standing on the board in a little memorandum book, studying the changes from the previous day's figures, searching for the repetitive patterns of market behavior.

Shortly after joining Paine, Webber, Livermore began frequenting bucket shops during his lunch hour to try his hand at the play. America in the 1890s teemed with shops that were ready to part the trader from his cash. They were to the stock market what the bookie today is to the racetrack. The trader did not buy and sell the actual stocks traded in the market but bet on the prices as they were reported on the quote board of the shop. The customer gave his money to a clerk and told him what he wished to trade in. He could bet either way, long or short. If he bet long and the market went up, he cashed in accordingly. If he bet on the short side and the stock tumbled, he made money that way. When the market turned against him, however, and the price went beyond the limit set by his margin, the deal was automatically concluded and the trader was cleaned out.

Livermore began playing the bucket shops and found that he had been born for the life. With a quick head for figures and an uncanny ability to anticipate price fluctuations, he presented an unusual threat to the shop owners—a customer who consistently won. This was unheard of and could not be tolerated, for the bucket shop owner was ordinarily as certain of coming out ahead in the long run as the croupier in a gambling casino. The very nature of the betting operation normally assured that he couldn't be beaten. And the shops practiced a variety of tricks to guarantee their edge.

It was standard practice for a shop to hold back from reporting sudden fast price moves on the Stock Exchange floor. If U. S. Steel, for instance, was selling at 90 and took a sudden climb to 100, the shop wouldn't announce this on the board immediately. It would let the stock advance only to 96 on a fake quotation, in the hope that some of the traders would be suckered into selling short, expecting the price to swing down again. After a few trades had been made at 96, the shop then would announce the rest of the run-up to 100, and the players who had gone short at 96 would be cleaned out.

But despite such sharp practices, Livermore continued to win. Gossip travels fast through the gamblers' grapevine, and in virtually no time most of the houses on the circuit were warned about him. Whenever Livermore walked in and plunked down his money, the clerks would stare at it as if they were hypnotized by the eyes of a snake. No one would lift a finger to take it. Livermore tried every dodge to force shops into letting him play. He took a fictitious name and traded in out-of-the-way houses. To allay suspicion he even tried losing deliberately on small stakes in the hope the house would let him get involved in big enough ones to make a killing. As more and more houses shut their doors, he had to travel further and further afield to get any action. But even under these handicaps, Livermore continued to win.

He had one consuming ambition—to accumulate enough money to enter the stock market as something more than a piker trader. And the day finally came when he was able to swing a big enough line for significant operations. He discovered that playing the stock market required a different strategy from playing the bucket shops. In the shops one bet on fluctuations of a few points, knowing exactly what price one was getting when one bought and when one sold. But the market was a different kettle of fish. The time that elapsed between the order a trader gave to buy or sell at the market and the actual price at the time of sale could vary sufficiently enough to wipe out his stake. Livermore found that while he was right more often than not in anticipating where a stock was heading, he was not making as much money as he should have because he was following the age-old psychology of the conventional trader—snatching at immediate gains instead of letting his profits ride. He took a 5-point profit only to see his stock continue up 15 or 20 points. He came to realize that the hardest thing for a trader was to put his anxieties on a leash. The market did not outwit the trader. He outwitted himself. The man who could sit still for as long as necessary for the market to confirm the accuracy of his judgment was a rare breed. The most important thing was to establish position, to keep one's eye on the long swing.

Livermore learned to play with nerves of steel. He had no predilections on moral grounds about going long or selling short. Frequently when he sold out a stock as a bull he simultaneously went short on it; for he reasoned that if it was poor judgment to continue to be long on a stock, it made equally good sense to turn bearish on it. He geared himself to make a profit coming or going.

Like other successful plungers, he seemed to be possessed of a mystical prescience. He had an instinct for foreseeing events in a way he could not explain rationally. Rumors spread among his friends that he acted on subconscious impulses. There were times when he just had to put away his golf clubs and rush to his broker's office to make a sudden short sale. There were occasions when he went fishing on which he put down his rod and hurried back to land and the local broker house to wire a buying order. His moods were unpredictable. At times he would move like lightning in his trading; on other occasions he would wait for months, doing nothing whatever, lying on the beach on the Riviera, 3,000 miles from Wall Street. And then, inexplicably, he would leap into action. Livermore himself disclaimed any extrasensory perception. And yet, some curious sixth sense divining the future led to one odd episode.

Early in 1906, Livermore took a vacation in Atlantic City. One morning he strolled along the boardwalk and sauntered into a brokerage office to see how the market was doing. It was climbing briskly. The Dow-Jones average was up several points. He looked casually over the quotation board until his eye lit on Union Pacific. The railroad stock was one of the market's star performers—deemed to be practically as invulnerable as the Rock of Gibraltar. The news about the road was overwhelmingly bullish. Livermore picked up a pad and wrote out a message for the office manager. It was an order to sell a thousand shares of Union Pacific short. The manager emitted a nervous little laugh as if to say, "That was a slip of the pen, wasn't it, Mr. Livermore? You meant *buy* a thousand shares." Livermore had no conscious reason for selling Union Pacific short. He had heard nothing about the road that everyone else didn't know. Its earnings' prospects were rosy. Freight and passenger revenues were on the rise. Its capital position was strong. And yet, deep within him, there was the feeling that all was not well.

He picked up a second order blank and wrote out orders to sell another two thousand shares short. He went out for a bite of lunch. When he had finished his coffee, he returned to the broker office and glanced at the quote board. The price of Union Pacific had climbed higher since his last sale. He was heavily short on a climbing market; yet he was strangely untroubled. The next day Union Pacific backed off a little. Livermore sold two thousand more shares short. That night he cut short his vacation and returned to New York to be closer to the action.

The following morning news came over the wires that stunned the nation. *San Francisco had been hit by an earthquake.* It was one of the greatest disasters in history. Whole city blocks had been leveled; hotels, office buildings and homes collapsed like splintered matchsticks. City Hall was demolished. The Grand Opera House and the entire financial district were reduced to ashes. Soldiers were rushed to the city with bayonets to hold in check the mobs. Livermore had acted on an uncanny premonition of disaster, for which there was no obvious ready explanation.

However, a curious thing happened. When the news reached New York, the stock market remained strong, yielding only a few points at first and then rebounding. The bulls who had been accumulating massive holdings for months weren't going to be dislodged easily. Although Union Pacific had miles of track in the disaster area and was bound to suffer, the stock refused to go down. Livermore was short almost a half million dollars, and his associates were gloomy over his prospects. A cataclysmic blow of nature had been unable to shake the Union Pacific stock. They urged Livermore to cover and take his losses before they grew heavier. But he held on. The hunch that had impelled him to sell in the first place continued to possess him.

And, sure enough, on the following day, as the details of the earthquake poured into New York and the full scope of the disaster became evident, the market began to slide. At first it was a measured, orderly retreat without any indication of panic. Then, twenty-four hours later, the break that Livermore had been waiting for developed. For several days now traders had been sifting the news from San Francisco to ferret out its implications. And at last they reacted; the market's critical threshold of resistance was penetrated and broken. At first, prices fell slowly; then they picked up momentum. Finally, the panic was on. Livermore doubled his ante; he unleashed wave after wave of selling and on the following day he covered, making a quarter of a million dollars on the play. He had held his fire until the last possible moment. He had learned through years of bitter experience a lesson that only the most successful speculators really take to heart. It is the most difficult thing in the world for one to keep himself on a leash, when he knows he is absolutely right in his judgment, waiting for the big swing. It is only on the big swing that the big money is made, but the market all too often takes an unconscionable time to behave as the astute speculator knows it eventually must. In the meantime, the trader has to sweat it out.

From then on Livermore's career as a short seller gained momentum. He became a master manipulator of the subterranean depths of fear, exploring the psychic caverns of sup-

pressed anxieties with a touch approaching that of genius.
He turned into an expert at sensing the nature and scope of
mass hysteria, the threshold levels at which different men
begin to panic. Everyone has some level beyond which he
loses control of himself. And Livermore became adept at manipulating the conditions necessary to bring his bull opponents to this point. Wrestling with one's adversary was
frequently a long, sustained cold war of nerves. Livermore
developed an infinite patience for waiting out the enemy, an
infinite cunning for accepting reverses and turning them into
opportunities, and the courage to wait without moving a hair
until the time was ripe for a decisive strike.

Utilizing these talents, Livermore was able to make a second killing within a year after the San Francisco earthquake.
In 1907 he had studied economic conditions carefully and
come to the conclusion that the money outlook was far more
critical than most people realized. Money rates were rising
ominously all over the world. Unemployment was growing
in the United States. Livermore concluded that the nation was
heading for a recession and that the stock market was bound
to react accordingly.

He went heavily short. At first, as in the case of Union
Pacific the previous year, the stocks he sold short stayed
strong; and once again his associates were skeptical about his
judgment. But Livermore was certain he was right. He felt
that the longer the market hesitated about going down, the
more drastic the final break would be. He sat through rally
after rally without turning a hair. And he continued to put
out heavier and heavier short lines. In the meantime, money
got scarcer and call rates rose. The market broke, and the
tumble accelerated as Livermore and other bears unleashed
waves of selling.

Morgan sent word through his emissaries to Livermore
and the other top bears warning them to let up or take the
responsibility for consequences no one could foresee. Livermore listened and was convinced. He had already raked in

over $1 million on paper. He was realistic enough to know that if the market became any weaker, he might be unable to turn these paper profits into cash. And if the Exchange were forced to close, this would freeze his assets.

So he agreed to let up on his pounding. Upon covering his lines, in one day alone—October 24, 1907—he took in over a quarter of a million dollars. And he never forgot—nor did Wall Street—that the market had been at his mercy and that of other big bears during its most critical hour. The bankers had been forced to come hat in hand to this onetime bucket shop trader because he had guessed right about the course of events against virtually the entire investment world.

Livermore emerged from the panic of 1907 a nationally known figure. Twice he had cleaned up by selling short in the face of prevailingly bullish prognostications by others. And his judgment had been confirmed by subsequent catastrophe. A number of editorial writers castigated him for growing rich by betting against the prosperity of America. It was immoral, they declared, to cash in on the shattered hopes of one's countrymen; to clean up on plummeting earnings, passed dividends, mass unemployment and bankruptcies. But Jesse Livermore was undeterred by such sentimental notions. He was playing the market with the detachment with which he had played the bucket shop. To him the entire game consisted of statistics on a ticker tape. He cared nothing about the stocks themselves, let alone the businesses they represented. The aspirations of the chairman of the board, the directors and the workers on the payroll meant nothing to him. His emotional commitment was only to the game of pitting his judgment against the world and proving he was right. The great gamble of the game was that he could also guess wrong and pay frightfully for his error. This he was sporting enough to accept.

When the First World War broke out, Livermore moved into the forefront of a tumultuous uptrend as the market reacted to the war economy. In 1915 and 1916, he raked in several million bulling U. S. Steel and Bethlehem Steel, Mexican Petroleum and American Sumatra. And then, with the intuition that was his hallmark, he became one of the first to sense the approaching end of the bull market. This had been his forte, this nose for trouble. He figured that the American economy, bulging with war contracts, faced a drastic shrinkage of business when the hostilities with Germany ended. Factories were dangerously overloaded with inventories. The returning soldiers would swell the labor force looking for jobs. Livermore decided that there was bound to be a sharp deflation. And his experienced reading of the market confirmed his feelings during the climatic stages of the boom. He had observed that key stocks that had constituted the advance party of the bull market offensive had stopped climbing. They fell back as other stocks continued their march into new reconnoitering ground. He became carefully selective, buying stocks which he surmised still had strong staying power and going short on the others. His judgment was untinged by the slightest bit of sentimentality.

He put out short lines on Atlantic Gulf, West Indies, American Sumatra and Mexican Petroleum. At first the stocks he sold short didn't react much one way or another as the market continued upward. But whenever a stock he was long on ceased to move forward, he sold out and went short on it. He did this with each stock in his portfolio the moment it had in his judgment reached the end of its tether. He was certain the next major swing would be downward, and true to his investment philosophy, he was positioning himself to take advantage of this move at the very moment the vast majority of people were still locked into a bullish posture.

And then it happened, as it was bound to; the whole market grew weak, buying support crumbled, and stocks began to slide on a wide front. Livermore doubled his short lines. But even now, with the end in sight, he kept himself on the leash, refusing to cover. He had staked too much on this struggle with the bulls to be satisfied with anything but the most complete triumph possible. The wise speculator has the patience to extract every last ounce of satisfaction from a tactically favorable position. Livermore had stuck by his guns to protect this position when time after time the stocks he had gone short on had rallied, exposing him to increasing peril. There had been the temptation during some of these rallies to cover and then to lay out new short lines, even though these would have been at a higher price. By refusing to take this less risky course, he was able to cash in on the maximum victory. Yet the bulls did not give up without a struggle. They continued to stage desperate last-ditch rallies in an attempt to recoup their fortunes. It was a terrible war of attrition. But as Livermore and his fellow bears let loose wave upon wave of selling, the bulls reacted less and less vigorously. Slowly, inexorably, Livermore was bringing them to bay like huge wounded whales on the points of harpoons. And experienced fisherman that he was, he refused to panic at their violent thrashings, realizing that these were a conclusive sign of the death struggle. Then, when he sensed that the moment had arrived and the market was able to absorb his entire line, he covered. He wasn't rash enough to try to cover at the rock bottom. Who could guess where that would be? But he was determined to lose as little money as possible in converting his paper profits into cash. As it was, he cleaned up over a million dollars.

So for the third time Livermore had made a ten-strike on a national calamity. And a floodgate of criticism was loosed upon him. Financial writers dubbed the beneficiary of the San Francisco earthquake, the panic of 1907, and the postwar recession a man with an evil eye. People feared his prognostications, his very presence.

However, the aura of terror the press had so assiduously built up around him served to enhance the psychological weapons he needed to carry out his trading strategy. When pressed by reporters, he vigorously defended his role as a bear. The speculators, he told Earl Sparling, a financial writer, were the stabilizers of the market. The short seller, by covering his line on a sliding market, provided a floor and kept prices from tumbling to an uncontrollable level. "Did you ever stop to think what might happen to the market some day if there were no buyers and some unexpected bad news arrived overnight? The shorts come to the rescue of everybody on bad days. They are the life-savers, a necessary evil. If we are going to have exchanges—and in my opinion we must have them—we cannot get along without the shorts."

When America entered the 1920s, Livermore was in his late forties, but he looked twenty years older. His hair remained ash blond, almost eerily white in color. His eyes were enigmatic, his bearing aloof. Only one mannerism betrayed the tension he was laboring under: he was a compulsive smoker, polishing off expensive cigars at a furious pace. He wore luxuriously tailored suits, liked his women and kept several of them in villas around the world. He drove a Rolls-Royce painted a gleaming yellow, wenched and fished and drank heavily aboard his yacht during the intense nervous spasms away from work that he called vacations.

He carried on his market operations from an unobtrusive office at Harriman & Company, the brokerage house. There was no lettering or number on the door to reveal his presence. He kept his eye on a huge silicate board hung on the wall, on which the prices of 30 or so of the more active stocks, as well as options on commodities, were displayed. Facing the board were three tickers—for stocks, cotton and grain—placed in such a position that he could read all three tapes at once by moving only a few steps.

In the early 1920s Livermore continued to make money selling short, playing in fast-moving, big-action stocks like Mexican Petroleum, Baldwin Locomotive and Crucible Steel. He made a killing in American Sumatra. He went short on Mexican Pete, selling it from 160 to 180 and covering at an

JESSE L. LIVERMORE, KING OF AMERICA'S BEARS. "WE
CANNOT GET ALONG WITHOUT THE SHORTS".
COURTESY OF THE BETTMANN ARCHIVE, INC.

average of 92. According to Clarence Barron, the financial editor, who had excellent sources of information, Livermore may have made several million dollars on this one deal alone.

His strategy remained bold and imaginative. In 1921, he told Richard Wycoff, another financial editor, that he didn't go into a trade unless he could see at least a ten-point profit, because he couldn't take on a line and get a decent run on short swings. He didn't use stop orders like some traders but closed out immediately at the market when he thought a trade was going sour. These days, instead of pyramiding—building up his purchases step by step—he customarily took his position all at once. With unerring instinct he sensed where the danger point was in a stock and tried to sell as near to it as he was able.

Such was the strategy with which Livermore entered the Twenties, an era when the manipulators of mass psychology would have a rare opportunity to display their talents. True, the times were predominantly bullish. Livermore had become stereotyped in the popular mind as an unswerving bear. But the image was unjust. He had no scruples one way or the other. He was just as ready to lead a parade of the bulls as to command a caravan of the bears so long as it led to the pot of gold. So Livermore joined the Durant brigade, offering his very considerable talents to the consortium.

Harnessing their combined skills, Livermore, Cutten and the Fisher brothers, put on a display during the latter half of the 1920s that for sheer pyrotechnics could scarcely be equalled. For four years the Durant syndicate systematically placed its millions behind key stocks which it bulled up to spectacular levels. And these stocks dragged whole areas of the market upward in sympathy. Thousands upon thousands of investors who until 1925 had not known what a stock certificate looked like followed Durant and company into the stocks they publicized. During the peak of his operations, Durant worked through fifteen brokers, contacting them at all hours of the day and night and from any part of the world he happened to be in. His calls from Europe alone cost over $20,000 a week. By 1928 he was handling more than ten million shares of stock, representing over a billion dollars; additionally, $2 billion were invested on his recommendation by individual members of the consortium. That year Durant paid one broker alone $4 million in commissions.

And yet it was by no means a one-man job. Gone were the days when the market could be manipulated by even a few men at the top. Trading had become too complex. Durant acted as a commanding general, supervising a vast chain of command that passed through corps of captains and lieutenants, who gave orders to a battery of stock specialists, who in turn carried out the actual trading on the floor.

The maneuvers of Durant's agents were imaginative and complex. To mislead the gullible they had to resort to all kinds of subtle duplicity. They did queer things—bought when they wanted to sell; sold when they wished to buy. In accumulating a stock at a bargain, they avoided attracting the attention of the public by camouflaging their operations. Once the price started to climb as a result of their buying, they would sell down again to keep the price low. But at the end of each session, each trader in the pool, like a master magician dealing with rabbits, had a few thousand more shares tucked up his sleeve than he had before. Day by day, as the stock stuck to their fingers like flypaper, the price rose naturally, for each day there was a little less stock available for buying. But the rise was so gentle, the trend was all but invisible to any but the most astute observer.

It was with such talent as this that Durant and his associates manipulated the great bull market. They played on it like an artist on a pipe organ, pulling out the stops here, pushing them in there, providing a caressing legato here and a booming crescendo there. They had a whole society under the touch of their fingers. Not just a few speculators but a whole nation responded to their tunes.

The Durant crowd became interested in International Nickel

and made it a major test of their virtuosity. International Nickel, a mining venture in Canada, wasn't earning much of anything but was long on promotional ballyhoo. The insiders who realized how leaky a vessel the company really was were cynical about the stock and were in the habit of using it as a football for short selling once the price had been run up to a certain target level. Durant's group moved in and pushed up Nickel 60 points. At first, as the price began to climb, the insiders, believing that once again it would fall back after reaching the usual target area, took their customary short position. They kept on selling and were horrified to discover that the Durant group grabbed all the stock they offered. They sold so much stock short in two days that Durant bought over 100,000 shares. Eventually the bears were forced to cover—at almost twice the price they had gone short, losing several million dollars to the Durant clique.

Then the syndicate tried American Smelters on for size. This seemed like another good speculative situation. Smelters had been sluggish for years, and the insiders were in an excellent position to manipulate the price back and forth, buying and selling short at will. They were convinced that they could sell without the slightest risk. The Durant group started accumulating stock, absorbed all the short selling that came its way, and continued to buy with the substantial funds at its command. When Smelters had risen 20 points, a friend of Durant who was a trapped bear rushed to him in consternation. What was Durant trying to pull? The stock wasn't worth the price he had pushed it to. Maybe not, replied Durant. But his friend had better watch out. It hadn't really begun to climb yet. And he moved it up another 250 points.

Then the group turned to even bigger game. Baldwin Locomotive was in bad shape. Its elderly president, Samuel Vauclain, had admitted that his plants were operating at less than 40 percent of capacity, and the story circulated that he had observed to friends the stock wasn't worth the price at which it was selling. Baldwin obviously was heading nowhere, and people in the know had been short selling it for years with aplomb. But one morning old Sam Vauclain woke up, took a look at the stock tables in his newspaper and almost choked on his cigar. Mysterious buying was taking place in Baldwin and it was moving up. Actually, the sudden interest in the stock was logical enough. The company was making plans to move its engine works from Philadelphia to Eddystone, Pennsylvania. This had been announced in the press, and tipsters were spreading reports that the Pennsylvania Railroad was considering buying Baldwin's Philadelphia property for its own expansion needs. Indeed, a number of astute investors were studying with interest that piece of Philadelphia real estate. They had made the discovery that its actual value was over twice the amount at which it had been entered in the books. To get this piece of real estate it would be smart to buy Baldwin, lock, stock and barrel.

Among those who had tumbled to the existence of this shining hidden asset were the Fisher brothers. They had quietly sent engineers out to the property to appraise its true worth, and the report they brought back whetted the Fishers' appetite. They began buying the stock for their own account, and shrewd Arthur Cutten, sensing that something was up, entered the lists. Together, the Fishers and Cutten rounded up block after block of Baldwin stock in an effort to buy control of the company.

The stock jumped from 94 to 233 as a raft of shorts, demoralized by the bull manipulation, desperately sought to cover their position. In August, with the battle for control approaching its climax and with the value of his stock hiked by over $20 million, Sam Vauclain blandly told the press that he was unaware of a fight for his company, that such rumors were only malicious gossip.

The final settlement was a compromise. The Fishers managed to grab over 50 percent of the common and wangled a couple of seats on the board. Cutten amassed a substantial

voting block and received a seat. But old Sam Vauclain managed to hold onto a piece of the company.

The stock had taken a ride to the amazement of thousands
of petty speculators who eagerly followed the price climb in
the newspapers. Although the company failed to earn any
dividends or show profits, this fantastic ride-up—this something for nothing—whetted the appetite of the average American. He wanted to get into action like this. The run-up of a
stock didn't have to have any relationship to the earnings'
prospects of a company, he concluded from the Baldwin experience. Run-ups like this awakened the greed in many an
honest breast.

The Durant group began roaming far and wide through
the stock index, picking up tempting situations to exploit,
and in one of their major maneuvers they enlisted the aid of
a stock specialist whose wits were of the sharpest. He was
Michael J. Meehan, a short, tubby, explosive Irishman with
rimless glasses, fluffy red hair and a superstitious horror of
wearing green ties on the floor of the New York Stock Exchange. Once he had taken a financial drubbing while wearing
a green tie and he swore off. "I don't need the green to identify
me. I've got Ireland written all over my face," he declared.

Mike Meehan started out in Wall Street as the manager of
McBride's ticket agency, which sold tickets for Broadway
shows to stockbrokers and investment bankers. It was difficult
to get good tickets for a hit play, but Mike Meehan arranged
for the Morgan partners, the Lehman crowd and Goldman
Sachs executives to obtain choice seats on the aisle in return
for profitable tips on the market. A top-notch salesman, he
became acquainted with all the boys "in the know," and he
decided to give up his $5,000-a-year job as a ticket broker
and become a broker on the Curb.

He was a substantial success. Within twenty-four months
he had forty private wires hooked in from his offices to banks
and brokerage houses all over the country. A born merchan-

diser, he hit upon the idea of trying out an ocean brokerage service. Market players often traveled all over the world, and Mike opened offices on Atlantic steamers so that his patrons would not be out of touch with Wall Street action even after they left the three-mile limit. He boasted that he was able to finish a trade for a customer within four minutes after the order had been wired.

Mike was a specialist for several stocks, but his chief baby was RCA. Radio was a magic name to Americans. In 1920, the nation had first become aware of the phenomenon of picking music out of the air. Several experimental stations were started, and enthusiastic hams tuned in and told their friends about it. By 1921 and 1922 everybody was talking about radio. Men would stop friends in the street and tell them how they had sat up until two the night before with earphones clamped on their heads, picking up jazz music coming in all the way from the West Indies or Canada. By the mid-Twenties radio had transformed the daily lives of millions. Amos 'n' Andy, Rudy Vallee crooning through his megaphone and the A & P Gypsies became national institutions. The Radio Corporation of America, parent company of NBC and the leading maker of radio sets, had first been listed on the Big Board in 1924, but it was a company that was still suffering its growing pains. Its promise was far greater than its performance, since it had not yet paid a dividend. At from 40 to 50, the range in which the stock hovered, it was fully priced; in fact, its earnings had been discounted for years into the future.

But Mike Meehan had unlimited faith in Radio. He buttonholed everyone who would listen, talked to them about its glorious promise, urging them to get aboard the stock before it was too late and soared out of reach. The former hot-shot salesman became the world's foremost ballyhooer for Radio. But though he extolled its virtues from the housetops, the stock refused to move—that is, until 1927, when William Durant and his associates and other cliques took a long hard look at it. Like Baldwin Locomotive and International Nickel, Radio provided a tempting situation by the very fact of its stagnation. The consortium noted that the bulk of over a million shares that had been issued by RCA was held by General Electric, Westinghouse and several other big corporations and had not been unloaded for trading purposes. The actual floating amount of the stock—that is, the amount that was being traded back and forth in the market—was a relatively small 400,000 shares. The stock had a glamorous name; it had struck sparks in the imagination of Americans. The chances for exploitation were ideal.

The Durant crowd—Billy, the Fisher brothers, Cutten— and several other interrelated pools began accumulating Radio stock. But as the stock began to rise and the company's earnings failed to strengthen—nor did the directors give any indication of when they would pay dividends—the bears, convinced that the stock was bound to tumble, built up a large short interest. The Durant group, as in past maneuvers, continued to buy everything the shorts offered, and the stock continued to rise. As the bears were forced to cover on their short selling, thereby pushing the stock even higher, the fascinated public, reading the daily stock prices in the papers, interpreted this to mean that the stock was continuing to have strong buying support. Few of the amateur speculators, in which the nation was in long supply, had the slightest notion of what short selling was. They were convinced they were being offered a big buying opportunity. In a matter of days, the short sellers had unleashed up to 300,000 shares; these were soaked up by the Durant people, and the man in the street tingled with excitement. As Radio continued to soar, fueled by the huge short interest and the feverish demand for shares to cover their lines, the supply of available stock ran out and an extraordinary situation developed. There wasn't enough stock to go around, and the bulls actually began buying the stock sold short by the bears. In the wild trading that was generated, Radio stock was being exchanged at the rate of 500,000 shares a day *although there were only 400,000 shares officially available.*

In March, 1928, the bull pool forced Radio into a technical corner. In four days the price had jumped 61 points. The entire floating supply had been cornered. Actually, the corner was only a technical, rather than an actual, one because there was a substantial supply of stock the manipulators did not control—the shares that were held by RCA itself, GE, and other major shareholders. Actual corners—a common occurrence in the Drew and Vanderbilt days—had long since been forbidden by Big Board regulations. When a corner developed, as, for example, when Allan Ryan in 1920 grabbed all of the Stutz Motor Company stock, and Clarence Saunders put a hammerlock on Piggly-Wiggly, the Governors of the Exchange stepped in and pried loose the stock.

Incidentally, the Piggly-Wiggly affair had a particularly larcenous note. Clarence Saunders, president of Piggly-Wiggly, a grocery chain in the Midwest had previously put substantial stock in the hands of the public, but he wished to make an additional offering. However, the market price for his stock was too low for his taste, and he wanted to have it pushed up to a level where his offering would bring in more money. He hired Jesse Livermore, an expert in such matters, to move up the price of Piggly-Wiggly. Livermore performed one of his finest jobs, creating exciting tape movement. A large short interest had developed as was usual in such cases, and as the price continued to go higher and higher under Livermore's manipulations, the bears began to sweat it out. Livermore did his job so efficiently that he managed to push up Piggly-Wiggly over 50 points in a single day, and then he found to his astonishment that he had unwittingly cornered all the available supply of stock.

When he relayed the news to Clarence Saunders, that worthy was flabbergasted. But then he rubbed his hands gleefully. With large numbers of bears caught short, he now saw opportunities for profit beyond his most sanguine dreams. All he had to do, he figured, was to cancel his plans for issuing more stock, as he had originally intended, and let the bears sweat to death. But when Saunders announced that he had changed his mind about a new public offering, the Governors of the Big Board stepped in and told him this wasn't at all cricket. They delisted Piggly-Wiggly stock and allowed the bears to settle at a nominal price. Saunders emerged from the operation with enormous losses.

But the fabricators of the Radio corner came to a happier ending. The corner, as noted, was only technical and did not call for Big Board action because there was a large group of shares the manipulators did not control.

For four days, beginning on March 12, pandemonium broke loose on the floor of the Exchange as the bears in Radio stock strove to work their way out of the trap. Radio skyrocketed and dove by turn and the floor was swept with rumors; nobody knew who held stock, who had sold it and at what price. An army of brokers pounced on Mike Meehan on the floor, frantically seeking advice about what to do with their own and their clients' holdings. Mike's shirt was torn to ribbons, his face battered by the people trying to get near him. Several times he left the floor at the end of a day's trading at the point of exhaustion. After one session, associates, waiting for him to appear in his office, went looking for him and found him collapsed on a runner's bench near the floor.

The trap was broken at the end of those four hectic days, but the artificial buying and selling between the bulls and the bears continued in the months ahead. Well into 1929, RCA stock continued to zoom higher and higher, luring in increasing numbers of innocents. Then, finally, like all speculative bubbles, it burst. To put it more accurately, it collapsed, not with the noiselessness of a bubble but with the crash of a thunderstorm. But before this, Durant and company had gotten out with their profits intact. Their accomplishment had been considerable. They had managed to bull up the stock of a company that hadn't paid a penny in dividends from 85 to 420 in 1928, and to 570 on a stock split in 1929. Then, within a matter of weeks after Radio hit 570, knowledgeable insiders who had gotten out near the top were able to buy it for $300 a share cheaper.

And so Durant, Cutten, the Fishers and Meehan ran rough-shod like the proverbial horsemen of the Apocalypse. But these capers were merely a prelude to what was yet to come. For as 1928 passed into 1929, the stakes were to grow even dizzier, setting the stage for a devastating turn in the wheel of chance.

9
PROPHETS AND PROFITS

A SECRET VISIT TO THE WHITE HOUSE AND A WARNING

$\mathbf{A}$s the nation entered the final year of the decade, 1929, its experience was to prove beyond the slightest doubt that the stock market is controlled at many critical moments not by a reasoned analysis of economic fundamentals, but by the spirit of national *hubris*, to borrow a term used by the ancient Greeks to describe a people feeling nine feet tall before a fall.

Durant and company and other syndicates continued to perform as Pied Pipers, and Americans continued to dance to their tunes. The impact of billions of dollars applied skillfully by pool operators to selected stocks provided lively bait for the mass of people. Those who responded to such ministrations had a definite motivation. What particularly excited their imagination was the leverage that Wall Street offered. People could buy stocks with less than 10 percent of their own money and hold it on a margin of 90 percent, figuring that as the stock rose in price this would cancel their debt to the broker. And, of course, the market was bound to go up and up indefinitely. This was an article of faith.

By the summer of 1929, over a million Americans held stock on margin. Not only was cheap credit available for individual stocks, but this leverage was powerfully magnified by the mushrooming of investment trusts which, holding a variety of securities, invited the public to move in and take a speculative joyride. The leverage of the trusts, generated by free-wheeling capitalization policies, was in many cases quite fantastic. Fueled by cheap credit, buying went up and up.

All over America legends grew. People told one another how hundreds of thousands of dollars could have been earned by anyone who had had the foresight to buy U. S. Steel right after the war and hold onto it. Clerks and stenographers in Wall Street kept their ears open to pick up the latest gossip about Montgomery Ward. Elevator boys hurried into the board rooms of brokers during their lunch hours to see what was happening to the shares they held in General Motors, into which they had poured their meager savings. The news of little people becoming rich overnight spread to every corner of America. Stories were told about the barbershop manicurist who had made $50,000 on stock tips handed out by her clients; the fireman who had bought Radio on the upward swing, making enough money to retire. Celebrated painters refurnished their studios to resemble brokers' offices, placing ticker tapes and price charts next to their easels. Doctors, musicians and professors of Latin spent their spare moments poring over stock tables and market letters with the enthusiasm of horse race addicts devouring form charts. Just a few months previously most of them had not even known what a ticker tape looked like. Now they spoke knowingly about the latest price rise in American Can, or the play the insiders were giving International Nickel. Referring to one's broker as casually as one mentioned one's bootlegger became the badge of membership in America's newest "in" group. Anybody who worked in Wall Street and had hot stock tips drew the lion's share of attention at social gatherings.

By the fall of 1928 the volume of trading had broken all records. Five-million-share days were ordinary. By the end of November volume had reached seven million shares a day. Large numbers of stocks were making new highs and shooting up 5 or 10 points daily.

Market-letter writers, investment analysts and an assorted company of financial pundits prospered on providing advisory services. A tidal wave of promotional literature assaulted the American stock buyer with advice on how to pyramid his profits. Brokerage houses issued bulletins in the morning, which were not content merely with analyzing market trends but, following the lead of racetrack touts, actually prognosticated for their clients which stocks would go up that day and how many points each would climb. Some promoters sent out telegrams alerting customers, for example, that at one-thirty in the afternoon special interests would take American Can or Wright Aero in hand and bull them up 10 to 15 points before the close.

And the public responded enthusiastically. Brokers' offices all over the nation were crowded from the moment trading began until it ended. In many board rooms it was impossible to get a spot from which to observe the quotes unless one lined up at the office hours before it opened for business. To feed this frenzied curiosity the number of ticker machines installed throughout the country rose from 5,500 to 7,000 in less than a year. The Exchange itself made herculean efforts to meet the demand. The number of trading posts on the floor were increased; a new system, using shorter abbreviations of stock names, was introduced to speed up the ticker service. The Exchange put its best engineers to work to plan an even speedier ticker.

The urge for speculation reached beyond the three-mile-limit. Brokers installed branch offices on transatlantic steamers to serve their customers during vacation travel. (Mike Meehan, as already noted, was one of the pioneers of this service.) During one trip in August, 1929, Irving Berlin, the songwriter, opened trading in a newly installed office on the *Île de France* by selling shares of a movie stock while cameras clicked and a crowd of fellow passengers queued up to make their own transactions.

The newspapers avidly reported every nuance of the boom and its effect on American living. In March, 1928, they blared forth how three hundred people had become millionaires within the last few months on their stock investments. The New York *Times* sent reporters out in the spring of 1928 to discover how Americans were spending their market winnings. A Packard dealer told the newsmen that car sales had been exceptionally good in recent weeks "due ... to the fact that a great deal of money had been made in Wall Street." A New York dealer in Cadillacs disclosed that March, 1928, had been the biggest business month in his experience. A Rolls-Royce agent disclosed that his sales showed a dramatic increase as a result of trading profits on the Street.

Officials at the United States Customs House reported that their figures indicated a marked uptrend in the importation of paintings and antiques. While it was not possible to actually pinpoint the effect of market winnings on the importation of art, they conceded, it was reasonable to suppose that the big bull market was a major factor in increasing America's store of valuable *objets d'art*. Manhattan dealers expressed the opinion that when the bigger traders finally got around to converting their paper profits into cash, the local art market would experience a boom that would make previous business seem pikerish. In the meantime, New York nightclubs and theaters were hustling with free-wheeling spenders. The owner of one night spot sent out 1,700 letters to members of the New York Stock Exchange, advertising the charms of his flesh-pots and he experienced an immediate jump in business.

Among the colorful phenomena commented upon by the

press was the large number of women who continued to flock into the market. Figures were presented indicating that 35 percent of market players were female, compared with less than 2 percent a decade previously. Some commentators looked upon this as the consummation of milady's efforts to be accepted on a basis of complete equality with men.

Pointing to the number of broker offices mushrooming up beside exclusive Fifth Avenue specialty shops, one female journalist, Eunice Fuller Barnard, writing in the *North American Review* in April, 1929, rejoiced in the number of smartly dressed women who stepped into their broker's office on their way to luncheon or their current events club to watch the progress of their investments. And she relished the idea that thousands of their less wealthy sisters in the hinterlands were also taking part in man's most exhilarating sport.

More and more, she wrote, the mystery was being taken out of the stock columns of the newspapers for the average housewife. Milady no longer thumbed past the stock tables, as if they were hieroglyphics, on her way to the woman's page. She was discovering that stock prices were quite as easy to comprehend as food prices in the corner grocery store. This mass indoctrination into the intricacies of Wall Street, she pointed out, was due to the radio, which carried the closing prices on Wall Street into the parlors of millions of housewives, while they were relaxing from their chores of washing the dinner dishes before going into the kitchen to cook supper. Over the radio, or in the newspapers that advertised the best stock purchase for the day, milady learned that American Can was going up, just as she discovered that fresh fish was now available and that strawberries were cheap. Indeed, said the writer, many stocks represented companies that were more familiar to the housewife than to her husband. The former had experienced with her own eyes the mass of customers thronging the chain variety stores whose stocks were being touted in the press. She had frequently shopped through mail-order houses whose stocks were making new highs in Wall Street. And she could well understand their prosperity. There was no doubt in Eunice Barnard's mind that the average housewife was equal to the task of playing the market and winning handsomely in this new era of riches that America had entered.

Not everybody shared this confidence in the perspicacity of the female trader. Some ungrateful denizens of Wall Street were less than enchanted with the onrush of women into their offices. The *Saturday Evening Post* assigned one female journalist, Elizabeth Frazer, to visit brokers in the fall of 1928 to find out how the "self-education of women in the speculative field was progressing." She browsed around a number of board rooms (in most instances, women were provided separate rooms where they could sit and watch the progress of the tape undisturbed by male joking and ribbing).

A woman in one board room hoped that the market would stay up since she was planning to buy a Pekingese dog and take a trip to Europe on her stock winnings.

Another confided that she was teaching her daughter how to speculate, figuring the girl might as well learn the game while she was young. All her girl friends were getting stock tips from their boy friends on where to put their money. The mother confided that she herself felt that speculation was somewhat harder than playing contract bridge; it was difficult to understand all that financial jargon. But she had a very patient broker who knew absolutely everything. It sent her head spinning merely to listen to him.

One female trader disclosed that she didn't have to take advice from a broker because she was psychic; she was unusually sensitive to the vibrations in the ether. Upon going to bed, she turned out the lights, crawled under the covers, purged her mind of distractions and murmured, "What stock should I buy?" By the time she awakened in the morning, the name of the appropriate stock had floated into her consciousness. She found that this system of playing the market was far more effective than relying on the fallibility of brokers.

Women got tips to buy or sell anywhere and everywhere. A distaff trader, the *Post* journalist learned, had attended a meeting of her current events club. Before launching into her topic of the afternoon, the guest speaker had swept her feminine audience with a grim eye, saying, "I hope nobody here has any tobacco stock." The shareholder perked up in alarm. "I have," she squealed. The speaker advised her in hushed tones to sell out immediately, since she had been reliably informed that they were in for a big fall. The shareholder rushed to the telephone and told her broker to unload her shares. The company was a sound one. The lady owned her stock outright. True, it had dipped but seemed due for a comeback. But milady sold and took a loss in spite of her broker's warning.

The *Post* journalist interviewed one mid-Manhattan broker who told her about a sweet young thing who insisted on giving him a buying order for a stock, together with an order to sell it as soon as it rose 30 points. The stock was a dud, and the broker was certain it wouldn't rise 30 points during the lady's lifetime. But he executed the order. A few hours later, just as he was about to leave his office, the phone rang. It was his fair customer, who inquired whether she could go out and take a walk; she had been staying home all day, she disclosed, afraid that the stock would go up while she was out and that she would miss the broker's phone call giving her the good news. The broker told her as gently as possible that she could take her walk with an easy mind, since the stock would not come to life this side of eternity. "If it does, I'll send you a telegram."

The flames of the orgy were fanned not only by the foolish and gullible but by top-ranking economists. Early in 1929, when stocks had jumped 100 points in twelve months and companies with scanty earnings and no dividend payouts were selling for thirty and forty times earnings, Professor Irving Fisher, a leading economist from Yale University, expressed the opinion that "the stock market will rightfully continue to

absorb credits in volume comparable to the recent past."
Another topflight economist at a leading university announced to the press that the traders bulling up stocks "are
among the best-informed and most intelligent people in
America." Another campus pundit, scoffing at the handful of
Cassandras who expressed alarm that the boom had gotten
out of hand, pointing to the fate of past speculative bubbles
to underscore their anxiety, declared derisively that "old standards are not only futile; they are childish."

A flood of books poured forth from publishing houses to
tell the American people it was its duty to contribute to the
forward rush of the economy by speculating in the great bull
market. The few voices that warned of trouble ahead were
drowned out by the cheerleaders who assured the public that
America had entered a new economic era in which past experience was no longer a valid guideline for the future. The
"most extraordinary phenomenon" which had made the current market different from all previous ones, wrote a financial
analyst in the *New Republic*, "is the extent to which the small
nonprofessional speculators and investors are participating in
the market." In the last seven years, a great increase in national
income, pointed out the writer, had gone mostly to families
earning $5,000 a year and over. Thousands of people now
had surpluses of cash to put into the market, and with this
foundation of mass purchasing power under it, the market
was bound to continue to go up.

Boasted the austere *American Banker*, "The fact holds
good that the public for once has been on the right side of
the market and has piled up some imposing paper profits."

John Moody, president of the august Moody's Investor
Service, in May, 1928, persuasively summed up the arguments
that America was geared for a future without precedent. In
the old days, he pointed out, bull markets never ran for more
than two or three years without ending in a crash. As soon
as the general public was loaded up with stock, the end of
climbing prices was at hand, and a prolonged decline set in.

But this pattern had failed to apply to the present bull market, which was continuing on and on despite all warnings. The bull market had been gaining momentum for five years "with the public getting in deeper and deeper, with the usual alarms being sounded and nothing happening." Obviously there was something present in the situation, declared Moody, that the traditional yardsticks couldn't account for.

Moody proceeded to analyze what these factors were. For one thing, World War I had decisively changed America from a debtor into a creditor nation, enormously increasing its productive capacity and its financial resources. Moreover, the Federal Reserve Banking system (organized under Woodrow Wilson) had succeeded in stabilizing credit and eliminating that historic breeder of financial panics, the old national banking system, which had stunted American financial growth. Also, said Moody, "The lessons taught by the crude financial errors of the speculative corporate period, extending from 1898 down into the war and through the deflation days of 1920–1, had been well learned by business and financial interests all over the country." Moody was virtually certain that the present pace of the boom would continue for another five years at least. While there might be minor reactions from time to time, the fundamental factors were likely, he thought, to sustain a continuing prosperity.

However, despite the complacency of Moody and company, as the momentum of trading in 1929 accelerated and Government statistics continued to show an ominous rise in brokers' loans on stocks, a growing number of financial people in and out of the Government began to get worried. The Federal Reserve Board took action to dampen the speculative spree. To block the relending of Reserve funds to brokers, in February, 1929, it asked the member Reserve Banks to stop diverting their funds to brokers carrying loans on securities.

But while the financial people in the Government were committed to tightening up money, the big market traders did not like this kind of thinking one bit. Their strategy of speculation was based upon the unlimited use of credit and the promise that it would be employed indefinitely. They could not attract a huge following into their stocks except under conditions of cheap money. And no group was more embittered by the Government's action than the Durant consortium. Durant himself was so concerned that he decided to call on President Herbert Hoover and lay before him vigorous objections to the Federal Reserve policy. Not wishing to attract publicity, he took extreme measures to keep his call a secret. Without informing even his secretary, he slipped out of New York one evening in April, 1929, using a taxi to take him to the train rather than risk attention by being driven by his chauffeur. When he reached Washington, he took another taxi to the White House, although he had a car of his own garaged there for his use. A little after nine he drove into the grounds of the White House and was ushered upstairs to the President's study on the second floor.

Durant warned the President that if the Federal Reserve Board did not reverse its policy of clamping down on security credit, a crash in the market was inevitable. He hinted very strongly that he and his friends would withdraw their buying support and that this could result in serious consequences.

The gist of what Durant is said to have told the President was afterward expressed by him in a speech to a financial gathering. It was foolish to assume, he declared, that anyone expected that the huge volume of stock issued in the bull market was to be sold for cash. It was to be distributed on credit. At the top of the Coolidge market almost three-fourths of loans to brokers, which the Federal Reserve Bank was now striving to curb, were not made with bankers' money but by business firms anxious to invest their money for the 12 to 15 percent return they were getting from Wall Street. There was no distinction, he argued, between credit extended for stocks and credit used to boost other types of business. And if the Federal Reserve Board wanted to curtail security credit, it might just as well compel all business to function on cash.

The financial health of the nation is based on credit. The huge volume of checks issued in the United States represented an employment of credit. The Federal Reserve Board in its tightening of security loans was killing the goose that laid the golden egg.

These were the arguments Durant had reportedly placed before the President that night in April, and Hoover had listened carefully. The man who founded General Motors and who represented powerful investment forces was a man entitled to a thorough hearing. Nevertheless, Hoover remained unconvinced. The Federal Board refused to retreat from its tight money policy, and Durant, true to his word, began laying plans to withdraw from the stock market.

The task of liquidating $4 billion was not an easy one. It was impossible to withdraw such a huge sum of money precipitously without causing a severe reaction in prices that would cut the ground from under Durant's own group. The most delicate maneuver in the entire art of speculation is the unloading of heavy holdings without collapsing the price of the market. Somehow or other, the stock must be unloaded quietly and skillfully in stages—unloaded in such a way that no suspicions are awakened and no panic ensues. Indeed, the essence of success is that large numbers of outsiders must continue to be bullish enough to take over the stock at a high price. To induce such bullishness, while the sellers are bearish, requires a psychological sleight of hand. It requires an expertly masked operation in which the right hand of the people (the millions of small buyers in America) is completely unaware of what the left hand (in this case, the Durant consortium) is doing. It was necessary for the Durant group to promote a feeling of optimism when it had privately become pessimistic. Unless these small buyers continued to float on their dreams, the Durant syndicate would be locked in with its holdings and unable to get out at a satisfactory price.

To promote a job of large-scale public relations, the Durant group turned to John Jacob Raskob. He was an old friend of Durant and a leading member of the DuPont interests, who had bailed Durant out of previous troubles and who had taken control of GM after Durant's retirement. Raskob had become the top financial officer of GM. And in 1928 he had left to direct Al Smith's campaign for the Presidency of the United States. As chairman of the Democratic Party, Raskob commanded national attention. During the Smith campaign he had been photographed continually, had been invited to speak at dinners all over the nation. Owning large blocks of stock in numerous corporations, Raskob launched a drive to create the proper climate for an extensive unloading of stock. As the Durant group began quietly to get from under, Raskob went around the country making speeches urging Americans to get deeper and deeper into the market, tossing out optimistic prognostications about the future of stocks as casually as a bridesmaid tossing out nosegays. In fact, even before the syndicate's withdrawal, he had been industriously bulling stocks. In March, 1928, just before sailing for Europe, he held a press conference at which he declared that GM stock, selling at the time for 187, could easily go to 225. Indeed, based upon his intimate knowledge of the company, he intimated, the 225 figure was a modest appraisal of its worth. Raskob's statement was hardly out of his mouth when it touched off a wave of buying. The following day the stock skyrocketed to 191⅞. It continued to soar, until it touched 200.

Raskob spoke on and on, and the Durant group stepped up its unloading operations. The evidence strongly suggests that Durant himself completed the final stage of his liquidation by May, 1929. On the first of June he was in Paris, where he addressed a group of fellow countrymen living abroad, members of the American Club. The speech was a highly pessimistic appraisal of the future during which he lashed out against Washington's tightening of security credit and the climbing rates of interest on borrowed money. It seems highly unlikely that Durant would have issued such a gloomy prognosis if he hadn't already extricated the bulk of his holdings from the market.

While the withdrawal of this buying support was a serious matter, it is obvious that the crash that followed in October, which wiped out over $40 billion worth of security values, was not due solely, or even primarily, to the withdrawal of Durant or any other group of traders. No one clique, no matter how large its holdings, could have had this impact. Indeed, it is quite possible that Durant, Raskob and company felt that they were hurting no one by their withdrawals, since the mass of Americans would continue to support stocks and hold up the market.

And indeed, the nation as a whole continued to remain optimistic. The economic soothsayers, and virtually everyone else, were lulled into security by the misleading appearance of things. The very duration of the bull market fooled not only the unsophisticated investor but many wise traders. Time after time, professional bears, convinced that the market had climbed to unsustainable heights and a reaction was bound to come, had put out heavy short lines, only to be clobbered as the market continued unaccountably to soar higher. Indeed, the incredible streak of misread signals, leading to one ill-timed bear sortie after another, was gleefully used by the bulls to spring the corner in Radio and other traps as the hapless short sellers persisted in their delusion that the bull market had outstayed its welcome. By the time the actual turn was at hand, the bear forces had been sharply reduced, thanks to their previous miscalculations, and there was not present the heavy backlog of short lines to cover which might have slowed down the slide when it did commence. Many a lifelong bear, convinced, after being burned time and again, that the bull tide would continue indefinitely, went long at the last moment, only to have his last fraction of savings wiped out in the downturn.

Moreover, the rank and file investor on the long side had

by the fall of 1929 become inured to market reactions and
no longer feared them, so that when the turn finally came,
there was no recognition, let alone concern, that the bull
market had come to an end. For, on their headlong rise upward, stocks had temporarily stumbled on several occasions
only to recover and resume their climb to a point higher than
the previous high. In the first week of December, 1928, for
instance, the market faltered and the averages tumbled 22
points. But then it righted itself and continued upward for
another 41 points before the next month was over. Then in
March, 1929, it slid back 25 points only to recover and boil
up 85 points by early September. These spectacular recov-
eries to heights previously unreached only served to confirm
the public's conviction that the market was bound to continue
upward on an irresistible tide.

One financial analyst, writing for the *Consolidated Press*,
summed up this widely held conviction: "The most astonish-
ing feature of the market is its wonderful vitality, its ability
to come back, to get up after being knocked down. It has
gone up to new heights in spite of the dearest money of the
year, the largest gold exports of the season. . . ." The "dearest
money" he referred to had been brought about by the Federal
Reserve's belated awareness that it must begin a squeeze on
credit to cut down the pace of market speculation. The "gold
exports" were indicative of the fact that America, as the world's
leading creditor nation, was making heavy loans to foreigners.

Moreover, characteristic signs of trouble that might have
alerted veteran traders and even the general public in time
were missing from the surface appearance of things. Alexander Dana Noyes, who was the New York *Times* financial
editor in the 1920s, in an autobiography recalling the events
leading to the crash, points out that in previous panics the
tightening of money and growing pressure on credit usually
brought about the bankruptcy of some overexpanded commercial enterprise, which waved the danger flag of serious
trouble ahead. For example, in the summer of 1907, Wes-

tinghouse Electric was pushed into bankruptcy, foreshadowing the subsequent money panic. The 1893 panic was signaled when the Reading Railway suddenly went into receivership. The panic of 1873 was heralded by the failure of a string of business concerns. These catastrophes, occurring from several weeks to months before the reaction in the stock market, alerted knowledgeable investors and choked off, to some extent, the pace of speculation. But in 1929 no bank or business failure, no bankruptcy of railroad or broker, occurred to flag the nation's headlong pace. Indeed, business corporations continued to float larger and larger stock issues up to the last moment. Sums up Alexander Dana Noyes: "The end of the great speculation came at the moment when the whole community seemed to have convinced itself that the end would never come."

10
THE CRASH OF 1929

THIS IS THE WAY THE WORLD ENDS

The fall of 1929 began like any other fall in the 1920s. There was no indication that before it was over life would be profoundly different. America entered the season in a swinging frame of mind. The nation was at the noontide of its fun and games. Broadway had launched a new season, and tickets for hit shows were as scarce as hen's teeth. *June Moon*, a musical written by Sigmund Romberg, with a book by George S. Kaufman and Ring Lardner, and Noel Coward's *Bittersweet*, billed as a new "operetta," were playing to capacity houses. Elmer Rice's *Street Scene* was smashing box-office records as the most critically acclaimed play of the year. Delighted audiences were flocking to see the urbane George Arliss in the widely heralded film *Disraeli*, and were standing in line to watch Harold Lloyd caper across the screen in his first talking picture. Across the street, Janet Gaynor and Charles Farrell, America's perennial lovers, were wringing the hearts of old maids and impressionable sweet sixteens in a sugary tidbit, *Sunny Side Up*.

That fall New York was in the throes of a heated three-way mayoralty race, with Jimmy Walker, who had taken office in 1926, running for reelection opposed by Fiorello La Guardia on the Fusion Republican Ticket, and Norman Thomas on the Socialist ticket. Thomas promised to cut the price of milk if elected. Jimmy Walker, for his part, angrily denied charges that he was a Tango Mayor, insisting that he had been in nightclubs on only three occasions since he had taken office, and then only to celebrate his wedding anniversary.

On the national front that October, America was celebrating the fiftieth anniversary of Thomas Edison's invention of the electric lamp. Henry Ford, Edison's close friend, had completely reconstructed the village of Menlo Park, New Jersey, as it had looked that night in 1879 when Edison had first pulled his switch. And now, with President Hoover and Henry Ford looking on, before a battery of newsmen and photographers the aged inventor stood over the battered worktable in his laboratory and rebuilt his incandescent lamp.

On the sports front that fall of 1929, football had arrived with its usual hoopla. However, the Carnegie Foundation for the Advancement of Teaching provided a jarring note by releasing a blistering report charging over 200 colleges with buying athletes, claiming that one out of every ten students competing in varsity sports was being secretly subsidized. Among those singled out for commercialization were such sanctuaries of learning as Harvard, Princeton and Columbia. The day after the report was released, Yale, which had received a clean bill of health, came to the defense of its beleaguered Ivy League brothers. The Yale *Daily News* in an editorial deplored the lumping of Harvard, Princeton and Columbia into the category of sports foundries. Mal Stevens, the Yale coach, retorted that if a Harvard baseball player wished to earn a little extra money peddling peanuts during the football season he had a perfect right to do so.

On the international scene, the papers buzzed with reports about an American actress, Lillian Foster, who, opening in the play *Conscience* in London, and receiving a withering review from the drama critic of the Sunday *Express*, walked over to him while he was dining in the posh Savoy Hotel and slapped him across the face as the roomful of diners looked on in shock. That fall Americans stormed the bookstores, snapping up *A Farewell to Arms*, the season's new best seller by the young writer Ernest Hemingway. Thousands more settled down with Mazo De la Roche's *Whiteoaks of Jalna*. And literary cocktail parties buzzed over a promising new novel, *Laughing Boy*, by Oliver La Farge.

The advertisers were busy as usual that fall. "Look Out for Sore Throats After Football Games," cautioned one copywriter. "Gargle With Listerine. It Kills 200,000 Germs in 15 Seconds." Paid testimonials by Social Registerites were *de rigueur*. "Princess de Braganza Will Accept No Substitutes For Cliquote SEC," boasted the proud makers of ginger ale, adding that the Princess had sent all the way from Paris to America for a shipment, instructing her American bankers to pay the New York distributor so that she wouldn't be without the precious beverage for a gala party she was planning.

For those Americans who had modestly resigned themselves to a simple interment, a New York burial firm offered a message radiant with good tidings. It could provide a private mausoleum with a suite of luxurious rooms within the reach of everybody's pocketbook. "From the Pyramids of Ancient Egypt, down the corridors of time, to the tomb of the unknown soldier, the mausoleum has always been chosen as the final resting place of kings and queens, statesmen and famous persons ... Now ... nestling in the beautiful hills of Westchester County, within an hour's ride of the crossroads of America's greatest center of population, a fitting monument, a symphony in marble ... is available to subscribers ... at less than the cost of a first class burial." This private mausoleum for everyone undoubtedly was the ultimate refinement in America's new age of affluence.

Other more prosaic but no less weighty events were reported in the nation's press. The Supreme Court ruled that under certain conditions Prohibition agents didn't need a search warrant to enter the home of a suspected violator to look for forbidden whiskey. In New York City, the Health Commissioner told a Conference of American Missionaries that he no longer considered leprosy a disease always necessary to be isolated, and that twenty-one lepers were at large in the city, working and living under the supervision of the Health Department.

That fall, millions of Americans gleaned some highly provocative tidbits from the world of science. A Japanese biologist, Dr. Yusaburo Noguchi, after fifteen years of experiments in the jungle, was reported in the press as claiming he had developed a surefire technique for changing the racial characteristics of human beings, even to the pigment colorings of the skin. By glandular control and nutrition, the scientist insisted, he could transform an Indian into a darker color with the physical characteristics of a Negro, or mold a Japanese so that he would have the same appearance as a white man. Within a short time, Dr. Noguchi prophesied, he would be able to change an infant virtually to order, making it tall or short, broad or slender, dark or fair.

In London, salty old Bernard Shaw told a party of American students that their countrymen were a barbarous people and were returning to red Indian life. "Your figures and faces are changing and your complexions get redder and redder. You treat your women like squaws and you are going back to feathers." When the professor in charge of the student group expressed to Shaw the hope that he would learn more about Americans if he would visit the States, the playwright retorted, "All Americans worth anything come over to see me."

It seemed then to be a characteristic fall. On the investment front the stock market apparently was scheduled to continue upward as it had been doing for the past five years. There was certainly no sense that trouble was imminent.

On September 3, 1929, the market had surged to new ground, and during the next two weeks went on to an even higher level. Then the market began a slight decline. But no one took it seriously; it seemed to be part of the normal pattern. No climb in a bull market has ever been perpendicularly up, but proceeds in a series of steps, with profit-taking causing brief reactions. The previous March, the market, as noted, had broken 25 points. The December before that it had tumbled 22 points. In both cases it had recovered to climb to new territory, winning much more ground than it had surrendered.

But as September progressed, the market did not follow the behavior of the previous March and December—that is, it did not decline sharply for a few days, slow down to quiet, listless trading, and then, upon catching its second wind, bounce back and boil up to new heights. On the contrary, during the week of September 19, stocks tumbled, knocking down the Dow-Jones averages by 19 points. This was followed by a half-hearted rally lasting two days. Then the market slid another 20 points in a week of heavy trading. By the third week in October, the averages were 50 points below the high mark reached in September.

Nevertheless, the public at large continued to be convinced that the reaction was merely a temporary one. The prices to which stocks had dropped were considered to be in highly attractive bargain areas at which it was thought to be smart to move in and get ready for the new surge upward. True, a disquieting note had emerged. A rising number of margin calls were being sent out by brokers to overextended buyers. The price of the stock which they held on margin had tumbled to a level at which they no longer had sufficient collateral. More cash was needed to keep up the account.

However, this sense of uneasiness was countered by more reassuring thoughts. Each day, as the market continued to give a little more ground, word was passed by market letter writers, customers' men and other financial pundits, reassuring Americans that the following day would see the development of organized buying support by big inside traders

who were poised in the wings, waiting to rush in. This com-
forting phrase, "organized buying support," was passed from
board room to board room. It was an article of faith that the
insiders who had gotten out were ready to enter, as they had
so often done in the past, to support prices when they reached
bargain levels. Organized buying groups would not allow a
further slide, so the argument ran, if only to safeguard their
own interests.

On October 21, stocks continued to tumble, and the pace
of the fall assumed disquieting proportions. Trading volume
rose to over six million shares and the ticker stumbled behind
the actual trading on the floor. It was the first occasion since
the break of the previous March that the tape was lagging so
far behind transactions. Investors all over the nation watched
the ticker with the realization that what they were observing
was actually several minutes behind the actual bid and offers
on the floor of the NYSE. True, the Big Board released every
few minutes spot prices on a list of the most popular stocks.
But this hardly assuaged the anxiety of investors whose stocks
were not so favored.

During the following two days the selling quickened. Much
of it was forced unloading on the part of shareholders who
had exhausted their margins and didn't have any more cash
to put up.

On October 24, the market opened steady, although on
a larger than usual volume. Twenty thousand block shares of
Kennecott Copper and General Motors sold off fractionally
and other losses began showing up on large blocks of stock
—Westinghouse, Sinclair Oil, Standard Brands, Packard, United
Gas Improvement.

Steadily the pressure grew during the first half hour. The
fall in prices gained momentum as layers of anticipated buying
support crumbled. Previously, when the market had tumbled,
it had been saved, at least temporarily, by the support of
professional short sellers covering their lines. However, the
army of short sellers had been virtually eliminated by staying

bearish too long in the bull upswing, and had been mercilessly whipsawed by the rampant bulls. Now, when the turn of the bulls had come, there just weren't enough bears around to constitute even a temporary floor for prices.

As prices hurtled downward, efforts were made to keep United States Steel above 200 because of the realization that if it crashed through this level, it would have a disquieting effect on the rest of the market. Briefly there was a struggle by specialists and floor traders around the Big Steel post, but the efforts to halt the break were useless. Before the day was out, Big Steel, which had opened at 205½ would have stumbled to 194½ before recovering somewhat at the close.

By ten-thirty the ticker had fallen fifteen minutes behind the actual trading on the floor. By eleven-thirty it was forty-eight minutes late. Prices were tumbling from 5 to 10 points. All over the nation Americans hovered over ticker tapes, stunned by the realization that the prices they were seeing were substantially behind the actual floor transactions. The Big Board tried to assuage anxiety by printing flash spot prices of a few favorite issues. But far from allaying nervousness, it intensified it, for the flash prices on some stocks were 30 points below the last quotes on the tape. This indication of how rapidly prices were falling sent chills up watchers from one end of the nation to the other. By noon, the suspicion dawned on Americans that *no buying support was going to be found at any reasonable level.*

Rumors leaped from coast to coast that the price structure of stocks had collapsed. The telephone lines were clogged with inquiries. But it was impossible to find out what the latest prices were. With stocks being unloaded in 40,000-share blocks and with the ticker tape hours late, no one could find out where he stood.

By noon demoralization had set in. Stocks were pouring in from every corner of the country for whatever they would bring. Phone calls came in ordering brokers "to sell at the market." Traders in board rooms angrily kicked over the ticker machines, breaking the wire circuits and throwing them out of commission. And still stocks continued to plummet—10, 20, 30 points. By one o'clock the ticker had fallen behind by 90 minutes. By two, it was 131 minutes late. By two-thirty it was 147 minutes late. By noon the scene on the floor had become one of confusion. With the ticker lagging, traders had given up all efforts to appraise prices and went "blind" in their trading.

By twelve-thirty so many people had crammed themselves into the spectators' gallery to look down on the scene below that officials ordered the galleries closed to further sightseers. One of those who had managed to squeeze in was Winston Churchill, the future Prime Minister of Britain, who was on a visit to America. Exchange officials posted at the Broad Street entrance to the visitors' gallery a notice that it was closed to further visitors. A messenger boy, running by, hurriedly glanced at the notice and erroneously spread word that the Exchange was shutting. The rumor swept through the streets before it was squelched.

As news of the disaster spread, crowds gathered in Wall Street. Commissioner Grover Whalen dispatched a heavy detail of police, but the crowd continued to snowball. It surged between the Exchange and the J. P. Morgan offices and overflowed onto the stairs of the U. S. Subtreasury building across the way. It was not so much hostile as stunned, not so much bitter as overwhelmed. Many in the crowd were women, some of them elderly, who stood with their eyes fixed on the Morgan building as though expecting it to produce a miracle and avert the catastrophe that was overtaking them. Scores of newsreel cameramen scrambled up the steps of the Subtreasury building and from their vantage point ground out movie footage of the scene. Later, Mayor Walker was to plead with theater exhibitors not to show newsreels of the crowds, for this would only further depress an already jittery nation. But this appeal went unheeded.

As the afternoon wore on and the scope of the disaster

became more apparent, the mob swelled beyond the confines of the Broad and Wall Street area. People stormed into offices high up in skyscrapers, to witness the scene from the windows. All kinds of rumors were passed—that the Buffalo and Chicago Exchanges had been shut down; that ambulances had been reported rushing to buildings where men had shot themselves because of market losses. At one point, a repairman working on top of a Wall Street skyscraper was spotted. Certain that he was a sold-out investor preparing to jump, some onlookers sadistically taunted him to take his life; others pleaded with him to reconsider his plans. Rumors of suicides continued to mount. The New York correspondent of a British paper, carried away by an excess of journalistic zeal, cabled that "lower Broadway was covered with corpses." The city editors of Manhattan newspapers were swamped with so many reports of people taking their lives they ran short of legmen to investigate them.

By mid-afternoon the financial district looked like an armed camp, with 400 policemen on guard to keep the crowd from getting out of hand. The following day Commissioner Whalen would keep his forces on the alert, warning brokers that there might be an outbreak of robberies.

In the meantime, inside the Exchange, trading finally came to an end at 3 P.M. As the gong sounded, brokers, sweat pouring down their faces, their collars and shirtsleeves torn to shreds, leaned against the posts. Some, their hands still full of unexecuted orders, stood entranced. But others, reacting like soldiers driven shell-shocked by a sustained bombardment, laughed and jumped about in hysteria, flinging handfuls of torn paper and memorandum pads into the air.

By the day's end, some 12.9 million shares had been traded. Four hours after the close the ticker continued to print out the prices. The bellwether stocks of the bull market were in ruins. Montgomery Ward had tumbled from 84 to 50; Johns Manville had gone from 180 to 140; Auburn Motors had fallen from 260 to 190; General Electric went from 319¾ to 302¼;

New York Central fell from 212⅜ to 197; AT&T slid from 274¾ to 265; National Biscuit plummeted from 209 to 193½.

Hours after the close the nation was still in a state of shock. Long after darkness set in, people sat in the board rooms of broker houses and watched the illuminated strips of glass on which the quotations continued to glide, marking sales that had been transacted hours before. The silence was broken only by messengers and delivery boys who, entirely oblivious to the ruined hopes of the watchers, went about joking and gossiping gaily as they changed the prices on the boards.

All that night Wall Street was ablaze with lights. Into the early morning broker houses worked to tabulate the final figures of the day's trading. Entire floors were reserved at downtown hotels so that office staffs could snatch a few hours' sleep before the opening of the next trading session. Delivery boys rushed through the Wall Street area, laughing and whooping, exhilarated by the drama in which they were engulfed. At 20 Broad Street, fifty runners seized a roll of ticker tape they found on the sidewalk and began tossing it around like a baseball. Brokers working in a nearby office on Beaver Street, hearing the noise and thinking that a riot had broken out, called the police, who chased the boys and confiscated the tape.

If brokers were jittery that night, it was because they had a painful job to do. They were calculating which of their margin customers had been wiped out in the day's trading and which still survived to be dunned with calls for cash. The volume of trading had been colossal; the bookkeeping process was slow. Numerous errors were made. Some brokers later confessed that they had sold out some customers twice. In many cases, the notice for additional margin didn't reach a client until his assets had already been wiped out. That night thousands of people went to bed and tossed around, wondering whether their brokers had been able to sell them out in time.

The nation emerged from October 24 in a mood of bewilderment. The promises of the financial experts had proved to be hollow. Americans had been continually told that organized buying would move in to stabilize the market if any serious trouble developed. Within the previous twelve months the investment trusts alone had marketed nearly $2 billion worth of securities. Their trading had been a big factor in pushing stocks up to unrealistically high levels. But now that the chips were down, where was the organized buying support—the well-publicized institutions, the big insiders, and other members of that magical fraternity that had been looked upon as a rescue brigade?

True, at noon on October 24, Wall Street bankers had held a meeting at the J. P. Morgan offices and decided to put up an emergency fund of $250 million to attempt to plug the "air pockets" in the market. The members of the pool— Lamont, the senior Morgan partner; Mitchell of the National City Bank; Wiggin of Chase; Prosser of Bankers Trust; Potter of the Guaranty Trust—had hoped to provide a temporary shot in the arm for a selected number of stocks with the hope that a rebound in these would induce people to move in with their own buying support. They planned to get out from under the stocks they had bought as quickly as possible and at the best possible prices.

And indeed, the market seemed to respond to their ministrations. Just before closing on October 24, Big Steel, reacting to the money, had rebounded from its low of the day and other stocks had followed up in sympathy.

On the night of October 24, after trading was over, a spirited campaign was launched to shore up the nation's confidence. It was felt by many officials in Washington and in the financial community that the worst was over. The break in the market had placed stocks in such a bargain area, they believed, that prices must inevitably rally. On Friday morning the New York *Times* carried the headline "Wall Street Optimistic After Stormy Day—Financiers Call Break Technical."

THE ENDING OF AN ERA.
COURTESY OF THE NEW-YORK HISTORICAL SOCIETY

The *Times* reported the opinion of brokers was unanimous that selling had gotten out of hand not because of any inherent weakness in the market but because the public had become alarmed over the steady liquidation during the last few weeks.

Over their private wires, brokers advised customers all over the country that the market was a "buy." Lists of recommended stocks were promoted as hot investments when the next session opened.

The bankers' pool would continue to exert a steadying influence, prophesied the experts. And the action of the market on Friday, October 25, seemed to confirm their hopes. Prices opened firmly and remained within normally narrow fluctuations all during the session. The trading was held to 5.9 million shares.

That Friday, following the break, an air of bravado swept the nation. The bankers' pool seemed to have definitely turned the tide. Many people felt oddly exhilarated by the historic drama. Operators of sight-seeing buses diverted vehicles from their regular routes to take crowds of tourists down to see the "excitement" in Wall Street, pointing out the Stock Exchange as the place "where all the money went."

The following morning the headlines were even bolder. Under the headline "Only Yawns Recall Big Day In Wall Street," the *Times* reported how the Street had its nerves completely under control again and how on Friday the only reminder of the hectic session of Thursday had been the yawns of brokers' clerks who had worked all night to get their records into shape. The New York *Herald Tribune* reported how one investor had walked into a broker office that morning and put $1 million into ten leading industrial, railroad and public utilities stocks to dramatize the confidence he felt in the future. It told how a leading Cleveland bank had instructed its New York representative to execute a $2 million buying order at current quotations.

Saturday was another uneventful day on the Exchange. The session was a short one, lasting until noon, and prices remained within a narrow range. The papers continued to carry reassuring headlines—"Hoover Says Business Is Sound." "Bankers Pledge Continued Support." The papers reported that the small investor was returning to the stock market with confidence, as indicated by the figures announced by odd-lot commission houses.

Americans entered the weekend apparently with much of their assurance regained. People crowded into nightclubs. Broadway audiences laughed heartily at the antics of Eddie Cantor in the Ziegfeld musical *Whoopie*, and stood in line at the Winter Garden to see the new film extravaganza *The Golddiggers of Broadway*, advertised as being "Entirely in Technicolor."

On Saturday afternoon, eighty thousand people at the Yale Bowl were witnesses as the Elis, trailing Army by 0 to 13, sent in a five-foot six-inch, 144-pound halfback named Albie Booth, who proceeded to slither and twist around and over the behemoths from West Point, scoring three touchdowns and adding all the extra points himself. Rhapsodized one sportswriter, "Over the cleat-scarred turf he tore, dodging one man here, sidestepping another there. . . . At times it looked as though he had been pinned to the earth, but just when you thought that, a little, bare-legged figure with a ball tucked tightly under his arm would be found suddenly shooting off at a tangent with the big and bulky Army men trying to surround him."

Superficially then, America seemed restored to normal. Few detected or cared to comment on the air of uneasiness that lay just beneath the surface. For the nation like a man having been shaken by the bounce of one shoe dropped by a perverse destiny, was waiting for the second one to drop.

On Monday, October 28, stocks once again opened unsteadily. U. S. Steel at 202¼ was off by ¼ of a point from the previous close. General Electric was off 7½ points; IT&T, 3 points. The opening quotes surprised many tape watchers around the country. After the widely publicized support by the bankers' pool and the two steady sessions that followed, the letdown indicated by the opening prices was keenly felt.

Actually, the market's lack of strength was logical. Over the weekend Americans had been provided with an urgently needed pause in which to review the situation in perspective, and many began to devote to the stock market the first hard thinking they had ever devoted to it. For many people, the last shreds of illusion had vanished. It was evident to them that the bankers' operation was meant to be only a temporary expedient and that no organized buying support could be counted on to bolster the market in any real strength. The hard truth dawned on them that what the majority of traders bought and sold most of the time were prices, not values, and that the hopes and fears of human beings were what determined these prices. There was no reason to believe that the market would be supported at any particular level if everyone wanted to sell and nobody was around to buy.

Now, over the weekend, the conviction that this was the time to sell gripped the minds of large numbers of Americans, and they proceeded to do the very thing that was guaranteed to destroy everybody.

From the sounding of the gong, the volume mounted, and once again a disquieting symptom developed: the ticker fell behind the trading. By ten-thirty, Big Steel had dropped through 200 again, and all through the list losses of 5 and 10 points were common. By eleven, wave after wave of stocks were being dumped at forced sale. There was a sobering new dimension to this sell-off. This market was not only destroying the little fellow—thousands of them had been wiped out in the October 24 break. It was demolishing the wealthy trader, the investment trusts and other institutional buyers. It was the big swingers who dealt in blocks of 100,000 shares, the movers and the shakers, the operators of pools, who were dumping their holdings for whatever they could get. These insiders were now being blasted by a market that was no longer a respecter of anybody, big or small.

When the closing gong sounded, that day 9.2 million shares had been traded, less, it is true, than the 12.9 million of October 24, but the drop in the averages was even more severe. In the final hour alone almost three million shares had been traded. The ticker was three hours late.

The following day—October 29—wave after wave of liquidation continued to sweep the Exchange. Within thirty minutes after the opening, it became apparent that the next four and a half hours would be the worst in Wall Street history. In the first half hour, stocks were dumped in up to 50,000-share blocks, with declines in prices of up to 30 points. In those first thirty minutes, 3.3 million shares reached the floor.

By afternoon, the ticker was an hour behind. Once, again, spot prices were flashed on the bond list, the Dow-Jones news ticker and the Wall Street News Bureau tape at ten-minute intervals. Again, men and women crowded broker houses to stare uncomprehendingly at the quotes. Many of them had long since been wiped out but they came back to sit and watch the figures dancing across the glass, like lost souls returning to haunt the scene of a crime.

By the time the session was over, despite a last-ditch rally fifteen minutes before the gong, $14 billion had been erased from securities values; 16.4 million shares had been traded. IT&T had dropped 17 points; Electric Autolite, 20 points; Fox Film, 18; Timken Roller Bearing, 19¾; Stewart Warner and Goodyear, 16 points; American Telephone, 28 points; Westinghouse, 19; General Electric, 28; United Aircraft, 19⅛. The American Exchange had been battered even more heavily than the Big Board. In the space of five hours, Aluminum Co. had tumbled 74¼ points; Electric Investors, 40 points; Standard Oil of Ohio, 30¼ points; Gulf Oil, 20⅞; People's Drug, 30⅛. And so on.

The hysteria produced events that would have been laughable if the circumstances had not been so grim. The containers in which buy and sell orders were usually deposited were inadequate to take care of the deluge of orders that poured in, and wastepaper baskets had to be requisitioned for the overflow. One exhausted trader overlooked a wastebasket crammed with orders that he had put away temporarily to make room for other orders and then had forgotten to execute. A *Herald Tribune* reporter unearthed an incident about White Sewing Machine. During the bull market, White had reached a high of 48. In Monday's session it had fallen to 11⅛. On Tuesday an astute page boy hit on the notion of putting in an order to buy it at $1 and he got it, despite the fact that for the third quarter alone White had reported earnings of $1.48 a share. Similarly, a stock called Sentry Safety Control dropped to $5, although its earnings for the year were substantially in excess of this. But in this mood of panic, equity values had been swept out the window. Reported the New York *Times*: "It was the consensus of bankers and brokers alike that no such scenes ever again will be witnessed by this generation."

The feelings of America were reported by journalists who were as stunned as the people they wrote about. The press brimmed with stories about the crowds who gathered about the ticker tapes during those final hours and who "like friends about the bedside of a stricken friend, reflected in their faces the story the tape was telling. There were no smiles. There were no tears. Just the camaraderie of fellow-sufferers. Everybody wanted to tell his neighbors how much he had lost. Nobody wanted to listen. It was too repetitious a tale."

One headline proclaimed: "Women Traders Going Back To Bridge Games; Say They Are Through With Stocks Forever." A reporter making the rounds of the broker houses wrote how women pushed their way into the board rooms berating brokers whom only a few days before they had deluged with buying orders. He told how one obese dame with prominent double chins stalked into an office and demanded from the broker a quote price on her stock. When he showed her how drastically it had shrunk, she exploded, "You might at least be a gentleman." Another white-haired lady, wearing four gold rings and chain-smoking cigarettes, went from board room to board room announcing she had lost $10,000. She walked up to strangers, reiterating her story in an odd display of boastfulness mingled with relief. One afternoon, after the market had closed, the reporter described how a little boy wandered into a broker office looking for his mother. Apparently, the lady had been in the habit of spending most of her waking hours in the board room and this is where the lad used to meet her after school every day. Now, despite the bedlam, he managed to find Mama. She took him by the hand and they started for the door. En route the mother began recounting her losses to a friend while the boy tugged at her, insisting on an ice cream cone.

Other stories poured in. The press reported how passengers sailing aboard the U.S.S. *Berengaria* just before the crash had used a broker office aboard ship to indulge in a buying spree. Then on Tuesday, October 24, when the news of the first sharp break came over the ship's radio, passengers were thrown into consternation. Over five hundred people tried to force their way into an office that normally held thirty to wire sell orders. One lady passenger who had lost $160,000 during the first few hours of trading managed to squeeze her way into the office and recover all but $40,000 during the rally that took place at the close, by buying stocks cheaply just before they started rebounding.

The newspapers recounted the plight of a jury that before the crash had been sworn in for the trial of a former State Banking Superintendent indicted on charges of bribery. Several jurors had heavy commitments in the stock market. They were under strict orders from the judge not to read newspapers or engage in any conversation with outsiders. Nevertheless, news of the debacle in Wall Street leaked in to them and they pleaded with court attendants to let them contact their brokers to find out how they stood. But there was nothing that could be done. One juror, while he sat in a sweat listening to courtroom testimony, lost $80,000.

Stories of market players who had shot themselves or disappeared mysteriously turned up in the press. The papers

CONCERNED CROWD GATHERS OUTSIDE THE NEW
YORK STOCK EXCHANGE BUILDING DURING THE WALL
STREET CRASH, OCTOBER 24, 1929.
COURTESY OF THE NEW-YORK HISTORICAL SOCIETY, NEW YORK CITY

reported how a woman from Mount Vernon, New York, asked
her attorney to help find her husband, who had last been seen
by a friend late on the afternoon of October 24, the day of
the first big break, walking near the Stock Exchange. According to the informant, he was tearing a strip of ticker tape into
pieces and scattering it on the sidewalk as he made his way
toward Broadway. He was not seen again.

On October 29, the owner of a coal business, David Karn,
dropped dead in a broker's office while watching the ticker.
That same day, a banker's son in Kansas City, Missouri, fired
two bullets into his chest at the Kansas City Club. He toppled

across a bed beside a newspaper that was open at the market page. As help was rushed to him, he mumbled, "Tell the boys I can't pay them what I owe."

In the midst of this America's wry sense of humor came to the fore. One columnist drew chuckles by referring to the Exchange as the "shock market." Vaudeville comedians got a laugh by telling what became the classic story of the sold-out trader who, unable to face his wife, went into a hotel and asked for a room high above the street noises. The clerk inquired whether he wanted it for sleeping or jumping.

Meanwhile leaders in Washington and Wall Street kept pouring out optimistic statements about how stocks had reached bottom and an upturn was inevitable. The majority of experts sincerely believed that the bear market had run its course and that the main job was to restore public confidence. At noon on October 29, during the worst of the trading, the Board of Governors had met and argued whether to close the Exchange. It was decided that the psychological impact would be too harmful. A compromise was adopted whereby the Exchange would stay open but go on shorter hours.

To demonstrate how optimistic they felt about business, the directors of U.S. Steel and American Can, meeting late in the afternoon of October 29, declared an extra dividend of $1 a share on their stocks. The next day a flock of companies followed suit. The press continued to grind out cheery headlines. "Bankers Optimistic To Continue Aid," ran a *Times* headline while the market was suffering its great convulsions on October 28. "Huge Funds Expected In Market Today For 'Bargain Buying'," the American people were told during their clobbering. On October 30, the *Herald Tribune* announced, "Fortunes Seen Awaiting Those Who Buy Now."

On the night of October 29, after the market had registered the greatest decline in its history, John Jacob Raskob, that *éminence grise*, conceding that he had been out of the market for months, insisted that stocks were now at an irresistibly low level and this was the time for people to start buying again.

But these verbal incantations were fruitless. The Big Board remained in session—and the market continued to fall; not with the pandemonium displayed in October, although there were several sharp breaks in the months ahead, but at a pace of steady, relentless attrition. This was to be death by slow poison rather than quick strangulation. All over the land, financial experts and political figures continued their optimistic predictions.

John D. Rockefeller, by now an octogenarian, announced to the press that "My son and I have been purchasing sound common stocks." And he hinted that he would continue to do so. The implication was that stocks had at long last reached a true bargain level. The shake out had been necessary and long overdue, and while it had been painful and had hurt a lot of people, the correction was a healthy one. Now the shrewd investor would be able to move in and snap up stocks at a much sounder level and start the market on its way up again.

The Rockefeller statement was issued at the end of October. In early November it was announced that the Rockefellers, to underscore their confidence, had put in an order for a million shares of Standard Oil of New Jersey, their own stock, at a price of 50. Before the crash it had sold for 83. There was no doubt, broadcast the experts, that the shrewd Rockefellers were bidding for the stock of their company at a bedrock level. So what happened? Down, down the stock continued its slide. In the next twelve months it went from 50 to 43. By April, 1932, it had slithered to 19⅞.

For the unhappy fact of the matter was that *far from reaching bottom in the crash of October, 1929, the market had only just begun its downward slide*. Only the surface had been scratched. Eight weeks of unprecedented panic selling, 147 points knocked off the averages by November, 1929, two years of bull market completely wiped out, sending the

averages to their lowest level since the summer of 1927—
all this had done no more than nudge the market in the
direction it was still to go. From November, 1929, until the
summer of 1932—a period of almost three years—the market
was to continue to slide and stumble day after day, month
after month, with a few upward flurries. It was to drop 86
percent below the level reached on Black Tuesday in 1929
before it finally settled on true rock bottom. And during the
course of this decline, traders who had been clever enough
to get out before the 1929 crash with their profits intact and
who returned in 1930 to snap up stocks at "bargain levels"
were to be wiped out. Before the debris was cleared away,
some of the most surprising individuals were found victims.
These included, through a stroke of irony, several of the leaders of the Durant consortium, which had called the power
plays during the bull market.

William Crapo Durant himself was a victim of the market's
whipsawing action. He got out, as we have noted, by May,
1929, five months before the crash, substantially ahead on
balance, thanks to the profits he had piled up during the years
of the boom. The dapper little man remained his buoyant,
jaunty self, ready as always with a quip or flamboyant gesture.
Interviewed in his office after the crash by Earl Sparling, the
financial writer, he leaned back from his desk and wondered,
if he started piling up the $40 billion worth of securities that
had been wiped out just how high into the sky the column
would reach. He took out a pencil, plunged into a mass of
calculations and then looked up with a smile of accomplishment. The stack of silver dollars would mount 100,000 miles.

Durant was an incurable salesman. Like many clever
plungers, he finally overfinessed himself. He had correctly
foreseen trouble in 1929 and withdrawn from the market in
the summer, turning his paper profits into cash. Believing,
after the crash, that the market had reached bottom and that
stocks were at bargain levels, he followed the tactics he had
pursued in the past; he plunged in, heavily margining his

purchases, waiting for the "inevitable" rally to occur. But the market unaccountably continued to drop. Durant was sold out by his broker in 1930. Forswearing Wall Street, he took what remained of his savings and plunged them into an auto company, Durant Motors, which he had in fact started shortly after being eased out of General Motors in 1920 and on which, now that the market was closed to him, he lavished his entire energy. But he couldn't buck the attrition of the Depression. Auto sales crumbled. His firm tumbled into the red.

In 1936, at the age of seventy-five, William Crapo Durant walked into court and declared that he was a bankrupt. He swore that he owed almost a million dollars and that all he owned were the clothes on his back. Earlier that year, several newspapermen, covering a beat in Asbury Park, New Jersey, had been amazed to see an elderly, stoop-shouldered man, with a mass of white hair, washing dishes in a lunchroom. They recognized Billy Durant, and they immediately flashed the story to their editors. In no time at all Americans were reading how the founder of General Motors, a man once worth $100 million, was reduced to such a lowly estate. Actually the reports were somewhat exaggerated. Billy was not completely a pauper. He owned the lunchroom in which he washed the dishes. But within a few months he was to lose even this.

There was no doubt that his Midas touch was gone. Still bubbling over with optimism, still the irrepressible salesman in his seventies, he was to try his hand at one speculative venture after another, hoping in one bold stroke to recoup his fortunes. He promoted a "cure" for dandruff, opened a bowling alley, buttonholed everyone within earshot to tell them how he would make a million dollars again. But it was too late.

In March, 1947, he died at the age of eighty-six flat broke. When the newspaper editors came to write his obituary, they recalled what he had said years before when he was at the height of his power: "Money, what is money? It is only loaned to a man; he comes into the world with nothing and he leaves with nothing."

Another prestidigitator of the great bull market, Jesse Livermore also played out a curiously allotted role. Like so many other leading bears, Livermore had been burned badly during the last few years of the bull market when he went short time and again, fully expecting that the bull market had outstayed its welcome. Finally, he turned into a bull just long enough to recoup his losses.

In October, 1929, as the market began to tumble, and men searched for the reason that no buying support was forthcoming whispers turned into a roar of accusation. There was no doubt of it. Livermore, who had made a fortune before out of catastrophe, was now ruining the bull market by selling his holdings short. It was he, they charged, who was driving the market lower and lower, unleashing stock in every category of the index. Threatening letters were sent through the mail to Livermore by people who vowed to kill him, kidnap his children, bomb his home.

Shaken by the outcry, Livermore issued a public statement, denying that he had been operating a bear pool to drive prices down. But still the letters poured in. He didn't dare to leave his office without a bodyguard.

Livermore came out of the crash comfortably; he was still worth several millions. He remained eerily inscrutable, his hair still blond, his manner unbending. But what goes on in the mind of a man who has incurred the wrath of a nation?

One evening in November, 1940, the tall, lean, aging multimillionaire walked into the Stork Club in Manhattan with his wife and sat down at a corner table. A photographer approached and asked whether he could take a picture. Jesse Livermore looked up and complied without a flicker of expression. For the rest of the evening he sat, while his wife danced with friends, absorbed in thought, oblivious of the nervous gaiety around him.

The following day he appeared without his wife at the

bar of the Sherry Netherland Hotel. He asked for a table by himself. From time to time while he ate lunch, he scribbled down notes in a little memorandum book. He ordered two cocktails, drank them leisurely. Then he rose, walked into the lobby, and entered the men's room. The place was deserted. He sat down in a chair. Ten minutes later, attendants found him slumped over, blood dripping from a hole behind his ear, a .32 caliber automatic pistol lying at his feet.

Mike Meehan, like Jesse Livermore, extricated himself with his fortune largely intact. But nimble though he was, he was unable to dodge his own special destiny. In November, a week after the crash, a close friend of his, James J. Riordan, the president of the New York County Trust Company, shot himself. Rumors swept the city that Riordan had been heavily involved in the market and that he had suffered particularly in RCA having failed to match Meehan's dexterity in getting out of the stock in time. There was ugly gossip that he had, in fact, been misled by Meehan, who had not informed him of the syndicate's plans for unloading the stock.

Mike Meehan denied that Riordan had been heavily committed in Radio. He denied that he had misled his friend. But the rumors persisted and Meehan became a haunted man. There was further trouble ahead. He got into difficulties with the Government, which charged him with stock manipulations.

In July, 1936, a stocky, bespectacled carroty-haired individual of forty-five entered the Bloomingdale Hospital for nervous and mental diseases, near White Plains, New York. His wife had made an application for his commitment. For four months not a word was leaked to the newspapers. The identity of the man remained a closely guarded secret. Finally, James F. McConnochie, a partner in his brokerage firm, announced to the press that the man confined to the institution was Mike Meehan. "He's not under restraint; he's been sick for about a year and has given no attention to business during the period. His condition is a matter of concern to his family and friends."

Bloomingdale was a tastefully built resort, with spacious, rolling grounds and an atmosphere of Old-World luxury. Closer study, however, revealed that the exquisite curlicued tracery that spanned the windows of the villas reserved for the guests was actually steel-springed bars and that the pretty young nurses who served the more severely sick patients so graciously were experts in jujitsu. And when the guests went to sleep at night, some of their rooms were bathed in a mysterious blue light that streamed in from a hole in the wall which permitted the attendants to keep them under constant surveillance.

Meehan was still a millionaire, and he could not give up his daily habits easily. He lived a life as close as possible to his previous one. He strutted with his old cockiness over the golf course of the sanitarium, puffing at a cigar and shouting greetings to the other patients in the booming voice he had used on the floor of the Exchange. Even now, he was willing to bet on anything with as much élan as he had plunged into bulling Radio. However, the currency here was not money but cigarettes. Mike Meehan had the privilege of carrying his own matches—a favor that was bestowed only on the guests who were tranquil and only temporarily interned. Mike gave away his cigarettes as freely as he used to give money to his friends and to charities. His favorite saying had been "There aren't any pockets in shrouds."

Meehan remained at Bloomingdale until June, 1937, in the company of others who had once been the movers and the shakers of the community. There was a professor of physiology; several lawyers, and a clique of businessmen who once strutted to and from their offices with springy step and an air of noblesse oblige enhanced by the aura of power. Now all of them had been thrust, at least temporarily, into the helplessness of childhood. As the writer William Seabrook, who was an earlier inmate, wrote, "We were a bunch of grown men, most of us mature, who had lost control of ourselves ... and who had to be controlled by others."

Such was the decline and fall of an era. As T. S. Eliot, the poet, declared, "This is the way the world ends.... Not with a bang but a whimper."

11
THE GREAT DEPRESSION

THE SCHEME TO ABOLISH MONEY—JOE KENNEDY LAUNCHES THE SEC; HE KNOWS WHERE THE BODIES LIE

The depression that followed the 1929 market crash lasted ten years. It took the outbreak of the Second World War to extricate the nation from the financial doldrums and nudge it along the road to economic recovery. For the 1929 crash had plunged America into a severe trauma. With large numbers of people impoverished overnight, sales of goods and services slowed down to a trickle. Businesses shut down, throwing millions out of work. In every city and town, the windows of stores and shops grew musty with disuse.

The Depression hit all classes. All over the nation, a vast army of migrants moved from city to city, sleeping in freight cars in their search for jobs. They lived on dandelions and wild roots, fighting savagely for the scraps from garbage cans. Gradually, stunned feelings gave way to anger. In West Virginia, housewives broke into stores and stole food. In the Midwest, when bankers foreclosed mortgages on farm homes, farmers organized posses and descended on the homes of bailiffs and judges threatening to lynch them if the orders for eviction were carried out.

Things got so ugly that when the Senate launched a debate over lowering the pay of Government employees to save money, President Hoover sent a secret memorandum, pleading with it to make an exception in the case of the Armed Forces since, in the event America were plunged into a revolutionary uprising, he didn't want to have to depend on security forces that were demoralized by pay cuts.

Among the grim absurdities surrounding the plunge of the world's wealthiest nation—with the most advanced industrial technology—into the severest of depressions, not the least were the political repercussions that developed. The Republicans inevitably had the albatross of the crash and the Depression hung firmly around their necks. Herbert Hoover was to spend a lifetime trying to live down his role as the Depression President. Yet the situation is not without its irony. It was leading Democrats who played a major role in the tragedy. They were the ones who masterminded the manipulation of leading stocks and spread much of the propaganda that stoked the great bull market. John Jacob Raskob, the publicist for the Durant consortium, led Americans deeper and deeper into the pitfall with his public pronouncements at the very time he was chairman of the Democratic Party and director of Al Smith's try for the Presidency. Had Smith been elected in 1928, Raskob would in all probability have become the Secretary of the Treasury, and would have presided over the collapse of the market and the plunge into the Depression. Al Smith himself was a close friend of the market manipulators who had engineered the technical corner of Radio in 1928. Had Smith won the election in 1928, the Democrats, not the Republicans, would have been blamed for 1929, and the subsequent political history of America might have been different. The luckiest thing that happened to the Democrats was losing the election.

In the early 1930s, with the stock market floundering, the economy in a state of collapse, and millions out of work, the American people eagerly grasped any straw that was offered them. A variety of individuals came forward with nostrums to serve as a psychological mustard plaster for the national headache.

One individual who peddled a "cure" for the Depression was Howard Scott, the owner of a paint and floor-wax business in Greenwich Village, in New York City. He was a spinner of social panaceas culled from an eclectic reading of economists and political scientists. He loved to buttonhole people, and talk on and on interminably about his theories for a better world; and now in this atmosphere of anxiety he suddenly found a nationwide platform.

Scott argued that the plight of America, possessor of the world's mightiest production plant, yet bogged down in a depression and loaded with an abundance of urgently needed goods rotting away in warehouses because people didn't have the money to buy them, was due to a basic aberration of the economy. The root of the trouble was the price system that the Western world had been living by for centuries. It was antiquated, outmoded and useless, Scott declared, for, thanks to the development of the industrial revolution, the machine had replaced man as the basic instrument for production. Goods are produced not by money but by machines, and energy, not currency, is the true basis of all material wealth. The profit system, which had been artificially and arbitrarily superimposed by bankers upon the labor of machines, was sabotaging the true might of America, Scott contended. If Americans were paid directly in terms of the output of the machines they operated instead of in financial currency, if they unleashed the full power of machines, producing all they were capable of turning out instead of being concerned with producing only the amounts of goods that could be sold at

"BUY MY APPLES!"
AFTER THE 1929 CRASH A WALL STREETER LAUNCHES A
NEW CAREER.
COURTESY OF THE NEW-YORK HISTORICAL SOCIETY, NEW YORK CITY

a profitable *price*, they would eliminate the curse of poverty, unemployment and depression. If we concentrated on providing everyone with the maximum output of machines, Scott calculated, the adult population in America would have to work only 660 hours a year to produce wealth that would be ten times above the gross national product of 1929. Moreover, thanks to the enormous productivity made possible by technology, the average American would be able to retire after working only four hours a day, four days a week for twenty years.

Let us throw away currency, Scott urged, and pay men for their labor in certificates measured in ergs and joules— according to the amount of work energy produced by the machines they operated. Instead of buying food, clothes and shelter with money, Americans should be given tickets punched out to represent so many joules and ergs, which would become the new legal tender. When units of energy replaced money, Scott insisted, the plague of stock market crashes and depressions would be eliminated. For, unlike the fluctuations in the value of money, work energy always remains the same in value. A dollar may be worth much more or less in buying power tomorrow. But the erg, the joule—the unit of work or heat—was the same in 1900, 1929 and 1933 and will be the same in the year 2000. Everybody desires to possess stocks, bonds and other certificates of paper—mortgages and so forth—which are thought to be wealth. But this is a basic fallacy, argued Scott. Actually, these claims are debts, not wealth. "A man," declared Scott, "if his wealth consists in bonds, stocks, mortgages, notes ... and so forth, is merely the owner of a collection of promises to pay. Even currency is in this category, for you will find on the face of a dollar bill the words 'Payable to the bearer on demand,' with no questions asked as to how he happens to be the bearer. The units in which these forms of debt appear ... are units of value. Value cannot be measured; it has no metrical equivalent. A pound of coal is always the pound of coal, but the weight of a dollar's worth of coal is seldom twice the same."

To adjust our economy to the realities of America's productive power, concluded Scott, the whole structure of society must be changed. Just as war is too serious a matter to be entrusted to generals, so the American economy was too fragile to be entrusted to economists, bankers and politicians. They must be replaced by a new ruling class of technologists—the scientists, engineers, and technicians who had developed America's industrial plant in the first place and who should be entrusted with the reins of Government and given the chance to bring reason and enlightenment into the affairs of men. The role of bankers and politicians had really been doomed, declared Scott, the day James Watt invented the steam engine.

Scott called his new social order "Technocracy." Borrowing liberally from the ideas of Thorstein Veblen, the sociologist, especially his work on engineers and the price system, and applying these to an America embittered by the breakdown of the capitalist economy, Scott and his theories overnight became the most widely discussed topic in the nation. He was given space for research work at Columbia University, launched an organization, putting ten assistants to work preparing impressive charts and graphs, and he lectured all over America using these layouts to illustrate his theories.

Technocracy fired the imagination of a large number of citizens, and it excited the antipathy of others. From coast to coast, bankers and bus drivers, professional men and laborers argued its merits. Newspapers and magazines devoted reams of print to the debate over the wisdom of abolishing money and whether industrialists, economists and politicians had indeed become relics of the past, and scientists and technologists were destined to become the new power elite.

Many Americans remained completely bewildered by the technical jargon and maze of statistics Scott flung at them. Will Rogers, the nation's folk humorist, declared he wasn't certain whether Technocracy was a corn plaster or a paint remover, but whatever it was, it sure had America buzzing.

For several months in 1933, the obscure paint dealer from Greenwich Village was lionized. And then, just as suddenly as it had burst upon the scene, the cult of Technocracy faded away. Americans lost interest in academic utopias and looked for more practical methods to fight the Depression.

However outlandish Howard Scott's wishes to abandon money and substitute an entirely different system of values may have seemed to many Americans, there was one class that had been so thoroughly whipsawed by the vagaries of the price system it must have been willing to at least lend an ear to anything that promised improvement. These were Americans who had been ruined not by the market crash, which they had shrewdly foreseen and avoided, but by the subsequent behavior of Wall Street stocks. For, as previously pointed out, what had happened to some Americans after the crash had been even more incredible than what had befallen most Americans during it.

Many astute traders had accurately called the turn in 1929. During the summer, the market looked extremely perilous to them and they withdrew, converting substantial paper profits into cash, taking shelter just in time from the hurricane. Then, still using their heads and following the time-tested maxims of classic trading strategy, they reentered after the crash, buying stocks at "rock bottom" levels in anticipation of the expected rally. And, sure enough, the market at first did rally and regain some of the ground it had lost in 1929.

Alexander Noyes, the journalist, recalls how in June, 1930, he took a steamer bound for Europe. Aboard were a number of Wall Street traders who had prudently escaped the crash and plunged into the market at its new low level. They were exuberant over the upward rally and were going on vacation completely relaxed, preening themselves on their wisdom. The atmosphere was gay and festive. Then, as the voyage got under way, the ship's radio began broadcasting ominous news from Wall Street. As the daily stock prices poured in, it became evident that the hope for an extended recovery was illusory; the market had resumed its relentless downward course.

Everyone aboard ship was gripped with the realization that the crash of 1929, far from being the end, was merely the first stage of the bear market and that terrible times were ahead. The mood turned to despair. Plans for a stay in Europe were canceled, reservations in hotels called off, tours rescinded. Urgent wires and phone calls were put in to brokers to readjust margin accounts, to shore up overextended positions, to salvage something while there was yet time. But the great distance made it virtually impossible to conduct these complicated emergency maneuverings. The passengers felt like trapped animals.

These were skilled professional traders, wise in their lore of the market, an astute minority that had accurately estimated the situation only a few months previously—and now they too were being destroyed by a market that simply refused to act according to any historic pattern or rational line of behavior. Truly, as one shrewd old trader had observed, "It isn't making money that is difficult in the stock market; it's *keeping* it."

Edwin Lefevre, a veteran financial writer who had been covering the Wall Street scene for thirty years and was personally acquainted with many of the top operators, conducted a survey in 1932 to find out just how the boys who had guessed right in 1929 were doing in 1932. Time after time he ran across men who had bought cheap stocks in 1930 and sold them at tremendous losses in 1931. There was nothing wrong with their theory about the market, only with their timing.

Lefevre reported on one unusually candid owner of a business that had been highly profitable during the boom. He had made a lot of money on the stock of his company and so had his employees. Several months before the crash, he had the intuition to get out. He knew the stock was selling way above its value, and he warned fellow stockholders to withdraw with him and cash in their paper profits. His associates scoffed, and when the stock continued to go higher after he had sold out every share he owned, he was the object of queer looks. But when the crash came, he had the last laugh—or to put it less brutally, the last smile.

Even after the 1929 break, when his stock had fallen to a ridiculously low level, this man still felt its price was too high and refused to nibble. But then it tumbled to the point where it was providing an 8 percent yield, and he bought a heavy block of it. Even so, he did it very conservatively, paying cash. He refused to have any truck with margin operations. The price continued to slide, and the stock skidded to a level at which it was producing a 12 percent yield. Then, and only then, did our man think it wise to take on another big block of stock. But by this time he had used up all his cash, and so he put up some of his other stock as collateral. The stock continued to fall. Down it went. Twelve months later it was yielding 20 percent. But by this time our man was not around to enjoy this dubious blessing. Having no more margin to put up, he had been sold out by his bankers.

Lefevre ran across another intelligent trader who had accurately foreseen the crash, who had forecast that business was going to turn bad, who had wisely refused to feel for the top of the market, knowing that this was one of the costliest operations to be practiced by traders. He got out before the crash with $2 million in profits. When his friends ridiculed him for being so cautious, he reminded them that he had his money in cash, that they had theirs only on paper, and that nothing burns up more quickly than paper once a fire starts.

Then, with an uncanny sense of timing, this trader moved in to cash in on the quick technical rally that followed the crash, making a million dollars; next, he went short and cleaned up another million as the market continued its decline. Then he took his entire holdings, plunged them into moving picture

stocks, for which he was certain there was a bright future—
and within the next twelve months he lost $5 million as the
market continued its decline. However, he took his loss like
a good soldier. He still had a little money left. But he was
determined to be extremely careful. Refusing to take any
more speculative chances, he put his money into "good safe
bonds." "If bonds like these are not worth more than I'm
paying for them," he told his friends, "then stocks are worth
nothing. Bear market or not, stocks must be worth *something.*" Within a year, many of the bonds he had purchased
were selling for considerably less than he had paid for them.
And he was bankrupt.

This highly intelligent trader had finally learned the bitter
lesson that, in all his wisdom, he simply could not previously
bring himself to understand. Much of the time, the vast majority of people do not buy and sell on a rational appraisal of
values. Before the crash of 1929, stocks that were selling at
ratios absurdly above their value were eagerly snapped up
by the public. In 1932, when many stocks had slumped to
one-third of their former price and when some were selling
for less than the physical assets of the companies they represented, brokers found it difficult to peddle them to the
public. True, America was in the midst of a Depression. But
its physical plant was still intact. The land, the machinery,
and the buildings had a value substantially beyond the price
some stocks were selling for. Stocks that were yielding 12 to
15 percent had no appeal for the timid.

In the summer of 1932, the stock market once again displayed its perverse penchant for doing the absolutely unexpected. Just as the majority of pundits failed to guess the top
in 1929, so now they were unable to guess the bottom. Suddenly, without the slightest warning, when business was at
its worst, when everybody was overwhelmingly bearish and
there seemed to be no hope, the market started upward again.
The low point of decline was reached on July 8, 1932. The
next day, stocks began to rally and *within the next sixty days*

the averages shot up 90 percent in the quickest, sharpest, most precipitous climb in history. For almost five years, during the depths of the Depression, the trend remained predominantly bullish—until March 10, 1937, when the market swung into a major decline again. As one student of the averages puts it, "The market is behaving most characteristically when it is proving the majority of the people to be wrong."

As for Edwin Lefevre and his observations about the quirks of human nature when the market was at rock bottom in 1932—his detachment was not typical. Most Americans in 1932 were in no mood for such niceties of analysis. The nation was in a temper for ferreting out scapegoats to assuage its frustration. And it fastened upon the most promising symbol of all—the short sellers. Since America had been plunged into a bear market, people reasoned it must have been due to the plotting of the professional bears. (The fact that relatively few bears were around in 1929 to cash in initially on the holocaust touched off by the bulls—although a number moved in when the panic was on—was not generally appreciated.)

Short sellers became the chief victims of the devil theory of the crash. President Hoover asked the Senate Committee on Banking and Currency to launch an investigation into the practice. Leading citizens demanded that the top bears be identified by name so that the people would know who were the public enemies of the nation. In the spring of 1932, Richard Whitney, the president of the Big Board, was summoned by Hoover to Washington to produce facts and figures on the short selling that had taken place during the crash. Ex-Ambassador to Germany James W. Gerard thundered to the press that selling short was nothing less than gambling and violated the New York State Constitution. Senator Arthur Capper, of Kansas, introduced a bill in the Senate to tax the profits of short sellers.

However, the big bad bears were not the only ones to be castigated. A cry went up against all professional traders. In January, 1933, the Senate Committee on Banking and Currency launched a marathon investigation. During the seventeen months of hearings, the great and near-great of the financial world trooped up to the witness stand to submit to an exhaustive questioning about their role in the market of the 1920s. J. P. Morgan, whose father had made an appearance before the Pujo Commission to give an accounting twenty years before, led the procession of witnesses, which included Charles E. Mitchell, chairman of the National City Bank; Otto H. Kahn; Albert Wiggin, chairman of the Chase National Bank; Arthur Cutten; and a host of other professional traders.

The appearance of Morgan occasioned tremendous interest. The crowd desiring to get into the committee room was so huge that motorcycle policemen, wearing revolvers and cartridge belts, were called out to keep order. Like his father, Jack Morgan had shied away from public appearances, and curiosity was high as to what he was like. He turned out to be an impressive-looking man, heavyset, with a big broad face and nose like his father's, and bristling black eyebrows that were dramatically set off against a head fringed with white hair. While he was being questioned under the heat of the klieg lights he was noticeably uncomfortable and he fidgeted in his chair. Drops of perspiration trickled down his chin and he did not bother to wipe them off.

During one of the sessions, the press agent for a circus threw the committee room into an uproar by bringing in a female midget, walking her up to Morgan and sitting her in his lap. Newsmen almost knocked people over in their haste to get pictures.

Morgan was dumbfounded as the tiny female, twenty-one inches tall and weighing twenty-three pounds, was dumped on him. But he recovered his composure and jiggled her on his knee in a fatherly fashion.

"I've got a grandson bigger than you."

"But I'm older," retorted the midget.

"She's thirty-two," broke in the press agent.

The midget gave him a sharp look. "I'm only twenty."

"You don't look it," Morgan observed. "Where do you live, little girl?"

"In a tent, sir."

Morgan put her down, and his business partners settled back in their seats, breathing more easily. The committee chairman rapped for order and the hearings were continued.

They lasted seventeen months and disclosed a widespread pattern of stock manipulation. On the basis of the testimony received, the committee came to the conclusion that during the 1920s and up to 1933 over 100 stocks listed on the NYSE had been actively manipulated by pools and that $25 billion worth of fictitious security values had been foisted on the public.

The committee disclosed how leading banks had plunged into stock speculations through banking affiliates that, evading the intent of the law, unloaded stocks with the missionary zeal of boiler shop operators on unwary investors. It revealed how top Wall Streeters avoided paying income taxes by transferring stock to their wives and how a number of financiers had violated their fiduciary trust for personal profits. It detailed how the Morgan group had put a select number of influential people on preferred lists, giving them stock below the market price. One of the recipients, William H. Woodin, later became Secretary of the Treasury under Roosevelt.

A choice bit of testimony was wrung from Albert Wiggin, chairman of the Chase National, who had been a member of the bankers' pool which was formed on the afternoon of October 24 in the much-publicized attempt to stem the fall of stock prices. It was disclosed that at the very moment Wiggin was publicly supporting the consortium he was quietly selling short—and selling short the stock of his own bank. By December 2, he had unloaded over 42,000 shares. Nine days later, he covered his lines and took in over $4 million. To add to the irony, Wiggin sold short five thousand shares to the banking pool that was trying to bolster the market. Then, when the time came for him to cover, his bank obligingly loaned him the money with which to buy back the stock. And he managed to avoid paying a penny in income taxes on his $4 million profit by doing the short selling through one corporation and buying it back through another he had formed for the purpose.

Under questioning, Wiggin and other top manipulators professed extreme ignorance about the working of pools. When asked by the committee what a "washed sale" was, Arthur Cutten looked at the questioner with a puzzled expression and said he hadn't the slightest idea. Another topflight manipulator admitted that while he had heard of the expression "pegging a stock," he understood the meaning only from what people had told him about it.

When the crash came and the seams of the economy fell apart, when the heavily margined speculator was unable to cover, and the gambler lost his opportunity to wipe out earlier debts that had come due, a number of skeletons fell clattering out of the closet into full public view. There was Samuel Insull, the public utilities' magnate, who had erected a labyrinth of holding companies, put together with highly leveraged financing and a prayer. Wanted by the police, he skipped to Paris and hurled himself under a subway train at Le Châtelet station. This financier, who had accumulated a fortune of several hundred million dollars on paper, who had built the Chicago Opera House as a hobby and spent a hundred thousand dollars on a favorite prima donna during an evening, had only a few cents in his pocket when his body was searched at the city morgue.

The path of scandal reached around the world. There was Ivar Kreuger, the Swede, who, scheming to achieve a global monopoly on a single important item of everyday use, had seized upon matches as his product—he called them "my little wooden soldiers." Dangling loans and other tempting private deals before politicians and Government officials in return for control of the production of matches in a country, Kreuger moved into Britain, the Low Countries and Germany;

J. P. MORGAN, JR., SON OF A FORMIDABLE FATHER, IS
INTRODUCED TO A MIDGET DURING SENATE
INVESTIGATION.
COURTESY OF THE BETTMANN ARCHIVE, INC.

he took over Scandinavia, most of the business in Japan and
the match production of India; he captured markets in South
America and even sold matches to far-off African tribal chief-
tains. And in a number of countries, once he had gained
control of matches, he spread out to take over the timberland,
mineral resources and chemical industries.

Obsessed with a Napoleonic complex—he built a terrace
to his suite in Paris, which was higher than the column in

the Place Vendôme, so that he could look down on the monument to the Little Corporal—Kreuger finally made the move of overextending himself. To broaden his position in the telephone industry, he purchased the top American telephone company in Europe, obtaining a loan from the Morgans to do so. But an audit disclosed that he had misrepresented his collateral assets. Kreuger's bankers in his native Stockholm undertook an investigation and found that the nation's "most celebrated financier" was an out-and-out crook. He had set up a score of phony corporations, forged piles of documents, created fake collateral, and kept afloat for years in glittering splendor, successfully hoodwinking the public (he had even been summoned to the White House by President Hoover as a financial advisor) by the simple expedient of robbing Peter to pay Paul. For years he had gotten by without suspicion—until the Depression hit not only his American but his world markets.

Kreuger was not around to answer the charges. On the eve of appearing before his bankers to explain discrepancies in his account, he walked into a firearms store on a Parisian boulevard, bought the most expensive revolver and killed himself.

His American investment agent, Lee Higginson & Company, was as shocked as everyone else. It had been kept completely in the dark about Kreuger's dealings. And the firm strove vigorously to keep the impact of Kreuger's defalcations on Americans to a minimum.

But a skeleton that fell out of the closet with an even greater clatter domestically was the collapse of the Van Sweringen railroad empire.

The protagonists of this odd chapter in Americana were Oris and James Van Sweringen, Cleveland real estate operators, who parlayed a shoestring investment into a $3 billion property and kept the headlines boiling with their exploits.

The brothers were a curious pair. Oris was two years older than James, but they lived and worked as though they were

Siamese twins. Both were unmarried. They occupied the same house, slept side by side in twin beds. Observed one social historian, "They were almost like two halves of a single personality."

Starting out, as noted, in the real estate business in Cleveland, the brothers got into railroading when their interest was aroused in the New York, Chicago and St. Louis Railroad, popularly called the "Nickel Plate," which had rights of way through Cleveland. Controlled by the New York Central, it was a desirable property, and the Van Sweringens heard reports that the Central might be agreeable to selling it. They put in a bid and got a controlling interest in the Nickel Plate stock for $8.5 million. Actually, the Van Sweringens didn't have $8.5 million to buy the property, but this trifle did not prevent them from acquiring it. They obtained a $2 million loan from bankers, using as collateral the stock they were *going to buy*, and this $2 million they handed over to the New York Central. For the remaining $6.5 million, they persuaded the Central to accept promissory notes that would come due in ten years. In short, the Van Sweringens acquired ownership of the Nickel Plate without putting up a penny of their own.

However, there was the little matter of the $2 million which they had borrowed and which had to be repaid to the banks. So they formed a corporation, the Nickel Plate Securities Corporation, and handed over to it the Nickel Plate stock which they had just acquired. The new company assumed the $2 million debt and the obligations on the $6.5 million worth of notes that were still outstanding. The Van Sweringens and several associates then purchased a block of preferred stock in the new corporation for $1 million (the brothers put up $500,000 of the money, which they managed to obtain from banks), and they obtained an additional million by peddling an equal amount of preferred stock to the public. As a result, they scraped together the $2 million to pay off the previous loan that was due the banks. The Van Sweringens took up all the common as well as 50 percent of the preferred stock, and since the common alone had voting rights, they owned the Nickel Plate Securities Corporation lock, stock and barrel, which in its turn tightly controlled the Nickel Plate Railroad. In short, for a $500,000 cash investment, most of which they had borrowed from the banks, they had themselves a railroad whose mileage was ultimately greater than all of England and the Netherlands combined, with shipping subsidiaries, dairy properties, trucking firms, mining properties, fruit orchards, transportation terminals, retail outlets, office buildings—a complex worth a total of $3 billion in paper holdings.

Using the same techniques, the Van Sweringens bought railroad after railroad. In each case they commenced with a small payment, usually borrowed from the banks, to take them over the hurdle of the initial hazardous stages of the financing. Then they met their indebtedness to the banks by unloading huge amounts of stock, bereft of any voting power, to the public. To annex a railroad, a hotel, a department store, they would conjure up yet another holding company. To amplify their leverage and dodge or whittle down taxes, they would sometimes launch several holding companies as the media through which to purchase a single railroad. Actually, no one method was used to build the labyrinthine empire. One holding company would sometimes be employed to control the stock of a second holding company. Or in a switch of tactics, the stock of a holding company would be controlled by a railroad. At the apex of the pyramid, tying the vast system into a single instrument for their personal control, they organized the premier holding company of all, the Allegheny Corporation.

The aim of the Van Sweringens was nothing less than to develop a railroad complex that would provide transcontinental passage of passenger and freight in a single system—something never before achieved, though often attempted, by American financiers. And the brothers might have succeeded in extending their holdings indefinitely if the Depression had not hit them. In the 1930s, finding themselves overextended, they turned to Wall Street for urgently needed capital; and to obtain loans amounting to $48 million from the Morgan syndicate, the brothers were forced to pledge virtually their entire holdings. By 1935 the Depression was still at its height, and they had not been able to bail themselves out of their financial difficulties. On May 1, 1935, they defaulted and the Morgan interests took over.

When the Morgan group foreclosed, it found itself in possession of properties with a paper value of $3 billion, which had depreciated to virtually nothing. The Allegheny Corporation, which was the key holding company controlling the system, was insolvent. The Morgans had only two choices. They could try to rehabilitate the empire or dispose of it at the best possible price. They decided on the latter course. For one thing, the American press was in an uproar over the shoddy doings of the Van Sweringens. The details of how they had picked other people's pockets on such a colossal scale had become the subject of bitter editorials and head-shaking all over the land. The Morgans decided it would not be fitting for bankers to try to operate such tarnished holdings. And since they did not believe they could get rid of them through the ordinary channels of investment, they took the unusual step of trying to auction them off.

Over the years there have been some rather bizarre means of distributing stock. There are securities that tumble so low no buyer can be found for them on any of the exchanges or through any conventional channels of trading. In such cases, the last resort is to unload them just like sticks of furniture under the hammer of the auctioneer.

A top specialist for over a hundred years in auctioning stocks was Adrian H. Muller & Son, of 18 Vesey Street, New York. Located across from St. Paul's cemetery, Adrian Muller lured groups of eccentric bargain-hunters—perpetual optimists ensnared by the hope that they would be able to buy a piece of "worthless" paper for virtually nothing and that the fortunes of the stock would change so drastically they would someday be able to sell it for a fortune.

It was to Adrian Muller that the Morgan emissaries came with an invitation to put the Van Sweringen railroad empire on the block. Miss Helen Collins, the brisk, businesslike woman who managed Adrian Muller, didn't flicker an eyelash when she was sounded out on this bizarre offer. She shrugged and decided she would have to put in a few hundred more chairs to take care of the bidders, the newspapermen and the host of spectators who were certain to descend on the premises.

The nation's press buzzed with rumors. Wall Street veterans and financial men all over the country were fascinated with the possibilities of this staggering rummage sale. People everywhere speculated over what bidders would show up and try to grab for peanuts this $3 billion railroad property with its maze of subsidiary corporations. It was known that anybody desiring to bid would have to deposit money with the Morgan group as a guarantee of good faith, but not even Miss Collins was given the names of the would-be purchasers until just before the auction began.

It was scheduled to be held on September 30, at three-thirty in the afternoon. An hour beforehand the crowd began to line up at the door of Adrian Muller. Armed bank guards arrived to provide security against possible rioters.

Shortly before three, the bidders themselves strode in. The Morgan group was led by its senior partner, George Whitney, tall, gray-haired, aristocratic, who wore a look of bored fastidiousness as he chain-smoked cigarettes. The Morgans were present purely in a protective capacity, to bid, if necessary, simply to keep the securities from going at a ridiculously cheap price. They were accompanied by an array of lawyers, headed by Frederick Schwartz, a slim, auburn-haired individual who walked up to the auctioneer's platform, presented his credentials as a bidder and handed over a bundle of portfolios containing the Van Sweringen securities.

Then he joined the Morgans as they took their seats to the right of the stand, placing himself next to Whitney, who continued to smoke one cigarette after another.

In a few minutes a second group of bidders entered and took their seats across the aisle from the Morgan group. The financial writers in the crowd perked up, recognizing three men—Colonel Leonard P. Ayres, a handsome individual with a shaggy mane of hair and a military bearing, who was a leading Midwest banker and an executive of the Cleveland Trust Co.; George Tomlinson, an industrialist whose face appeared frequently in the financial pages of Midwest newspapers; and George Ball, the multimillionaire owner of a canning jar factory. The financial analysts plunged into lively speculation as to whether Messieurs Ayres, Ball and Tomlinson were planning to bid on their own as individuals or were acting as the front for somebody who represented the real power.

The hands of the clock moved slowly toward the time of the opening. Both groups of magnates, flanked by a phalanx of lawyers, clerks and messenger boys, alerted themselves for the struggle. They whispered instructions, last-minute evaluations, advice. Documents were taken hastily out of briefcases and read over again; notes were passed on memo pads. The clerks had with them a battery of portable calculating machines on which they punched out streams of arithmetical calculations on the basis of which the bids would be placed. Finally, the hand of the clock reached half past three, and Miss Collins' assistant, a Mr. Kingston, stood up to open the auction.

Suddenly, people sitting in the rear of the room were astir. A short, rotund individual with metallic gray hair slipped in and took his seat in the back. Several newsmen could hardly believe what they saw. But there was no doubt of it. This was Oris P. Van Sweringen, the older of the brothers, whose default was the reason for the auction.

What was he doing at Adrian Muller's? It wasn't possible

that he had come to try to win back his property. Quite apart from the arrogance involved, there were serious legal difficulties. The Van Sweringens could not bid for property they had welched on through a repudiation of their debts. Moreover, they were flat broke and they owed the banks $40 million.

The reporters, along with the Morgan group, who had spotted Van Sweringen, were nonplussed. The bizarreness of the room added to the incongruity of the situation. It was a very old chamber that looked like an art student's studio out of Henri Murger's bohemia. Apart from the auctioneer's stand and folding chairs, there were no furnishings. The ceilings were punctuated by shabby old skylights, which looked as if they had been poked into place capriciously without any reason or pattern. The walls were yellowed with age and plastered with broadside notices of auctions, forced rummages and legal foreclosures that had taken place over past decades. Hanging next to several of these broadsheets were signs of a newer vintage, warning against conspiratorial bidding and other fraudulent tricks of the trade. This bare interior was bathed in the glare of naked electric bulbs that hung from the peeling ceiling.

It was three-thirty. The bell of St. Paul's Church tolled out across the way when Mr. Kingston opened the proceedings. The properties were to be auctioned off in four major packages, but the key offering was the one that included a heavy proportion of the securities of the Allegheny Corporation, in which the control of the empire was vested. This package contained a block of 456,000 shares of Allegheny bonds, 34,000 shares of preferred stock and 2,640,000 shares of common that represented voting control of Allegheny.

Mr. Kingston began by holding up a parcel of the less important securities. "What am I bid?"

Immediately Mr. Schwartz was on his feet. He put in a protective rock-bottom bid for the Morgans. Colonel Ayres speaking for the Midwestern bidders, responded from the other side of the room with an offer that was a little higher. Several other minor packages were offered; and the same routine was followed. The Morgan people sang out a bid, Ayres upped it. And when no one else spoke, the auctioneer's hammer closed out the sale.

Finally, the key package containing the controlling shares of Allegheny was reached. Kingston grasped the bundle, and held it up.

"What am I bid?" Fred Schwartz for the Morgan group sang out, "Two million, eight hundred and two thousand, one hundred and one dollars."

Colonel Ayres countered, "Two million, eight hundred and three thousand dollars."

"Who else do I hear? Do I hear another bid?"

No one responded. The hammer struck the stand. The deal was closed.

The reporters crowded around Colonel Ayres and ferreted out an amazing story. The real victors were the Van Sweringen brothers. The Ayres-Ball group had been bidding on their behalf and through a legal façade had enabled the brothers to buy back their property on a shoestring.

Several weeks before the auction, Oris Van Sweringen, in a desperate attempt to win back control, had sought out George A. Ball, the wealthy Cleveland manufacturer, and pleaded with him to bid for the securities. He took the canning jar tycoon out for a ride in the countryside, wined and dined him, drove him up a lovely mountainside, and having put him in a relaxed mood, launched into a discussion of the huge potential worth of the Van Sweringen properties, the bright future they could enjoy if they were rescued from the grip of the Morgans and rejuvenated with new capital. Van Sweringen succeeded in inducing Ball, a man in his seventies, to form a holding company, the Midamerica, and to dip into its treasury to raise $3 million to bid for the property. Moreover, Ball was talked into offering the brothers an option for 55 percent of the railroad's stock, once it had been repurchased, to last for ten years (for which the brothers would pay a mere $8,250 of their own money) on the understanding that within this period they would settle all their debts with their creditors. In other words, the Van Sweringens were handed back 23,000 miles of railroads, a network of coal mines, office buildings, streetcar railways, suburban real estate developments, trucking companies, a department store, a hotel and the Allegheny holding corporation for the princely sum of $8,250.

Oris Van Sweringen was confronted by reporters before he could slip away through the door. But he was too overwhelmed with emotion to make a formal statement. Over and over again he nodded his head and muttered, "I would have rather paid the bill." He was referring to the fact that even with the proceeds of the auction, the Morgan interests were over $40 million out of pocket as a result of the brothers' default on their loans. Finally, Oris managed to push his way through the crowds to the door; he climbed into his three-year-old Chrysler and was driven off as he sat reflectively in the rear seat, his chin cupped in his hand.

Fate continued to play slyly with the Van Sweringens. Years of financial aggravation and hounding by creditors had broken them. Ninety days after winning back the property, James Van Sweringen died; the next year his older brother, Oris, followed him. And George Ball was left with a mountain of headaches.

The collapse and manipulative comeback of the Van Sweringens, together with the Insull and Kreuger scandals, and other outcroppings of financial hocus-pocus, heightened the public's disgust with the nation's investment banking system. The Congressional investigation that had been launched to find the reasons for the market crash added its evidence to the record. It seemed essential that America's methods of credit utilization and capital financing be revamped to make publicly owned companies more strictly accountable to the public and to protect the rights of the stockholders. It seemed obvious that operations like the Van Sweringens' must never be allowed to be repeated if the people's confidence in business was to be revived.

Actually, even before the grotesque Van Sweringen bankruptcy and comeback which was merely the final chapter of the shoddy story, the Roosevelt Administration had prepared and introduced four pieces of legislation designed to correct abuses.

One condition that, in the opinion of experts, had led to the unhealthy situation of the 1920s was the practice of commercial banking firms operating in the investment banking business. In the former role they took deposits and financed commercial enterprises, and in the latter they were chiefly concerned with underwriting and using the capital of their depositors to finance their stock ventures. To eliminate this conflict of interest, Congress passed the Banking Act of 1933, which required that institutions previously engaged in commercial banking and investment banking must henceforth confine themselves to operating in one field or the other. As a result, the investment banking profession was completely restructured. J. P. Morgan, the leader, for instance, chose to leave the underwriting field and confine itself to deposit operations. A new firm, Morgan, Stanley & Co., was organized to take over its investment operations.

A second key law passed by Congress was the Securities Act of 1933. The aim of this "truth in securities" bill was to furnish the public with a complete disclosure of all significant facts about a company it bought stock in. The Act denied the use of the facilities of the U.S. Post Office or of interstate commerce to anyone desiring to sell stock who had failed to enter a registration application with a Government body. Neglect to do so entailed criminal as well as civil prosecution.

The Securities Act was broadened by a new bill, the Securities Exchange Act, passed the following year, which provided for the setting up of a Securities and Exchange Commission of five members, armed with the powers to regulate operations on the Big Board and other exchanges. Under the law all stock exchanges were required to register with the SEC. Manipulation of stock prices was outlawed. The Federal Reserve Bank was given the power to regulate margin-buying requirements. On the touchy question of short selling, the law took an equivocal position. It didn't prohibit it but erected restrictions around it. Henceforth no short sale could be made in a stock except at a price higher than the last previously recorded transaction. The theory was that if a trader were prevented from unloading at prices placed below the market, he could not so readily manipulate a stock downward by systematic short selling. In the following year, 1935, Congress passed the Public Utility Holding Company Act, designed to eliminate the employment of the holding company as a tool for speculation in the manner made celebrated by Samuel Insull.

Wall Street reacted ambivalently to the New Deal legislation. On the one hand, the old guard stoutly resisted any attempts at reform. Richard Whitney, who had been elected president of the Big Board in May, 1930, led the fight against it. When Ferdinand Pecora, who headed the Senate investigation committee looking into trading practices, sent Whitney questionnaires to distribute to members of the Exchange to elicit information, Whitney refused to hand them out. The president and his cohorts had to be subpoenaed to answer questions under oath.

However, Whitney's group was challenged by a liberal wing of Big Board members who were convinced that reforms were overdue and that it was necessary for the Exchange to change its image fundamentally if it desired to restore the confidence of the American people in it. A committee consisting of liberal-wing leaders was established to study the question of reform. It suggested that the Board of Governors be enlarged to include men other than those who were solely members of the Exchange, and that these nonmembers should be drawn from outside of New York. Traditionally, the pres-

ident of the Big Board had been paid only a nominal fee and
had been permitted to engage in other business activities.
But the committee recommended that a president should be
elected who would divorce himself from other business connections, in return for which he should receive a salary large
enough to compensate him for this full-time commitment.

The resistance of the Whitney group collapsed when
Whitney himself was indicted for fraudulent stock dealings.
On March 17, 1938, he was expelled as president; he was
later sent to jail. The liberal group took power and voted to
reform the Board of Governors in accordance with the suggestions of its committee. William McChesney Martin, the
secretary of the committee, was elected the Big Board's first
salaried president.

In the meantime, many rank and file members of the business and investment community, suspicious of the New Deal
legislation, particularly the setting up of the Securities and
Exchange Commission to regulate trading, had gone on an
investment strike, refusing to come to the market with new
underwritings. This was a serious matter, since the nation was
still in the throes of the Depression and the economy badly
needed private capital to create jobs.

Indeed, in 1934, Roosevelt had been faced with the tick-
lish job of naming as head of his newly established Securities
and Exchange Commission a man who on one hand could be
relied upon to administer the role of policeman vigorously
and on the other hand restore the confidence of conservative
business elements. There were not many men in America
who qualified, but Roosevelt settled upon an individual who
was brilliantly equipped for the job—Joseph P. Kennedy.

Kennedy (the father of the future President of the United
States) had made a fortune as a Wall Street trader and had
ingratiated himself at the same time with the New Dealers
by becoming one of the leading financial backers of the Democratic Party. The choice of a Wall Street plunger as chairman
of the SEC shocked Pecora and other liberals. But it made

good sense. One of France's legendary detectives was Vidocq, who had become chief of police after a brilliant career in the underworld. His success as a policeman was due to his intimate knowledge of the psychology of his former associates. He knew where the bodies were. While the analogy to Kennedy is somewhat exaggerated—the latter made his fortune by perfectly legal methods, adhering to the rules as they then existed—nevertheless, the selection of a man who knew where the Wall Street bodies lay was a shrewd stroke.

Kennedy was too restless to remain at his post as SEC chairman for more than a year. But during that period he fulfilled his mission skillfully. The investment community, apprehensive about the regulatory powers of the SEC, had been sulking like Achilles, refusing to come to the market with underwritings. Kennedy approached his old Wall Street associates. He talked turkey, laid down the law, cajoled and threatened. And he got urgently needed capital flowing back into investment channels. When he handed over his post to his successor, the crisis of confidence was largely over.

With reform elements in the saddle at the Big Board and Washington ensconced in a supervisory role, the image of Wall Street began losing its tarnish as the end of the 1930s approached. The outbreak of war in Europe, which turned America once again, as in 1914, into a major supplier of combat hardware, gave the economy a massive shot in the arm and lifted the nation finally and decisively out of the Depression.

When war threatened, the stock market did not behave as it had in 1914. Then, the prospect of combat had caused uncertainty and timidity. But now traders remembered the prosperity that the first war had touched off, and upon the news that Hitler had invaded Poland, the Dow-Jones averages climbed 20 points over the next three days. On December 7, 1941, when the Japanese attacked Pearl Harbor, the averages were at 110; in the next five months, gripped by temporary investor uncertainty, stocks fell to 92.29. But as America's war strength began to be felt, they started a long upward move, reaching 212.50 by May, 1946.

And as America progressed into the postwar era, the past would gradually be forgotten by many. Once again, the financial pundits would begin telling people that the nation's economy could no longer be judged by the criteria of the past; that the vast purchasing power generated by rising consumer incomes, the increasing affluence of the middle class and the organized buying strength of investment funds insured that the stock market would continue to go up and up; and that a severe crash such as occurred in 1929 was impossible.

And, perhaps, once again, the end would come, at the very moment the whole community had "convinced itself that the end would never come."

12

THE CORPORATE RAIDERS

THE BATTLE FOR 20TH CENTURY-FOX— THE RISE AND FALL OF A TEXAS FINANCIER

It took a world war to eject America from the rut of the Great Depression. And this it did with a vengeance. When General MacArthur signed the peace treaty with Japan aboard the battleship *Missouri*, bringing final victory to U. S. arms, Americans reached for the luxuries of life that had been denied them during the war and the Depression. The nation went into an inflationary spiral. Before the 1940s were over, the wage of the average workingman had leaped over 50 percent above that of the Depression years. With the rise in wages came a surge in Sybaritic living. Sales of goods and services ballooned. Hotels, nightclubs and restaurants were jammed.

Once again America had entered an age of affluence; but this was one with a difference. It was far more substantial and enduring than that of the 1920s. Then the workingman was largely unorganized and he worked for a fraction of what

he was to earn, even in terms of real wealth, during the 1950s
and the 1960s. Legislation under Roosevelt had laid the foundation for social security, minimum wages and other measures of welfare that freed millions from the specter of
breadlines in the event of unemployment. The Keynesian
philosophy of building consumer spending to a high level as
the key to insuring prosperity had replaced the old notion
that America's investment community had the first claim on
the nation's concern.

But even though this prosperity was more widely based
and had greater roots with the rank and file American, the
age was a curiously ambivalent one. It was an era of plenty
spiced with somber international developments. The first atom
bomb had been dropped on Hiroshima. Russian armies had
seized Eastern Europe, turning it into a Soviet satellite. The
Reds had launched a blockade of West Berlin, forcing Americans into retaliating with an airlift to supply the hungry population. Across the Continent contending troops glared at
each other, threatening to turn the slightest incident into a
new global conflict.

In the United States, Americans enjoyed themselves with
the febrile gaiety of children who whistle to allay their tension
as they pass a cemetery in the dark. On the one hand they
jitterbugged to the catchy rhythms of the musical *South Pacific*; on the other they sought release from restless anxiety
by reading Rabbi Liebman's *Peace of Mind*. A shocked nation
focused its attention on Capitol Hill, where Alger Hiss was
denounced by Whittaker Chambers for being a Soviet spy and
went to jail for perjury when he denied the charges under
oath. President Harry Truman, with his left-wing support shot
away by Henry Wallace, who headed up a Progressive Party,
and his right wing taken over by the conservative Democrats,
who broke with his welfare legislation, nevertheless won an
upset election over Thomas E. Dewey. A popular soldier,
Dwight Eisenhower, was biding his time as president of Columbia University before moving to Washington.

In the meantime, the New York Stock Exchange, under the stress of the war and the new conditions posed by the subsequent outbreak of peace, had been undergoing changes of its own. During the war, the shortage of manpower had caused the Big Board to take a revolutionary step. Girls were hired to be pages on the trading floor, in place of boys going into uniform. Early in the war, William McChesney Martin, the Big Board president, resigned and entered the army as a private, and Emil Schram, the head of the Reconstruction Finance Corporation, took over as president.

When the war was over, the Exchange launched a large-scale campaign to induce the rank and file to invest in a slice of America. The idea was to soften the aloof, austere impression of Wall Street, to bury forever in the popular mind the image of J. P. Morgan and his imperious eye and substitute the atmosphere of "just plain folks."

However, oddly enough, when the shooting ended in 1945 and a pent-up demand for consumer goods was released, the stock market did not initially respond to the surge of the economy. Stocks backed and filled for three years after V-J Day as investors remained uncertain about the effects of inflation. The outbreak of the Korean War added to this uncertainty, and the market remained uncommitted to a major line of action. Not until the election of Eisenhower would stocks launch a really sustained march upward.

This was an age of material abundance for the majority of people. And so they had developed a sophisticated new attitude toward abundance. Once, in earlier times, a visitor, meeting Andrew Carnegie, the multimillionaire, criticized him for having so much money and suggested he distribute it more fairly among his less fortunate brothers. Carnegie thought a moment, and then said to his secretary, "Get me the latest figures on my wealth and on the world's population." When the data was brought to him, he made some quick calculations with his pencil and instructed his secretary, "Give this man two cents. That's his share of my money."

As America emerged from World War II into an era of explosive economic expansion, the masses of people, far from criticizing the wealthy or opposing them as a class, tended increasingly to identify themselves with their aspirations. They wanted a great deal more than the two cents per person the socialists might have been able to wrest by confiscating capitalist wealth and redistributing it.

And the rich, like the poor, were still with us. Indeed, *Fortune* magazine found in a survey that the possessors of the older fortunes made in Wall Street and finance—the Harrimans, Vanderbilts, Whitneys and Mellons—despite F.D.R. and New Deal taxes—had managed to hold onto their money and increase it substantially.

In many instances the descendants of the Very Rich retained the attitudes of their forebears with regard to their wealth. The new generation of proper Bostonians was just as abstemious as the old. It couldn't care less about elegant clothes. It repaired the soles of its shoes and proudly showed the patched up holes. "It is *better* to be a frump in Boston," declared one chronicler who was highly sensitive to the nuances of fine breeding.

A Bostonian who stood midway between the new and the older generations was ninety-six-year-old Godfrey Cabot, who, while possessor of about $90 million, preferred to walk places than take a cab. When Harvard bestowed an honorary doctorate in classical languages on him, the nonagenarian celebrated the occasion by making a concession for just this one day. He took the subway from Boston out to Cambridge to attend the ceremony. But when a friend invited him to return home with him in a cab, the parsimonious old gentleman turned on him with a scandalized look and didn't speak to him for months.

A questionnaire sent by the editors of *Fortune* in 1957 disclosed 155 Americans who had fortunes of $50 million and over. Many of them lived with surprising frugality. Half of those questioned disclosed that they had only one house or apartment. The average number of servants was three. Most did the bulk of their entertaining at home, spending very little for socializing at clubs. And the clubs they did frequent were not the most posh ones in town. The Eagle Lake Club, operated by the second generation of Houston's Very Rich, was a barn-like, dingy building full of beds with broken springs. Forty percent of the $50-million-and-over class sent their children to public schools. Lavish living in this age of affluence apparently was indulged in only by vulgar upstarts with a few million dollars in their pockets and not by the oligarchs whose fortunes were almost too large to count.

Many of the harvesters of great fortunes found it was psychologically difficult to be rich in this post-Roosevelt age. For, while their fortunes grew, the possessions of value they were able to acquire steadily decreased in an age of cheap machine-made goods. Pointed out William Gilbert, the Victorian satirist, "When everybody is somebody, then nobody is anybody."

And yet, despite these negative factors, the possessors of great wealth have been amazingly tenacious about clinging to their fortunes and nursing them into even greater ones. Indeed, the *Fortune* survey of 1957 disclosed that F.D.R. and the New Deal, despite dire prophecies, hadn't confiscated the great American fortunes at all. By the 1950s the wealthy in postwar America were thriving as rarely before. Thanks to ingenious investment tactics, conceived by imaginative lawyers, the effective rate of taxation for individuals in the $50-million class and up was no more than 65 percent and in many cases under 50 percent.

To ward off the Internal Revenue Bureau, the survey showed, the typical member of the Very Rich kept up to 30 percent of his money in tax-exempt securities. In 1957 these earned a heady 3 percent (equal to a 30 percent return on taxable income in this bracket). The Very Rich were heavily in growth, rather than big-dividend-paying, stocks. They were constantly seeking out investments in oil and mineral resource companies, where up to 27.5 percent of their income was tax-free thanks to depletion allowances. One favorite device used by the Very Rich to cut down inheritance taxes was to buy undeveloped oil lands and sell them to their children at the low purchase price. If the lands, under development, greatly increased in value, the income was laid away for the children. If the land proved to be a dud, the father bought it back and assumed the loss for tax purposes.

Many of the big American oil fortunes have been nursed to burgeoning proportions by an uncanny skill displayed by the owners in the leveraging of money. J. Paul Getty, who in the 1950s came to the attention of Americans as one of the world's richest individuals, gained his wealth, estimated at a billion dollars, through an astute use of leverage. He laid the foundations of it by wildcatting for oil, and he enlarged it by finding himself in the classic position of having hard cash during the Depression, when most other people were broke.

Reportedly unhurt by the market crash or the treacherous years that followed, when so many traders went bankrupt on declining stock prices, Getty bided his time, and when the Depression was at its peak he began buying stocks heavily. He picked up stock in Tidewater Oil Company, eventually winning control of the oil firm; and he added other imaginative investments. One of his agents on Wall Street was Ruloff Cutten, the nephew of Arthur Cutten, who had learned the economics of the stock market from one of its shrewdest teachers, his uncle, and who became a valuable member of the Getty team.

Getty was a curious person. The epitome of success in the materialistic world of the present, philosophically and aesthetically he yearned for earlier ages when making money was not the supreme aim in life. A supreme activist on the one hand, he embarked on an elaborate withdrawal into the past, becoming an authority on French antiques and tapestries, Greek and Roman artifacts, Oriental rugs. He wrote monographs and uncovered facts about art that eluded the research of scholars. Capable of surrounding himself with the splendors of a Renaissance prince, he lived in and worked out of small hotel rooms as he traveled around the world on business.

This widely publicized billionaire received thousands of letters a month from strangers who bombarded him with demands for money. In an age of mass production, corporate anonymity and the synthetic public relations image, Getty remained a rugged nonconformist and an admirer of other nonconformists. He admired the man who, as he put it, has the nerve to "wear a green toga" instead of a gray flannel suit; who drives about in a "Kibitka" rather than a Cadillac; drinks "yak's milk" instead of a martini and votes "the straight Vegetarian Ticket."

Another expert in the art of financial leverage who had built his fortune on oil was the Texan Clint Murchison. In the 1950s, when he was at the height of his career (before he retired and handed over the reins to his sons), Murchison had already become a legend. Despite a fortune estimated at $300 million, he went around in an old battered hat and homespun shirt. He was self-effacing in the extreme; whenever he was pointed out to a visitor in Dallas, the reaction was, "That fellow worth $300 million? Impossible!" Murchison had a leathery face, etched with furrows, a squat nose and glasses. He looked like a high school teacher and he spoke in so low a voice it was sometimes difficult to hear him.

Yet, at the height of his career, he owned a network of cattle ranches in the United States and Mexico, controlled a string of chemical and public utilities companies and banks, operated drive-in movie theaters and a silverware factory; owned Henry Holt, the book publisher; and he rounded these out with a network of shipping, newspaper, bus and real estate operations.

Murchison and Getty were striking examples of multi-millionaires self-made in our times. Most of the Very Rich in the 1950s, however, were people who had made money or inherited money made in days that can never be recaptured. With the 1929 crash there disappeared the last of the speculators cast in a heroic mold. That mold was broken when the trading of the market was reshaped by the Securities and Exchange legislation. And yet, while in postwar America the lone wolf trader—of the breed of Harriman, Baruch and Livermore—has become increasingly more rare, he is not entirely extinct. Since World War II there has been a handful of plungers who, if not exactly cast in the grandiose mold of their predecessors, have walked with élan in their own smaller shoes.

With trading regulations on the Exchange considerably more stringent than before the crash, the most successful of these postwar plungers sensed that their major opportunity no longer lay in manipulating stocks, but in manipulating the companies these stocks represented. In these times, the big killing was going to be made, they felt, by owning an electronics concern, a movie company or a coal producer and speculating with its assets.

In this respect, they were abetted by a new social trend developing in America, which gained rapid momentum in the 1950s. The fanning out of national prosperity lifted new millions into the middle classes and created a broadened interest in stock ownership. But while a growing number of Americans became investors in the nation's major corporations, this ownership was diverse and unorganized. Thousands of stockholders, scattered from coast to coast, who were strangers to one another and without any common aims, allowed the control of their companies to fall into the grip of small groups of activists, who, owning 15 percent of the outstanding stock or less, actually controlled the company. At the same time, many private firms during the 1950s went public to raise money for capital expansion. The more stock they issued, the greater the risk they ran of an outsider, or a syndicate of outsiders, buying up the stock in the open market, gaining the controlling interest, and in some cases pushing the incumbents out.

Many of the proxy fights of the postwar period, of course, were entered into for highly legitimate reasons, often to unseat incompetent management and give the shareholders a better opportunity for profits.

In any event, a complex technology of proxy fighting was developed; highly skilled specialists turned up to draw the blueprints. A proxy fight could be expensive—a good-sized one could run to over a million dollars in expenditures by insurgents to overthrow incumbent management. Studies were made by raiders to determine just what type of company was ripest for the plucking. It was generally agreed that a management holding 15 percent or more of the stock was unassailable. For one thing, in a costly struggle, the incumbent could call upon the corporation to pay the expenses of its fight to stay in office, using the resources of its treasury as its war chest. The insurgents had to furnish their own financing. True, if they managed to unseat management, they could then ask the stockholders to reimburse them for their expenses, but if they lost, the money had gone down the drain.

So a new breed of speculator arose—the dissident stockholder who moved in on the complacent incumbent to wrest control on the promise of running the company more profitably.

The overthrow of management frequently caused a rise in the price of the company stock as the contestants, in wooing the shareholder, outbid one another with promises of juicy dividends or tempting stock rights. In some cases, the rise of the stock was enough to pay off the expenses of the insurgents' battle, even if they failed to defeat management. (Some skirmishes were started with the sole purpose of pushing up the stock for personal profit.) In any event, once the fight was launched in earnest, the grass-roots stockholder was king of the roost while both sides wooed him for his vote.

The right of a shareholder to vote his stock in his company's affairs is the Magna Carta of our industrial democracy. Under the laws of most states a stockholder not only has the right to send in his proxy to whomever he designates to represent him if he cannot attend the annual meeting, but he may send in his proxy as many times as he desires during the course of a proxy battle. The reason for this is that as he continues to be bombarded by letters and proxy material loaded with claims and counterclaims, he may very well change his attitude and switch his support. He is allowed to change his proxy up to the actual moment of voting. Proxy battles must be waged according to strict rules supervised by the SEC. Neither side can send out proxy material until it has been approved by the SEC.

Often in a proxy fight, all the devices of political and psychological warfare are enlisted. Both management and the insurgents mobilize an army of experts. Public relations firms are hired to function virtually as espionage and counterespionage agents, spying on the opposing camps, and reporting on enemy activity. Private detectives are recruited to investigate the background of each candidate named as a director on the opposition slate, with a view to obtaining damaging information on his public or personal life. Wire-tappers are employed to listen in on conversations, to snoop around the boudoir as well as the executive suite. One misstep that an opponent may have made, one financial peccadillo or an unsavory affair with a woman may be exploited to blackmail the opposing camp into surrender. A bombardment of letters is issued from command headquarters, hammering away at the opponents' sins of commission and omission. Whispering campaigns are started about the incompetence, the senility, the venality of the opposition. Phone calls are made at night at sudden intervals to strike fear and paralysis into the enemy camp. Motivational research experts plot subtle campaigns, aimed at the psychic needs of the stockholder, to induce a favorable response to their clients. Crisis huddles are held

288 —— THE PLUNGERS AND THE PEACOCKS

every hour of the day and night. There are no holds barred; all the arts of modern propaganda are brought to bear in the modern proxy struggle. Outwardly, the contest has the smell of a carnival, the showmanship of a Hollywood extravaganza. And all this is paraded under the banner of democracy—the appeal to the stockholder's vote.

A key figure in the struggle has been an individual strictly of twentieth-century vintage—the Madison Avenue public relations man. This new breed moved into Wall Street with its astuteness for creating public images for individuals, institutions and trends. Some public relations houses specialized primarily as experts in proxy soliciting, others in promoting personalities. Still others were expert in Government-private business relations, or became students of the international business field.

One resourceful pioneer, fascinated by the psychology and logistics of proxy fighting, was David Karr, who previously worked as an assistant to Drew Pearson, the columnist. Opening a public relations firm, Karr became one of a handful responsible for raising proxy fighting to the level of a philosophy. Indeed, he wrote a book which is an astute guide to the art. One of the major battles Karr took part in, a fight at Loew's Inc., is described by Louis Nizer, the legal counsel for the incumbent management, in his book *My Life in Court*.

Karr teamed up in several insurgent struggles with a gifted Washington lawyer, Alfons Landa, who contributed formidable legal skills to the science of proxy fighting. Landa was born of a Spanish upper-class family and he spent his youth toying with a number of vocations. He went to Vienna, where he reportedly studied with a view to becoming a psychoanalyst, but he subsequently settled for the law, becoming a top-drawer Washington attorney.

Landa entered into a series of proxy fights that became a landmark of strategy. Together with Karr and others, he perfected the technique of counterinsurgency; that is, when called upon to defend a management that was being threatened with overthrow, he launched a counterattack upon the insurgents to topple them from their own position of strength. When Leopold Silberstein, the president of Penn-Texas, unleashed a battle to take control of Fairbanks, Morse, Karr was asked to defend the Morse management, and Landa provided the legal strategy. Aware that Silberstein, although he was president of Penn-Texas, owned relatively little of the firm's stock personally, Karr and Landa calculated that the best defense of Fairbanks, Morse was a countermove to uproot Silberstein from Penn-Texas. The strategy paid off. Indeed, Landa and Karr ended up in control of Penn-Texas and of Fairbanks, Morse as well, when their client sold out his holdings to them.

There were other proxy strategists who generated notable struggles during the 1950s—Albert List, for instance, the financial wizard who, having dealt himself into control of a coal empire, a movie chain, and a network of retail establishments, tried to take over the Endicott Johnson Corporation, a shoe manufacturer, but aroused the townspeople in three communities in upper New York State to rally to its support and keep the firm in local friendly hands. There was Louis Wolfson, the ex-football player from the University of Georgia, who launched a bold effort to wrest the $700-million Montgomery Ward chain from the grip of the aging Sewell Avery, its chairman, and missed victory when his plan of strategy badly backfired. There was Tom Evans, a distant member of the Mellon clan, who took over the Crane Company of Chicago, the sleeping giant of the plumbing industry, and touched off furious attacks in the newspapers when he proceeded to dismember the labor force. There was Louis B. Mayer, the retired lion of MGM, who made a dramatic but unsuccessful bid to win back control of the company he had dominated for years. And there was George Lloyd who tried to snatch Decca, the record manufacturer, from the control of Milton Rackmil. Rackmil countered by charging that Lloyd was being supported by Serge Rubinstein, an unsavory financier with a jail record. An alliance with Rubinstein was the kiss of death. Lloyd denied the allegations, but Rackmil's ploy successfully swung the stockholders behind the incumbent management.

One scrapper who sprang from neither a legal background nor the synthetic environment of Madison Avenue was Charlie Green. Bantam-sized but gutsy, he started in business as a wholesale distributor. But he soon found his métier was stalking companies whose managements, he felt, were not giving their stockholders a square deal.

Green's fights with the incumbents were no tea party affairs. The boys could get pretty rough behind the ballots and SEC-scrutinized proxy statements. In 1949 Green mounted a successful attack against the management of Minneapolis and St. Paul's Twin City Rapid Transit Company. But insurgent forces, shortly afterwards, launched a palace revolution and ousted him as president.

Looking around for other issues, Green toppled the management of United Cigar-Whelan and then tackled the behemoth of the movie industry, Twentieth Century-Fox. This was in 1952. Television had erupted on the scene and jarred the complacency of the movie-makers. People were staying away from the cinema palaces in droves. Like the other studios, Fox had taken an earnings tumble. And stockholders were apprehensive. Hollywood executives, who for decades had been lulled by easy prosperity, now scrounged around for ways of winning back movie-goers.

The time was ripe for an assault on the movie-makers by dissident stockholders. But the incident that touched off the battle for Fox was a relatively trivial one. In 1952, Green was a minority stockholder, owning his shares as an investment. During a trip to Hollywood, he and his wife wanted to watch a movie being made, but the couple was barred from the lot. It was one of the costliest rejections a studio employee ever made. Charlie Green quietly girded himself with blocks of Fox stock, and he moved in to do battle for control.

At the time, Fox was run by a strange duumvirate, who

had made an even-handed division of the spoils. Spyros Skouras was president and directed the distributing end of the organization from New York. Darryl Zanuck was vice-president and headed picture production out of Hollywood. Both men were highly gifted, idiosyncratic, uncompromising. They were supremely powerful in their spheres of influence. According to Hollywood scuttlebutt (which may or may not have been apocryphal), they brooked no intrusion from one another; they didn't write or telephone one another but communicated only through their lawyers. The system worked beautifully, so reports went, until one day their lawyers stopped speaking and there was a complete breakdown in communications.

The two moguls had reached their eminence through different routes. Skouras, the second of three brothers who had emigrated to America from Greece, entered the movie business in St. Louis just after the nickelodeon era, put together a string of movie houses and, through an astute display of business daring, rose to the top. Zanuck started out from the relatively humble position of movie scriptwriter. He was a diminutive fellow who played an expert game of polo, was an avid health food advocate, stalked game in the African veldt and swaggered through life as though it were a perpetual *commedia dell'arte*.

In assaulting the Fortress Fox, Green aimed at splitting Zanuck from Skouras by offering the production boss the presidency if he joined the fight to unseat Skouras. But Green did not understand the psychology of show business. The relationship between Zanuck and Skouras was an ambivalent one. Much as they battled to preserve their prerogatives, they were brothers under the skin in the business of making movies, and they couldn't tolerate the "audacity" of an outsider trying to wriggle his way onto the throne of one of Hollywood's royal dynasties. Zanuck lined up solidly with Skouras.

Strategy meetings to counter Green's ploy were held in Fox's offices. It was a curious place, according to reports.

Surrounding the executive suite were steam closets, rubbing tables and shower baths, where the Fox VIPs relaxed in ancient Roman splendor. The elegance of the establishment suggested that Twentieth Century-Fox had fallen under the spell of one of its own technicolor extravaganzas. Here, ensconced in vapors of steam while a masseur methodically slapped their buttocks, if one is to believe the Hollywood columnists, the Fox high command lolled around with its battery of lawyers, financial advisers and public relations experts and planned the strategy to be employed to hold onto the loyalty of its stockholders.

In challenging Fox, Green had run up against a quality of opposition he had never before encountered. The pooh-bahs of Hollywood were unquestioned virtuosos at public relations; and since promotional ballyhoo was a key to a successful proxy fight, Green found he was carrying coals to Newcastle. In a letter to Fox stockholders he wrote scathingly about the movie-maker's skidding earnings, and he contrasted this with the lavish salaries the Fox high command was paying itself out of the treasury. Skouras and Zanuck retaliated by charging that Green was an opportunist who had made a career of muscling into companies where he didn't belong; who knew nothing about the motion picture business and who, if elected president, would close up the Fox studios and sell off the assets to enrich himself.

The Fox high command realized that the great vulnerability of their case, which ballyhoo could not gloss over, was dwindling motion picture receipts. For several years, Fox and other studios had been searching desperately for a technological breakthrough that would restore glamour to the silver screen and lure Americans from their television sets. Recently, Fox had been experimenting with a novel way of widening the screen beyond its usual size. It called the process CinemaScope, and it had plunged over $15 million into the venture, but as yet it had not completed a full-length picture in the medium.

However, Green's attack forced its hand. The Fox brain trust realized that the surest way to capture the imagination of its stockholders was to rush CinemaScope to completion. It leased the Roxy Theater in New York, had it converted to a CinemaScope screen and sent out invitations to financial writers, investment bankers, movie reviewers and other opinion-makers to attend a gala private showing. It presented scenes from three films that were in production—*The Robe, The Twelve-Mile Reef* and *How to Marry a Millionaire*. The showing was a big hit. The press went into rhapsodies over the promise of CinemaScope, and the Skouras-Zanuck slate wound up getting four times as many votes as the Green slate.

But if Green lost the battle, he had won the war. His message had been thoroughly digested. Whenever he and Mrs. Green went to Hollywood, they were treated like visiting royalty. The Fox high command thereafter ostentatiously asked Green for his advice on corporate matters.

The Fox battle was a rough, colorful battle. But an even more significant one—one of the bitterest in Wall Street history—was yet to come. This was the attempt by Robert R. Young, a financier from Texas, to capture the New York Central Railroad.

Young was an enigmatic man who would have made a fascinating treasure trove for psychologists. A throwback in some ways to the great market plungers of the nineteenth century, Young was a man of culture with a love for the humanities and, some of his adherents were to insist, an idealism that was conspicuously absent from other financiers of his type.

Standing only a little over five and a half feet, the son of a Texas cowpuncher who became a small-town banker, Young came east during the First World War. He had inherited money from his mother, had lost some of it in an unsuccessful business venture and had plunged the rest of it into the stock market, selling Mexican Petroleum short. The stock rose over 50 points and he went broke. At one point he was down to his last suit of clothes and he had to stay in bed while his wife mended it before he could go out job-hunting.

Then his luck changed; he managed to get a post with General Motors, starting at $100 a week. Thanks to his talent for figures, within eight years he rose to the position of assistant treasurer. Weekends, he buried himself in financial reports to prepare himself for intelligent stock trading. Irritated by the licking he had taken in Mexican Pete, he vowed that he would never again enter the market without thoroughly knowing what he was doing. He studied Moody's reports, soaked himself in all the investment literature he could get his hands on. Later he was to boast that during these years he was able to recall from memory the net profits and amount of capitalization of every major stock listed on the New York Exchange.

His diligence paid off. From 1922 on, he played the market steadily and won on balance. In the meantime, he was advancing rapidly at GM. In the course of his work in the treasury department he came to the attention of John Jacob Raskob, the chief financial officer, who got to think so highly of him as an investor he let him handle the bulk of his own market operations; and in 1928, when Raskob resigned from GM to manage Al Smith's Presidential campaign, he asked Young to join him and take care of his financial enterprises, so he could concentrate on politics.

By 1929 Young is reported to have made over a million dollars in the market. Months before the crash he had turned bearish and sold out. In 1931 he left Raskob and struck out on his own as a broker. He specialized in a highly speculative field, buying the stock of tottering businesses for a song with the purpose of rehabilitating them. He developed an uncanny nose for hidden values, pouncing on seemingly unappetizing properties, accumulating stock in them and bobbing up on the boards of directors to nurse them into lusty new money-makers. He became an expert in the intricacies of proxy fighting, buzzing around like a gadfly to exploit rivalry and dissension, ferreting out the gripes of disgruntled dissidents, darting about for insurgent stockholder suits to latch onto.

And he brought a new dimension to the struggle. In a battle to gain control of Allegheny Corporation against the opposition of the Morgan interests, he grasped that there was a sociological context in which his fight could be waged. Thanks to their control of railroad bonds, through which they ran the roads and pushed through policies, the Eastern bankers epitomized in the minds of many Americans that traditional bugaboo, Financial Monopoly. Young seized the opportunity to portray his battle as a struggle between the grass-roots stockholders, most of whom were Americans from the Middle West, and the oligarchical bankers of New York.

He hired publicists, experts in psychological motivation, students of the science of hidden persuasion; and he oiled up a vast proxy-soliciting organization that enlisted thousands of small shareholders in a crusade against the banking interests. During one appearance before a Senate committee on railroad financing, he delivered an impassioned speech for the grass-roots investor before a fascinated group of lawmakers. When he finished, Max Lowenthal, the committee counsel, declared wryly: "This man Young seems just like an evangelist—perhaps a self-deceived evangelist? But it's the evangelists who are making all the money nowadays."

Bit by bit and battle by battle, Young snapped up a railroad empire almost as extensive as that owned by Vanderbilt, Harriman or Hill. By the time he was fifty he was a multi-millionaire. The son of the former Texas cowpuncher bought a mansion in Newport. He had cast his eye on Fairholme, which was only a short distance from the Breakers, the showplace built by William Vanderbilt, the Commodore's oldest son; with his nose for a bargain he had been able to buy the estate (erected originally at a price of $150,000) for under $40,000. This was during the height of the Depression and real estate values had tumbled. Sacrosanct Newport was wide open to a man who had hard cash to spend, whatever his origins. Young also bought a house in Palm Beach, Florida. Winter he spent there; summer, fall and spring at Newport. He hobnobbed with the bluebloods, gave his daughter a coming-out party that was lavish even by Newport standards. As a social *coup de grâce*, he invited the Duke and Duchess of Windsor to be his guests. In recent years he had become close to the former King of England. When asked by an irreverent newsman how he squared his role as a spokesman for the underdog with his zest for entertaining royalty, he replied, "It's perfectly simple. I like the fellow, that's all."

Like many of his predecessors in finance, Young had a curious streak of mysticism. A believer in extrasensory perception, he was convinced that there was a world of spiritual dimensions beyond reach of the physical senses. He had an obsession for going off by himself in order to "feel a truth." He had deliberately picked a home in Newport that overlooked the sea, taking frequent walks along the three miles of rocky cliff and winding paths that towered above the Atlantic, accompanied by a dog and a pair of binoculars. From time to time he'd pause to peer through his glass at ships limned against the horizon, or seagulls swooping gracefully over the billows. It was during these walks that he laid out his strategy for a key business operation, planned a critical acquisition, developed a new insight into a financial situation that opened up powerful leverage possibilities. The cliffs that rimmed the Atlantic were his peripatetic headquarters, the nerve center from which extended the ganglia of his business empire. Here he experienced his most audacious insights, this sad, whimsical man, to whom the sea was most appealing when it wailed with the melancholy of bagpipes.

Young remained an enigma even to his close friends. They could not understand the storm that lurked within him. No one seemed more amiable than this little Texan—until he was crossed. Then his pale blue eyes turned to ice, and people had a sudden, awesome glimpse of what lay within.

Skillfully using financial leverage, Young bought control

of the Van Sweringen empire, the $3 billion property which, as reported previously, had been built, lost and then regained by the Van Sweringen brothers. Shortly thereafter, the brothers died, leaving it in the hands of George A. Ball, the Midwestern industrialist. Young formed a syndicate to bid for it, and won control.

Then he cast an eye on the New York Central. For years he had dreamed of doing what no other financier had succeeded in accomplishing—putting together a transcontinental railroad system. A major step toward the realization of this ambition would be to acquire the New York Central, which would extend his routes from the Far West to the Atlantic Seaboard. The Central was the nation's second-largest road (after the Pennsylvania), with lines extending from the New York terminal westward to Chicago and north into Canada.

The Central was richly embedded in American history. It was the child of Cornelius Vanderbilt, America's legendary captain of wealth, who had poured his lifeblood into its veins, pushing its growth in one historic brawl after another. The descendants of the Commodore had held on to the road through thick and thin, and even now a Vanderbilt sat on its board of directors.

The idea of snatching the New York Central possessed the mind of Young as he paced the cliffs of Newport. His purchase of a home, within a stone's throw from the Vanderbilt mansion, the Breakers, was a deeply symbolic gesture. For years Young sat in the shadow of the bigger, more lavish home, planning how he might move into the Vanderbilt executive suite.

Yet, there was more to Young's ambition than mere sentiment. There was the very practical consideration that the acquisition of the Central would add strength to his holdings. One of Young's subsidiaries, the Chesapeake & Ohio, was an originator of coal haulage, the nation's largest, plying its way through the West Virginia mining territories. The Central was one of the world's biggest terminators of coal freight. It would, in short, beautifully complement the C & O's operations. Moreover, the Central was sliding downhill in operating efficiency and this made it particularly vulnerable to a takeover. Indeed, the road had been losing ground for over twenty years. Before World War II, it had barely escaped going into bankruptcy. It was saddled with heavier debts than most railroads and weighed down with a high proportion of unprofitable trunk lines. Its passenger business had become pretty much of a drag.

Quietly, Young began buying Central common stock until he had accumulated a sizable interest. Then, in January, 1954, he emerged into the open. He informed the Central management that he had a commanding block of stock and asked to be appointed to the board of directors. He wouldn't be content with an ordinary seat, he said. He expected to be made chairman of the board.

The request raised the hackles of Bill White, the Central's president. A descendant of Dutch immigrants, White had started in the railroad business when he left high school, and he had worked all the way up, becoming president in 1952. Financial observers on the whole felt that White's stewardship was a competent one.

White's reaction was positively visceral. "If Bob Young is looking for a fight," he told newsmen, "it will be bare knuckled . . . and no punches pulled. We're not pushovers and we're not punching bags."

So the battle for the Central was joined. It was to become one of the most savagely fought proxy battles of the 1950s. Both sides prepared to use the fullest resources of the press, television and stump oratory. The in-fighting and the jockeying for votes were almost as intricate as the maneuvering of politicians to line up blocks of power behind one candidate or another in a Presidential campaign. In a play for the woman's vote, Young asked Mrs. Lila Acheson Wallace, the co-owner of the *Reader's Digest*, to take a place on the board of directors he was naming to challenge the White slate. "We need a woman's touch on the railroads," he said. Mrs. Wallace accepted the nomination, replying, "I think everything needs a woman's touch."

The press had a field day with local color stories. It told how eleven shares of the Central had been willed by a recently deceased stockholder to the city of Akron, Ohio, and how the Mayor, Leo Berg, announced that Akron would vote its shares for Bob Young. However, the courts ruled that a city could not legally vote shares of stock and so Berg's good intentions were nullified.

Young carried his case over television. He posed at his desk in his office in the Chrysler Building with a Confederate flag at his side, the epitome of the gallant rebel, wrapped in the banner of dissent against the Yankee bankers. For years Madison Avenue had been cheerfully exploiting God and motherhood, but this was undoubtedly the first time the Confederate flag had been hauled out to sell a personality in a proxy fight. Other props were used effectively. As the campaign moved toward its climax, Young's workers blossomed out wearing red and white buttons with the inscription "Young at heart."

The eye of television focused on the principals, Young and White, in a confrontation on the widely watched show *Meet the Press*. Upon entering the studio, the adversaries shook hands, but when photographers asked them to repeat the gesture for pictures, they demurred. Lawrence Spivak, the moderator of the show, flipped a coin to decide who would address the audience first. Young won. Twice more the coin was tossed for the benefit of the photographers. Each time Young was the winner. He said he had a knack of calling coins correctly, thanks to his powers of extrasensory perception. The photographers weren't sure whether Young was pulling their leg, but the little Texan didn't crack a smile.

The tension built up steadily as May 26, the day for the annual meeting of the Central, approached. The final stage of the struggle was to take place in the 10th Regiment Armory

on Washington Avenue, in Albany, where the Central shareholders would gather to vote on the contesting slates. Those
who attended would drop their proxies into the ballot boxes
in the Armory, while thousands of others would mail them
from home.

Both sides grew increasingly apprehensive. There was no
telling what might take place at the meeting. On similar occasions, contending sides in a proxy battle had been known
to organize demonstrations on the floor in an effort to stampede
the vote. Each side now made preparations against the possibility of rioting on the floor. The White people mobilized
a number of Central railway police to stand guard at the
entrance to the Armory. Young contacted the chief of police
in Albany to have a detail on hand to protect his supporters.

The atmosphere was so charged with emotion that three
individuals who had been designated inspectors to count the
election returns sent in their resignations at the last moment.
An emergency search had to be made for replacements.

Finally, May 26 arrived. Over a thousand shareholders
from all parts of America converged on Albany by auto, plane
and bus. In the crowd were brisk, young suburbanites, representatives of America's increasingly affluent middle class;
elderly pensioners; and that ubiquitous contingent of "little
old ladies in tennis shoes" who oohed and aahed, determined
to exploit this day for all it was worth. The Vanderbilt clan
was represented by Harold Vanderbilt, a great-grandson of
the Commodore, and the old ladies marched up in a phalanx
to pump the hand of the bearer of the celebrated name.

The following morning the counting of votes was begun
behind bolted doors in the Ten Eyck Hotel. Three professors
of law—John Hanna of Columbia, Bob Miller of Syracuse and
Covington Hardee of the Harvard Law School—had been selected to do the tallying; and seventeen other lawyers were
present to advise on any knotty legal question that might
arise. The tabulation was a slow, tedious business. All the
proxies voted had been challenged by one side or the other,

resulting in numerous technicalities that had to be ironed out. Since each stockholder had the privilege of changing his mind by sending in a new proxy during the months preceding the meeting, it developed that some of the proxies had been voted as many as a dozen times.

The tabulation took two weeks. And when it was over, Bob Young emerged the winner. He had won 60 percent of the 6.5 million shares declared valid.

But while Young emerged victorious, the ingredients of his triumph were paradoxical. Time and again during the campaign he had declared that he was out primarily for the support of the small shareholder, the "Aunt Janes," as he called them. Indeed, he made much ado about allying himself with the grass-roots voter. As a matter of fact, he had quietly plotted a different course of strategy. He had concentrated his major financial resources on going after the bigger stockholders, those with 1,000 shares and up. He was shrewd enough to realize that his greatest appeal lay with the large Wall Street trader. Most of the votes held in the broker houses were owned by the smart money boys, who were convinced that Young, successful in a long series of previous deals, would bring new glamour and profits to the Central. They were convinced that, at the least, a Young victory would result in a speculative rise in the stock.*

And the White-Vanderbilt interests, for their part, blundered into the trap Young had laid for them. They believed they could automatically count on the support of the big traders but that it was necessary to woo the "Aunt Janes" for victory. So they concentrated the bulk of their propaganda efforts on the grass-roots voter—and won him, but lost the election.

The little Texan had taken over the Central on the public promise of giving it back to the grass-roots stockholder, but

*This feeling was strengthened by the fact that Murchison and Richardson, two leading oilmen and experts in leveraging operations, had been prominent backers of Young with big blocks of Central stocks.

the shareholders, small and large, were in for a sobering experience. Stimulated by Young's victory, Central common stock rose at first, from 23 to 49½. Young raised the dividend to $2 annually from the $1 paid out by the White group. But then the stock, as it ran up against rock-ribbed facts, began to slide.

Young had made a major miscalculation. He had bet against the American future. A deeply rooted romantic, he was trying to revive the past, to restore the railroad to the dominant position it once had held. But he couldn't buck dynamic new trends in America's living habits.

America, thanks to the automobile, had been put on wheels. Increasing numbers of people after World War II moved into the suburbs, away from railheads, using automobiles for getting about in; and a whole new concept of Suburbia, U.S.A., sprang up for sociologists, economists and fiction writers to ponder over. To keep up with the move to the suburbs, retailing establishments moved from downtown locations into suburban shopping centers, and they turned to trucks, which were able to make quick door-to-door delivery.

In the meantime, with the mushrooming of chain retailing, a rising number of discount houses and one-stop shopping centers began stressing a rapid turnover of inventories. They refused to store or hold backlogs of goods, demanding that manufacturers supply them with their needs on a moment's notice, delivering directly to their back doors. Trucks, in effect, became moving warehouses, eliminating costly standing installations.

At the same time, growing consumer affluence generated a rising demand for sophisticated goods—hi-fi and stereo sets, fancy household appliances, precision cameras, electronic gadgets—all of which spurred the use of truck trailers specially designed to carry them. While the Central and other roads would retaliate over the next few years with aggressive new management and equipment to win back much of the ground they had lost and rebound with healthier profits, the day when they were the dominant arm of American freight haulage was over.

In addition, Central continued to be plagued with its own complex of corporate problems. The stock continued its downward slide. Young's boast during his campaign that under his regime it would go ultimately to 100, with dividends soaring to $8 annually, turned into a pipe dream.

Beginning in 1957, Central's earnings had entered a serious decline. They fell from $6.02 a share in 1956 to $1.30.

Young showed the strain. He had become prematurely old. His thin shoulders were stooped. His pride had been struck a severe blow. Not only was the Central experiencing rough going, but his business associates were also taking a financial drubbing, for as Central's earnings went down, their investment in the stock continued to tumble along with them.

Young too was not spared. The stock he had personally purchased in Central was slumping, and in addition, he was being harassed on other fronts. A large part of his investment was in the Allegheny Corporation, of which he was still chairman. He attempted to recapitalize the Allegheny by issuing new preferred stock in exchange for the outstanding preferred, a large percentage of which he held. But a former business associate, Randolph Phillips, irritated by a previous business dealing of Young's, went to court to block his action and succeeded in obtaining a decision that prevented Young from using his Allegheny stock for trading purposes.

Fundamentally Young remained a trader to the end, and the bulk of the collateral for his trading operations was in his Allegheny stock. Now in effect the shares were frozen, and he was unable to borrow on them. As Central common stock continued to plummet, the banks called on him to rearrange collateral of their outstanding loans, and he was forced to unload more and more of his stock as the value of his collateral shrank.

From 1953 until he had won control of the Central, he had personally accumulated a little more than 100,000 shares of Central common, and now he was being forced by the banks to sell his holdings while the price was tobogganing. He had bought his 100,000 shares at an average of $18 to $22 a share. By 1957 the stock had plunged to $13.50. To raise the cash demanded by the banks, Young sold virtually all his common stock in Central and Allegheny. By year's end he had been forced to reduce his holdings to a mere 1,200 shares of Central common, and he was left with 17 shares of Allegheny common. True, he still held a substantial block of preferred stock in his properties, but the forced divestment of virtually all his common, especially in the holding company that controlled the Central, was a severe blow.

On Monday, January 20, 1958, the Central's board of directors met at Young's house in Palm Beach to discuss what to do about the dividend. There was little to assuage their anxiety. 1957 had been a bleak year, marked by a continual slide in earnings. The talk was dispirited; everyone knew what the decision would be. The board voted to pass the quarterly dividend for the first time since Young had taken over direction of the railroad. He had been unusually quiet at the meeting, so much so that a director phoned him afterward to find out if he was well.

On Saturday, January 25, Young arose early in his Palm Beach home. The rest of the household was still asleep. He finished his breakfast and headed toward the billiard room located in one of the towers. It was a warm day. The sun was already climbing in a sky of sparkling blue. He walked into the gameroom. In one corner, next to the billiard table, stood a collection of firearms. For years, Young had enjoyed hunting small game and he had become an excellent shot. Now he looked carefully over the rifles and picked out a 20-gauge shotgun from the rack. It had two triggers. He loaded both barrels. Then he sat down, placed the butt of the shotgun on the floor and bent his head so that the muzzles nestled against his temple. He pressed the triggers. Blood spurted out from his mouth and fanned like a crimson napkin over his body.

The body was taken from Palm Beach in the private railroad car Young had used for trips—Central Car 28; and it was carried to Newport, where the funeral was held. Several years previously, his only child, Eleanor Jane, who had been one of Newport's most attractive debutantes, had been killed in a plane crash. Now her father was buried beside his daughter by the sea they both had loved.

Years before, when he had entered middle age, this complex man, who had written verse and fragments of an autobiography in his spare time, had penned lines expressing his bitterness and anxiety that were especially revealing:

Sad are my thoughts, for I am forty,
Sad as the drifting leaves this autumn day. . . .
Until today it seemed my path led upward,
But now I find myself upon a constant downward
*   slope*
Which gains in pitch until I see
Dim, distantly, a void
From which departed friends have turned tired
*   faces,*
And love has lost its zest,
The quest of fortune ended,
While none but liars house the halls of state.

Young's suicide was a highlight of the postwar period of proxy fighting. There would be other dramatic episodes but none that revealed more tellingly the helplessness of personal ambition when one is handed the wrong cards in a game with the Weird Sisters.

13
THE PLUNGERS
AND THE
PEACOCKS
TODAY

THE COMPUTER
REVOLUTION COMES TO
WALL STREET—THE
CRASH OF 1987

Wall Street has not changed much physically since that day in September, 1920, when it survived the holocaust of the terrorist bombing. Today, as one walks down the Street, starting from Trinity Church, in whose graveyard Americans of Colonial and Revolutionary times lie buried, and enters into the canyon of stone and steel buildings two blocks down at the corner of Broad and Nassau streets, he will pass the former Subtreasury Building, where the statue of George Washington, which survived the bombing, stands as inscrutably as ever. Along the way he will encounter soapbox orators haranguing knots of passersby, as they have done for decades, warning about Jehovah's readiness to hurl his thunderbolts down upon this conclave of money changers. But as the walker strolls down toward the East River, he will be greeted with the aroma of mobile food stands instead of the tangy smell of coffeehouses mingled with the odor of fish markets that assailed the senses of the casual browser during the prosperous 1920s and the depressed 1930s.

But while the physical aspects of the Street itself have remained pretty much the same, there have been widespread changes in the social structure of the market. At the end of World War II, the Big Board launched an energetic public relations campaign to deemphasize its snob spirit and lure the humble from Podunk, Keokuk and Timbuctu. To put the seal on this folksy image the Board of Governors selected as the NYSE's President Keith Funston, the former head of Trinity College, who had spread the message of good fellowship in countless after-dinner speeches throughout the land.

At the same time, brokerage houses like Merrill Lynch, which was founded by experts in chain store retailing, brought the psychology of mass merchandising to the peddling of stocks. Giving free investment advice, setting up monthly investment clubs, the broker set dead aim at the little old lady from Dubuque.

After backing and filling for several years following World War II, and through the Korean War, stocks moved into a sustained bull market beginning in 1954, under the Presidency of Dwight Eisenhower. The Dow-Jones averages went through the ceiling of 311.9 first reached in August, 1929, and which for the following twenty-five years had been considered well-nigh impregnable. Then, when the market began to falter in 1958, along came Sputnik, the first satellite to be launched into space by the Russians; and America, in a vigorous effort to catch up, embarked on a crash program of its own, touching off a burgeoning boom in electronics stocks and other space hardware. Up went the market, past the 500 mark, soaring toward the 1,000 level.

Meanwhile, Wall Street underwent far-reaching changes.

WALL STREET AFTER THE SECOND WORLD WAR.
GEORGE WASHINGTON STILL PRESIDES PROTECTIVELY
OVER THE NEW YORK STOCK EXCHANGE FROM THE
SPOT WHERE HE WAS INAUGURATED PRESIDENT IN
1789. BUT THERE ARE VAST NEW DEVELOPMENTS. THE
COMPUTER ERA HAS ARRIVED AND THE FUTURE IS UP
FOR GRABS.
COURTESY OF THE NEW YORK PUBLIC LIBRARY

For the first time, women in significant numbers entered the Street, which had been one of the last bastions of male enterprise, rising to high executive positions in investment banks and brokerage houses. A woman became the head of one of Wall Street's best-known investment houses and purchased a seat on the New York Stock Exchange. Another served as a commissioner of the Securities and Exchange Commission and went on to become a member of the prestigious Board of Governors of the New York Stock Exchange itself. A third became the investment manager of one of the nation's largest pension funds, with over $40 billion to invest. Still another ended up as president of a highly successful arbitrage firm, aggressively involved in the corporate takeover game.

One trend emerged that would have especially fascinated the old-time speculator on Wall Street. There was a systematic effort afoot to take the *speculation* out of human risk. The aim of the new intellectual age—to control precisely what can be measured and made quantitative—would have been greatly sympathized with by James Keene, Edward Harriman and Jesse Livermore. And, at the same time, they would have treated it with a great deal of skepticism, for they strove for a lifetime to calculate statistical probabilities, seeking the surefire system for rigging things, the foolproof way of manipulating affairs so as to come out consistently on top. And they never found it.

The question asked by the master speculator is, "Can it really be done?" The answer was that for the first time man was embarked on a mighty scientific effort to try to do it. Throughout the long history of his struggle upward, what has distinguished *Homo sapiens* from the machines he developed has been his ability to remember and to learn. But engineers discovered how to make machines that actually remembered and learned; that possessed sense organs equivalent to eyes, ears and fingers; that, like men, adjusted their future behavior in the light of previous experience. In short, they developed the computer.

The birth of the learning machine took place at the beginning of World War II, when Britain stood alone to defend herself against the scourge of Nazi air raids. The tight little island had been plunged into a struggle for its survival. England and her American ally studied the problem of how to develop the most efficient defense against the Nazi bombing planes.

Because of the great speeds the bombers generated, it was necessary to come up with an antiaircraft defense that took into account the fact that after an artillery shell was fired, the attacking plane would move a considerable distance from the point at which the gun had sighted it originally and that to bring it down successfully, the arc of the gun's bullet would have to intercept the arc of the airplane's flight over this distance. Therefore it was necessary to find a way of predicting automatically where the plane would be at the point of impact to adjust the firing range and focus of the gun.

To predict the plane's behavior by scientifically determined means, avant-garde mathematicians—Norbert Wiener, Julius Bigelow, Arthur Rosenbluth—teaming up with physicists and electronics engineers, developed an antiaircraft system that enabled Britain to survive the saturation air bombardment dealt out by the German Luftwaffe.

However, Wiener and his colleagues soon realized that they had seized upon something with implications far beyond the single application of antiaircraft defense. They had, in fact, come up with the key to unlock a whole new frontier of technology. By utilizing the techniques of feedback and memory processes analogous to the physiology of the human nervous system, game-playing computers were built that were rudimentary learning machines able to improve upon their performance by exploiting their own past experiences.

Not surprisingly, the emergence of the computer as a supreme calculator of odds was zestfully pounced upon by Wall Street. The game-playing machine entered the contest of picking stocks, and pitted itself against traders who used only their judgment.

Intriguing changes took place in the *dramatis personae*. Engineers, mathematicians and computer programmers invaded the Street. In austere old firms on Wall and Broad, where tradition had not been tampered with for generations, a new executive arose. Bearing the curious title of Computer Applications Specialist, he served as a coordinator, synchronizing the efforts of a battery of security analysts and computer programmers—the latter assigned to turn the thinking of the former into mathematical symbols to be fed into the computer for analysis.

All over Wall and Broad streets, students of the market hunched over stacks of huge steel boxes that—bristling with panels of small, blinking lights and batteries of switches breathing forth heat like some antediluvian monster—spewed out utterances to questions that were being asked it, in some quarters with a reverence once reserved only for the Delphic oracle.

Enthusiasts of the computer pointed out that Wall Street deals with heaps of numbers; they change constantly, and the relationships among them are complex. The computer, which can do billions of statistical calculations in seconds and instantly recall thousands of facts stored on its magnetic tape, can eliminate much of the statistical tasks a security analyst has to labor on, liberating him for more creative thinking. By performing studies on the historic earnings trend of companies or comparing the market behavior of a stock to the averages under a variety of previous conditions, the computer, said these advocates, can screen out of the huge universe of stocks those worth further looking into, dramatically narrowing the field the trader has to examine, so his judgment can be more effectively focused.

Computers began to move into the subtle, still largely unexplored regions of human psychology as it manifests itself in trading strategy. Mathematicians commenced to block-diagram many of the thought processes that actually take place in the mind of a trader as he moves forward to his investment decisions. Professor Geoffrey Clarkson of MIT joined the officer of a large-sized trust fund who, in studying what stocks to buy and sell for his portfolio, called on a number of companies. The professor spent several months studying the officer's habits of research, making note of the root questions he put to company executives—for instance, "Does this firm have enough promise of earnings growth to justify my putting my clients' money into it?" Clarkson drew up a schematic diagram of several hundred of these key queries and fed them into a computer to determine what stocks the electronic brain would select. The computer chose over ninety percent of the securities that were actually selected by the officer for his portfolio. In short, the machine had simulated over ninety percent of the actual thinking process embarked on by the officer in arriving at his decisions.

Wall Street was increasingly becoming an arena in which traders, armed with computers, were being pitted against one another in high-stakes, ultrasophisticated combat. The electronic brains were being employed not only to sharpen a trader's own strategy but also to track the footprints of those on the other end of the sell-or-buy position. Computers, using complex mathematical formulations, were being programmed not only to determine what a stock was worth but also, equally important, what other traders were planning to do about it. In the old days J. P. Morgan and his associates would acquire inside information about a company and secretly begin to accumulate its stock. Their buying would not be visible to outsiders until the price had been put up to where the smart-money people wanted it. By then it often was too costly to get in.

For instance, a plunger bent on a hostile takeover of a company would accumulate its stock at as low a price as possible, camouflaging his operations to avoid attracting the attention of the public. Once the price started to climb as a result of his buying, he would sell down temporarily to keep the price low. But by the end of each market session he would have quietly raked in a few thousand more shares, making less stock available for buying in the market. The rise in price would be so gentle it would be undetectable to outsiders.

On the other hand, a plunger having accumulated large holdings was faced with a problem: Now that his stock had been pushed up to a high price level, how could he unload it without so depressing the market that it couldn't absorb his stock at a decent profit? He did this by intermingling his selling with buying flurries so that the initial stages of his unloading were successfully masked. Indeed, as we recall, the old-time plungers frequently made their financial killings not on the way up but on the way down, unloading on declining prices.

But now computers, programmed to spot unusual trading through price-volume studies, could frequently pick up at the earliest stages the first faint traces of accumulation by insiders. Previously, the precise stage at which such buying and selling patterns began was undetectable to the outsider. He was like a bystander watching an auto race by. All he could do was estimate its velocity. But now he was in the driver's seat; he could *feel* when acceleration or deceleration began, as well as how rapidly the vehicle was gaining or losing momentum.

Early on the computer was put to still another test. It emerged as the means of automating the quotation network of the huge, amorphous market for over-the-counter stocks, representing publicly owned companies that weren't listed on the NYSE or Amex. Hidden in the hills outside the sleepy town of Trumbull, Connecticut, fifty-eight miles northeast of Wall Street, a compound of buildings mushroomed up to house two giant Univac computers and their satellite equipment, which flashed electronic messages over twenty-five thousand miles of a high-speed transmission belt. This complex functioned under the most rigid security measures. To be admitted into the computer headquarters a person had to obtain a card from a security guard and insert it under an electromagnetic eye for the door to open to him. The windows were designed so that operators inside could scrutinize outsiders but no one could look in. This compound bristled with heat-sensitive devices that warned of the merest change in temperature. If someone lit a cigarette in a forbidden area, alarm bells rang. Fortress NASDAQ, as this headquarters was dubbed, automated the market for OTC stocks, thrusting it into the high-tech world of the twentieth century. The electronic brains of the speedy computers enabled the OTC market-makers to flash bids and offers to their opposite numbers onto television desk screens, where quote figures were constantly updated as the bid and offer bargaining heated up.

True, the best-laid plans of mice and men often go astray, and in one case, a rodent triumphed over high technology. An adventurous squirrel emerging out of nowhere squeezed its way past the surveillance monitors, the heat-detection sensors, and the security guards and crept into the complex labyrinth of high-tension wires, creating a sudden power failure that blacked out the NASDAQ automation system. Thousands of stock dealers lost contact with one another; trades that were in the process of being consummated went dead. Conversations between traders and the exchange of quotations stopped in midair. Millions of shares of stock that would normally have been traded were lost before workers, frantically exploring every nook and cranny, discovered the offending squirrel lying dead in a tangle of wires. Meanwhile, another version of the computer bobbed up on the New York Stock Exchange through the so-called DOT system, which vastly speeded up buying and selling operations. The American Stock Exchange introduced computerized equipment of its own.

Other significant changes were taking place in the structure of Wall Street. The stock market was being transformed from an auction arena, dominated by individual traders, into a market where institutional traders were rapidly becoming the dominant force; for, paradoxically, while rank-and-file shareholders had been increasing in numbers, the amount of stock they controlled was steadily on the decline. The bulk of common stock was passing from private investors into the possession of institutions, and along with this, there was a shift in investment power.

The reasons for this had to do with changing patterns in America. Since World War II, many people who had accumulated fortunes in the days before Roosevelt and the New Deal reached the end of their allotted years. Their estates passed into the hands of widows and children who, inexperienced in investment matters and desiring ready cash, sold blocks of their inherited stock to institutions. With securities in increasingly short supply and institutions eager to add to their portfolios, the latter vigorously snapped up stocks from all classes of investors.

Accelerating this impact was the shifting of many institutions from conservative to aggressive trading postures. Mutual funds who acted for investors entered a race to outperform one another, and this was having a profound effect on the trading patterns of the stock market.

Acting as market-makers for growing numbers of institutional investors, several old bond houses added equities as a service to their new clients, functioning in the role of block traders. Unlike individual traders, the new block houses frequently did not go to the floor of the stock exchange to trade through the traditional stock specialists. They traded with one another off the floor, often "crossing" blocks.

Also, the structure of the brokerage business was changing. Heeding the hue and cry of institutional traders who chafed at having to pay the broker's commissions charged to individual traders, the SEC eliminated the practice of fixed brokerage commissions. Henceforth traders dealing in block volume transactions were free to negotiate their own fees, opening the doors to aggressive new competition for customers. With fixed commissions eliminated, not only for institutions but also for individual traders, a number of discount broker firms moved into the arena, eliminating the advisory and other additional services to clients provided by the traditional broker. They confined themselves simply to carrying out their client's trading wishes, charging in return a discount commission.

With a massive pool of investment money available, institutional trading skyrocketed. By the mid-1980s, block trades of 10,000 shares and up constituted over half the total trading on the stock exchange. Over 18,000 pension funds with $1.3 trillion available for investment controlled more than twenty percent of all the shares on the exchange. The NYSE had not been organized to handle this kind of trading. Big Board officials in their wildest fancies had never imagined the day when a trader would be able to buy or dump $1 billion worth of stock at the push of a computer button.

Thoughtful observers watching the growth of the institutional market with its computerized trading strategies began to ask disturbing questions. What would happen as computers increasingly took over the action in the years ahead? Would this lessen or increase the risk for everybody? Would the powerful institutional swingers, using vast pools of other people's money, be less prone to back off from a sharply falling market? Would they stay in with their tremendous cash reserves to prevent the market from falling apart?

Meanwhile, the democratization of Wall Street had definitely arrived. More Americans were involved in the stock market than even during the highly popular bull market of the late 1920s. Wealthy Americans always had realized that it was far easier to make money by allowing it to work for you than to labor for it. But now, thanks to the spread of the new investment populism, this strategy had become apparent to the grass-roots American.

Spurred by new tax deferment incentives, millions of wage and salary earners commenced putting money aside in Individual Retirement Accounts and Keogh Plans, and this, combined with a burgeoning of mutual and corporate pension funds, generated a new pool of cash that helped fuel a boom in securities investment. By the 1980s there were over six hundred mutual funds—not counting money market funds—available to Americans, covering the investment waterfront, ranging from the conservative fixed-income variety to speculative vehicles for options and futures trading. Financial institutions catering to the needs of small investors blossomed into giant money managers serving as one-stop investment "supermarkets," which flashed their message through high-powered promotional programs to Americans everywhere. Advertisements trumpeted the notion that because the investment field had become more complex and changes were taking place with increasing rapidity, it was important for people to be aware that they could no longer safely stash their money in a bank account or even in a stock or bond and forget about it. They had to be ready to shift their funds over a spectrum of investments as the economy expanded or declined and as interest rates rose or fell. One had to be able to deploy and redeploy one's financial resources in the most profitable manner possible at any given time.

To serve this vast grass-roots clientele, the profile of Wall Street was changing. The larger brokerage firms and other financial institutions embarked on acquisitions and mergers to broaden the financial services they offered. Some grew big enough to function as department stores of finance. In addition to providing stock trading services, they began offering checking accounts, credit cards, mutual funds, life insurance, and unit investment trusts. While a handful of major firms catered only to the richer investors, others began wooing customers with $5,000 and under to invest, providing them with personalized services. Ranking in size below these Wall Street houses were hundreds of firms who were not members of the New York or any other exchange. Many of them were small, one-office operations. Since they were not members of an exchange, they were not bound by its regulations. Relatively few of them offered securities research, confining themselves to trading services. For investors who aimed primarily to save money on commissions and who didn't require advisory services, these discount brokers were becoming an increasingly significant force in the stock market.

At the same time, the public was being bombarded with books telling it how to invest in the stock market, what strategies to use, how to pick growth stocks, how to employ technical analysis to build a better stock portfolio, and how emotionally to handle one's investment losses. Manufacturers launched, with much promotional fanfare, computers for home use and sounded forth on the value of using them as tools for sharpening one's sophistication in the stock market. Computers were turned out that could be programmed to perform technical analysis using the same concepts as those employed by the technical chart or graph plotters with a pencil, but these computers enormously speeded up the process of analysis, digesting a tremendous universe of statistics. The computers monitored the action of far more stocks and picked up market trends much more rapidly. The investor could buy an abundance of trading programs for his home computer or if he were clever enough could even write his own program for it. Merely by hooking his desk computer into a centrally located data bank he could, within seconds, receive statistical material from financial and business publications, annual reports, daily and historical records, on the entire universe of stocks, bonds, and commodities.

All the while, traders continued to seek riches in trendy investment plays. During the early 1950s uranium stocks had a speculative allure as new uses for atomic energy made the business headlines. This was followed by a high-technology boom that thrust IBM, Transitron, and Texas Instruments, among others, into the investment spotlight. In the 1960s the stocks of financial, health care, and franchise retail operations had a vigorous play, followed in the 1970s by the real-estate investment trusts that experienced a spectacular run-up followed by a crash landing.

At the same time, Americans became increasingly interested in investing overseas. One reason was that a number of domestic industries had reached maturity, resulting in a flat growth level, while businesses abroad were still rapidly growing. Although an obstacle to foreign investment had hitherto been that many overseas companies were unwilling to disclose as much information about themselves to the public as U.S. companies were required to do, an increasing number, canvassing for U.S. investors and a New York Stock Exchange listing, began to comply with the Securities and Exchange Commission's requirements for full disclosure of their operations.

Ironically, a chief beneficiary of this new interest in foreign investments was Japan, America's old wartime adversary. Japanese stocks in particular became a favorite of American investors as Nipponese technology began penetrating markets around the world.

It had all begun, ironically enough, in August 1945. During the holocaust precipitated by the explosion of the world's first atomic bomb used in a war, on Hiroshima, a miracle occurred. A Jesuit priest who ran a mission, after having been blasted into unconsciousness, opened his eyes, got to his feet and found that his mission was still standing although everything else was in shambles. He stumbled into the house and was amazed to see an attaché case lying on his desk exactly where he had placed it before the explosion. Trembling, he opened it and found it was still crammed with the money he had collected for his mission. A hundred thousand people had been killed, sixty thousand buildings had been destroyed, yet this attaché case had survived, undamaged, loaded with the paper yen he had raised for the Society of Jesus.

The survival of this bundle of cash amidst the atomic ruins was a dramatic omen of an even greater miracle, the rejuvenation of the Japanese economy which, surviving the atomic bombing, became one of the world's mightiest. Japan's defeat in the Second World War provided the very opportunity for its economic rebirth. Reduced to a shambles, it was compelled to start from scratch and, with considerable financial aid from Uncle Sam, it built a highly advanced state-of-the-art industrial plant. Under the umbrella of U.S. military protection, it devoted most of its budget to large-scale development of high technology and financial know-how.

The flood of Japanese exports that resulted, inundating markets all over the world, aroused concern, especially in the United States. As one trade official expressed it, "The Japanese are still fighting the war. Only now instead of a shooting war, it's an economic one." Once Nipponese soldiers had advanced relentlessly through China and Indochina, reaching the Philippines. Now Japanese businessmen, armed with briefcases instead of rifles, were advancing just as doggedly throughout the world, using the same human-wave strategy that the Japanese high command had referred to as *senjitsu*.

By the early 1970s, Japanese steel products were engulfing California. Honda motorcycles were bobbing up on highways coast to coast. Fords and Chevrolets were embroiled in a bitter, competitive struggle with Datsuns and Toyotas. Japanese traders had pushed into the midwestern commodity pits. Japanese-controlled banks emerged on the Pacific Coast. American homes from Maine to California sported Sony televisions and transistor radios, and U.S. astronauts on their voyages into space used videotape recorders turned out by the ubiquitous manufacturer.

Sony, which had started business on an investment of less than $600, in an abandoned Tokyo department store hit by American bomber planes during the war, had subsequently blossomed into an international colossus, and it became the first Japanese company to distribute its common stock to Americans via ADR receipts deposited through Morgan Guaranty's Tokyo agent. Each ADR, when originally issued, was worth 10 shares of Sony stock, and American shareholders received their dividends in dollars. In less than a decade, Americans owned a third of Sony's outstanding shares, and they found the investment to be highly profitable.

In ensuing years Japanese capital was to acquire stakes in some of Wall Street's most prestigious financial institutions. This trend was triggered by a change in Japanese law that permitted Nipponese firms to invest more of their pension and other institutional money outside Japan. The fantastic success of the Japanese as world traders, coupled with the country's traditional culture, which generated a high savings rate, created a huge pool of investment capital, larger than Japanese industry was able to invest at home.

Meanwhile, in the 1960s America embarked on a war in Vietnam, and the nation was torn by dissension. As the prices of goods and services soared, precipitated by the Johnson Administration's policy of providing both guns and butter— i.e., increased spending for the war without a commensurate increase in taxes to pay for it—inflation took off with a vengeance. People's attention was drawn to the growing instability of the U.S. dollar. The generations of Americans born after the First World War had never fully appreciated the possibility of a serious deterioration of their currency, although those folks living abroad who had been plunged into wars, revolutions and dictatorships had suffered painful experiences with inflation and currency collapses.

Now, as domestic prices took off and the purchasing power of the dollar skidded, the prospects of a steady growth economy based on a stable currency began to be seriously questioned by many. Advocates of a "sound" currency asserted that the dollars people tucked into their wallets and pocketbooks were not money at all in the traditional sense. Paper dollars were no longer guaranteed, as in the past, by their equivalent worth in gold or silver. The value of the paper dollar was determined by the amount that is printed. Specifically, America's banking system, led by the Federal Reserve Board, argued the "sound" money people, created paper dollars through a series of sophisticated bookkeeping maneuvers that the banks arbitrarily accepted as money. The holders of paper dollars may believe they have a legal claim on physical assets, but they really don't, asserted the skeptics, for the Fed's excessive expansion of the paper money supply had led to a situation where the outstanding claims of the people far outweighed the nation's tangible physical assets. The current dollar was in effect a government IOU that Uncle Sam hoped to pay off by going still further into debt; and this procedure of servicing debt by issuing more debt would continue on and on in the way a compulsive spender, deeply in hock, keeps on handing out IOUs all over the place until the roof falls in.

The fear that the nation could become unable to stabilize the purchasing power of its currency and that this could lead to runaway inflation seeped into the awareness of Americans with a shock. In the face of this threat, inflation and the management of money were no longer preoccupations solely of the economic experts. They had become "in" topics of discussion.

Participating in these discussions were growing numbers of women who, to an even greater extent than in the 1920s, were taking part in the money management game. Concern over inflation even filtered into the consciousness of that epitome of America's upward aspiring young woman, the *Cosmo* girl. Proclaimed a contemporary advertisement for *Cosmopolitan,* expounder of feminist chic for the millions: "How does a smart girl fight inflation? . . . You start reading everything you can put your hands on about managing money. . . . *Nobody* can afford to be a dumb-dumb these days. My favorite magazine calls inflation a challenge. . . . Says I am to meet it like all the other challenges I've faced and come out a better, more interesting person at the other end."

A number of factors conspired to stoke inflation. In the 1970s the Arab oil nations wrested from the big foreign oil companies the right to own the production reaped from their soil. They banded together in OPEC, which functioned as a cartel that successfully kept down production. As a result, the prices of oil skyrocketed, provoking a further round of inflation in America and other countries dependent on oil imports to power autos and heat homes and businesses. Moreover, wealthy Arab sheikhs spent their money lavishly on the good life in America, pouring oceans of cash into U.S. banks and fueling inflation even further.

A cult of doomsday books and articles spewed forth from the presses, cautioning Americans about the coming collapse of the dollar and prescribing what steps the reader should take to protect himself. Investors moved into various hedges against inflation. One tempting practice was investing in *objets d'art*. Sophisticated people pointed out that paintings by the old masters were one of the few gilt-edged securities available in periods of political and social unrest. With the value of paper money deteriorating, the masterpieces of sculpture, painting, and antique furniture functioned as highly negotiable currency in London, New York and other world capitals. Another vehicle investors moved into against shaky currencies was diamonds. A Pacific Coast exchange, which traded commodities, launched an experiment in trading diamond futures contracts.

But the most attractive inflationary hedge was gold. The aureate metal always had exerted a potent mystique for people everywhere. Gold is accepted universally as a measure of exchange. At times, paper money may not be. Throughout centuries of warfare, revolutions and economic disasters, the possession of gold in times of crisis has meant the difference between eating and starving for many. In various parts of the world, hoarding gold was a veritable way of life. In Asia, for instance, smugglers risked sneaking the precious metal over borders even though the punishment for being caught was jail or execution. Buddhist monks and Indian gurus hid gold in the folds of their robes, and peddlers concealed the metal in containers of dried milk. Browsing through the winding, foul-smelling streets of Bombay amidst the panhandlers, a visitor would come across an array of shops stocked with gold, bracelets and religious charms for the natives who bought them for the same reason Americans collected insurance policies.

In the 1970s U.S. citizens joined the world fraternity of gold traders when for the first time in forty years they were permitted to own gold legally, a right that had been wrested from them when President Franklin Roosevelt took America off the gold standard and prohibited owning and trading the precious metal by its citizens. With the shackles removed, there was a rush to buy the yellow metal reminiscent of the spirited trading in Gilpin's Gold Room during the Civil War, when purchasing gold was employed as a hedge against possible defeat of the Union armies. At that time some of the gold plungers amassed fortunes that launched them into positions of power in post-Civil War America, enabling them to become the nation's foremost captains of industry and the founders of illustrious family dynasties.

Just as traders in Gilpin's Gold Room had fixed their eyes obsessively on an indicator that displayed the price of each transaction, so sophisticated modern traders focused their attention on London, where precisely at ten-thirty each morning five traders representing Britain's leading gold dealers stepped into an ancient room at the Bank of Rothschild in St. Swithin's Lane and, settling into faded green chairs behind which hung a portrait of the last Russian czar, began a spirited exchange of bidding and offering, marked by each man's raising or lowering a tiny Union Jack on his desk, thereby signaling his trading intentions, and setting the price of gold at which most transactions around the world would be made that day.

Some American zealots (who were dubbed "goldbugs" by the irreverent) hoarded gold bricks in underground storage rooms, muttering that if runaway inflation broke out, resulting in a crash of the dollar, they could be the only "bankers" surviving to do business.

A growing number of Americans came to fear that inflation was indestructible because of the social values America lived by. It had been operating since the New Deal on the premise that if a choice had to be made, full employment was a more acceptable goal than keeping prices stable. The problem was admittedly complex. Obviously, governments needed to expand the paper money supply to meet legitimate social needs. But to what extent and where must the politicians call a stop?

The bleak reality, said the skeptics, was that throughout the ages what had given money its worth was its scarcity. The gold that traditionally backed money was limited in supply. But once money had been unhitched from gold and printed at the whim of politicians, and the more pockets into which it was distributed, the less valuable it became. Unpalatable as the idea was to idealists, if paper money issued via the printing press was made as freely available as the air we breathe, it would become just as cheap.

The great paradox was that despite stubbornly persistent pockets of poverty, never did the great bulk of Americans have it so good from a material standpoint. The age-old dream of the Utopian philosophers of redistributing the wealth of the world from the rich few into the pockets of the many had been taking place at a striking pace. However, as the doubters pointed out, there was a hidden trap on the road to Utopia. As the average man continued to win an increasing share of the world's material possessions, the money he received was relentlessly shrinking in value. The end result could be a grim mockery, for if the masses of the human race ever succeeded by some miracle in getting their hands on the whole of the world's wealth, they could find that it had turned to ashes. The masses, overloaded with worthless paper money, would be as rich as Croesus—sitting on a garbage dump.

However, as Americans entered the 1980s, the nation's economy, as far as inflation was concerned, took a surprisingly favorable turn. Thanks to infighting among the members of OPEC, the price monopoly of the oil cartel crumbled. Beginning in 1982, the rate of inflation was rolled back to a more tolerable level, and the appetite for gold buying abated. However, potentially inflationary bias remained and threatened to erupt again. As government spending soared under President Reagan's military programs and as Congress continued to earmark money freely for social programs while failing in the face of Presidential resistance to provide the taxes to pay for them, the nation plunged deeper into debt.

In the meantime, a new breed of Plungers and Peacocks emerged to try their luck under the changed conditions that had unfolded. One of the earliest and most colorful of these was a pioneer of the mutual fund concept, Bernie Cornfeld, who was an odd mixture of dreamer and pragmatist from the environs of Brooklyn. Starting out as a social worker and backer of Norman Thomas, a Socialist candidate for the Presidency, Cornfeld ended up as a cult figure in the investment world. In a little over a decade he accumulated over $100 million by launching IOS, Ltd., a mutual fund that aimed to make the masses of middle- and lower-income people prosperous through the blessings of professional management. "We're in the business of literally converting the proletariat to the leisured class, painlessly and without violence," Cornfeld enthused. "It's revolutionary and goddamn exciting."

Cornfeld's profit-sharing Utopia seemed feasible. The stock market in the years since the war had been climbing with only a few minor reverses. Cornfeld was convinced that prosperity was here to stay. The market was no longer a roller coaster. Like the space ships headed for the moon, it had nullified the laws of gravity.

Hammering away at the theme that the masses could make money in the market without any particular skills of their own by hiring experts to do their masterminding, Cornfeld piloted IOS into a global behemoth. He operated out of headquarters in the tax-free Bahamas, from where he could pour money into the stock market unhampered by SEC rules. He applied another astute notion. Instead of having his fund invest in stocks directly, he used IOS to invest in other funds that did the actual investment in stocks, squeezing his leverage to the utmost. He referred to his flagship enterprise as the Fund of Funds, borrowing the legendary appellation of Solomon, the King of Kings. To promote his venture with maximum ballyhoo, Cornfeld assembled as his subalterns a galaxy of top celebrities.

Cornfeld also trained his salesmen meticulously. One of his colleagues who indoctrinated IOS recruits told a story that, while it may be apocryphal, certainly illustrates the mood. A veteran IOS salesman took a rookie on house-to-house canvassing. A family invited them to lunch. During the meal the sales pro suddenly unlaced his shoe, took off his sock and methodically proceeded to clean his toenails with his dinner fork. The trainee's stomach turned a somersault. But no one reacted visibly. Indeed, the salesman inked the family to an IOS contract, explaining to the recruit afterward that he had demonstrated to him that a person could achieve anything on earth if he had enough nerve.

As he zoomed over the fast track of international finance, Cornfeld took on the snappy *persona* of a global swinger. He drenched himself in lavish scents, had his suits made by Pierre Cardin, had his thinning hair coiffed by Vidal Sassoon. He maintained sumptuous quarters in London's Belgravia and in a chalet in Switzerland that had once belonged to Napoleon. Here Cornfeld maintained an exuberant entourage that partied from dawn to dawn while majordomos fawned before it as if this were the Winter Palace of the Russian Czars. Yet despite his lavish caperings, Cornfeld never lost touch with his homely Brooklyn origins. While his guests dined on *filet de boeuf mirabeau* washed down with vintage Madeira, Cornfeld guzzled Coca-Cola and munched on pastrami sandwiches shipped from Manhattan's Lower East Side.

Cornfeld's high-flying career ended in a crash landing. Several irresponsible officials plunged IOS money into highly speculative ventures, exposing the fund most dangerously in case the stock market, which had been so obliging to it, should turn around with a back-of-the-hand slap. And this is what happened. The bull market that had been supporting IOS's euphoric dreams suddenly went into a tailspin, resulting in a prolonged bear market. This drop clobbered the value of the IOS investment portfolio, and this, coupled with management's skyrocketing expenses and shaky bookkeeping practices, doomed the enterprise.

Meanwhile, as his troubles mounted, Cornfeld confronted them with a jaunty bravado. He went about tirelessly bolstering the morale of his entourage, sending it into paroxysms of laughter with his quips and belly jokes, that scattered the gloom.

The end was ironic. The board of directors dropped Cornfeld from the enterprise he had founded and that had given them riches beyond their dreams, calling in outsiders in a frantic effort to salvage the carnage.

The poet Robert Browning wrote, "Ah, but a man's reach should exceed his grasp, or what's a heaven for?" Cornfeld failed despite his basically good intentions because his aims outspanned his grasp in trying to reach his private heaven. However, the wants of society he sought to meet were genuine and his concept was valid. The great masses of people needed a vehicle that pooled their money and put it into investments that would protect them in an economy threatening to be undermined by insidiously creeping inflation. Cornfeld had been the first to prove on an impressive scale how a mutual fund, armed with mass purchasing power from grass-roots investors, could wield decisive might in the councils of international finance.

Another individual who popped into the business news during America's growing concern over inflation was Charles Engelhard, the head of Engelhard Minerals & Chemicals Corporation. A mover and shaker of the precious metals trading market who ran a global hedge against the falling value of the world's currencies, Engelhard was a portly, heavily jowled individual with a lined face and fringes of prematurely white hair who walked with a cane and reminded some people of Sydney Greenstreet in one of his espionage thrillers. Indeed, Ian Fleming, the creator of secret agent James Bond, knew Engelhard socially and was so mesmerized by his personality that when he came to write *Goldfinger,* the author is said to have based his fictional character on the real-life industrialist. However, Engelhard, far from being a spiritual descendant of Jay Gould, the "goldbug," was a solid citizen. He was a major financial supporter of the Democratic Party, a backer of John F. Kennedy when he ran for the presidency and a close friend of President Lyndon Johnson. Ironically, while the Johnson Administration during the Vietnam War preferred to unleash a flood of paper dollars instead of risking the political consequences of raising taxes to foot America's war bills, Engelhard was busy running a company dealing in precious metals to protect itself against the consequences of such a reckless printing of paper money. His business operations, Engelhard insisted, were valuable "as long as we must live in a world economy that is basically inflationary in nature."

Meanwhile, on the corporate front, other significant developments had been taking place. American industry, fueled by sturdily rising stock prices, exploded with a rash of mergers and acquisitions. A new kind of gamester bobbed up, putting together conglomerate businesses that raised the merger technique to the nth power. In an ordinary acquisition, an entrepreneur bought a firm in the same line of business to expand the scope of his operations. In putting together a conglomerate, however, management acquired firms in totally unrelated fields. The aim in many cases was to show a quick jump in earnings and boost the price of one's stock on Wall Street. In crazy-quilt fashion, high-tech firms merged with catfood makers, food processors with funeral parlor operators, makers of auto parts with movie producers, insurance firms with shipping companies. The word "conglomerate" was decidedly apropos, since it signified a variety of irregularly clustered components pressed together in a mass (or mess).

Free-swinging conglomerate-builders based their strategy on the magic concept of "synergism," according to which two and two, if added up creatively enough, could equal six. The word "synergism" was alleged to have been dreamed up by a professor who described it as the process of mixing strong black coffee with slugs of Irish whiskey. The impact could be something one hadn't bargained for.

Into this Alice in Wonderland of conglomerate-building stepped an enthusiastic financier, James Ling, who, parlaying a few thousand dollars into an industrial empire, emerged for a brief time as a leading sage on Wall Street and then went broke when his dizzily leveraged enterprises came crashing down. Another swinger was Ben Heineman, who acquired the Chicago-Northwest Railroad and added a dazzling array of enterprises. A sudden drop in the stock market ended his dreams.

One particularly brilliant player in the corporate takeover game was Charles Bluhdorn, a Viennese immigrant who started out by making a fortune in the commodity pits and subsequently began trading companies as he had formerly peddled corn futures, ending up with the goliath Gulf + Western Corporation, a firm that dealt in sugar, filmmaking, real estate, metals, and auto parts manufacturing. Bluhdorn built so well in his own eccentric fashion—he was called the Mad Austrian by friends who were bewildered by his hyperkinetic personality—that his conglomerate enterprise became a thriving superpower.

Still another plunger who hit the jackpot—in this case by hitching his wagon to the star of high technology—was a former professor of psychiatry at Yale who, abandoning his studies of Freudian behavior in order to make money on Wall Street, programmed a computer to work out a gigantic global strategy for trading gold and silver. During a single fabulous week, when virtually every other trader in the world was paralyzed by a sudden currency crisis, this ex-psychiatrist emerged as the only dealer who, thanks to the calculations spewed out by his computer, was willing to risk making a market in precious metals. He was rewarded by becoming a multimillionaire, something neither Freud nor IBM could have foreseen.

In this madcap Maytime of adventuring, a particularly profitable ploy turned out to be in the venerable field of ranching. A major incentive was the tax advantage Uncle Sam offered for building up the quality of the nation's herds through cattle breeding. Out on the range where Wyatt Earp once galloped with his six-shooter, a new kind of cowboy rode tall in the saddle. "I'm an old cowhand" became a popular ditty with a new stripe of Plungers and Peacocks, nurtured on Park Avenue and in Chevy Chase, who didn't step within a thousand miles of Matt Dillon territory yet profited as absentee cowpokes. Not only did cattle breeding via hired managers prove profitable for these dudes, but also ultrapotent bulls who performed legendary feats as breeders and exacted fancy prices became highly prized by speculators operating in their own special bull market. Those bulls who won reputations through their sexual displays were housed in special quarters festooned with plaques signifying the awards they had reaped for their mating exploits, and they were showered with the reverence usually reserved for charismatic movie stars. An ultravirile bull was often owned by several traders eager for a piece of the action, each buying a stake in his seed.

The delicate task of mating a bull with the most suitable paramour was handled by sophisticated computers in whose electronic memories were stored a mass of statistics on the track record of bulls from celebrated sires. When a super-potent bull was ready to be mated, his statistics were flashed electronically to a terminal, where a battery of computers sifted through a heap of statistics on heifers all over America and came up with an ideal *inamorata*. Once this was calculated, the two lovers, sad to relate, didn't meet. They joined forces through the technological blessings of artificial insem-ination, thanks to which vials of frozen sperm were shipped all over America. Computer breeding became so lucrative that a small army of speculators got into the act and bull semen became an avidly sought-after commodity. Swingers entered the game, grabbing up as many vials of frozen semen as they could lay their hands on. Some traders literally measured their wealth by the vials they owned. One jaunty risk-taker, exuberant over his success in the bull market, an-nounced a research center to breed champion racehorses through computerized lovemaking, and there were some who quipped that breeding humans by computer was just around the corner.

Not around the corner but very much here today was Florida, historically the scene of land scams, booms and boon-dogles and which became the site for a new kind of game-playing. The Sunshine State was lavishly endowed with orange groves, and a slew of pitchmen bobbed up to sell them as a tax shelter. The planting of orange groves appealed not only to money-thirsty Americans but also to well-heeled foreign-ers, many of whom had never tasted an American orange. Investors from France, Greece, Germany and even trust fund managers from canny, tightfisted Scotland rushed into Florida citrus grove ventures. One illustrious *grande dame*, de-scended from Hungarian nobility, became an ardent booster of Florida oranges, sinking her family wealth into them, and prominent American athletes gave their ringing endorse-ments in ads that touted the blessings of tax-sheltered orange juice.

One firm, American Agronomics, was organized to issue stock on Wall Street to trade on the assets of grove purchases. However, battered by sliding profits and lawsuits, the owners gave up, and new management took over. Suddenly two individuals bobbed up, a husband and wife in Florida, who started buying the firm's stock heavily. The spectacle of these individuals avidly snatching up sizable amounts of stock in a company whose prospects were clouded by tumbling earnings and years of stockholder litigation seemed to defy reason. Then word surfaced that a West Coast lawyer was also energetically gobbling up shares in the firm.

The reason behind this was piquant. As the firm's troubles with the SEC and the investors' lawsuits became widely publicized, a clique of professional bears on Wall Street had begun selling the stock heavily short, expecting prices to tumble still further. The husband-and-wife team in Florida and the West Coast lawyer, carefully scrutinizing the company's balance sheet, concluded that there would not be enough floating stock around to allow the short sellers to cover themselves by buying back their shares. Short sales had zoomed to 90,000 shares and the total floating supply was less than 350,000 shares.

In short, the possibilities seemed to be present for something that had not occurred on Wall Street for generations: an old-fashioned attempt to corner the market of a stock. Corners, as the reader will recall, had been a regular practice of the old-time Wall Street pool operators. But experts had insisted they could never be accomplished under present-day conditions. However, the husband-and-wife team in Florida and the West Coast lawyer, acting in partnership, decided to prove the pundits wrong. The SEC speedily moved in and the raid was throttled. Nevertheless, the attempt to corner the market was a telling symptom of the audacity of the times. Speculation had hit a pitch at which wheeler-dealers were overreaching themselves in trying to emulate the nineteenth-century robber barons.

One plunger who most definitely overreached himself was Ivan Boesky, referred to in the press as the grand monarch of international arbitragers. He was caught red-handed in an illegal insider trading operation, sentenced to jail for three years and banned for life from the U.S. securities industry. The son of immigrants, Boesky had risen to become an *éminence grise* in financial quarters, whose arrest, according to the United States Attorney, opened "a window on the rampant criminal conduct that has permeated the securities industry in the 1980s to an extent unknown to this office." While awaiting sentencing, the mercurial financier turned sharply from the pursuit of mammon to washing the feet of the poor. Specifically, he commenced working with homeless derelicts and told the judge he was "trying to understand how I veered off course. I would like the opportunity as I go forward to redeem myself and leave this earth with a good name." Such was Boesky's transformation from humbuggery to humility as he passed from the Gold Coast to Skid Row.

As investors were lured increasingly to Wall Street, the professional gamesters continued to stoke a saturnalia of speculation. Adding to the witch's brew was the conjuring up by fertile minds of clever new devices to be used by the "pros" to make money faster through even fancier leveraging. As early as the mid-1970s several ambitious deal-makers who operated exuberantly on the Chicago Mercantile Exchange had seized on the notion of trading currencies the way corn, wheat and pork bellies were peddled in the commodity pits. The technique spread to stock index futures, enabling traders to bet on the direction of an entire index of stock prices instead of individual stocks. From such concepts evolved an even shrewder notion, portfolio insurance programming, which took advantage of the price differences between stock index futures and the groups of stocks represented in these indexes. Variations occurred sometimes because of the different psychology of commodity and equity traders. Computers monitored the slightest price variations. When the stock prices rose significantly above the futures prices, the computers signaled selling the stocks and buying the futures and vice versa. (The trader bought the cheaper and sold the higher-priced of the two.)

By the mid-1980s at least $80 billion were involved in program trading operations. The Big Board had become dominated by the financial institutions, many of which were too huge to be able to wrest a significant profit simply by buying shares in individual companies. An institution with a portfolio of billions of dollars couldn't find stocks with a sizable enough market to provide a meaningful return on its investment, so it tried to beat the market as a whole by buying and selling basketfuls of stocks through the indexes. During the early 1980s other fancy techniques came into fashion—for instance, use of junk bonds to achieve highly leveraged corporate takeovers. A junk bond is a corporate debt instrument not fully secured by assets or a predictable flow of income. Traditionally regarded as a low-quality, noninvestment-grade security, it now became used in massive amounts to finance hostile takeovers.

Prominent among the financial panjandrums who made hay in this leveraged-buyout era were Sir James Goldsmith, an Anglo-French tycoon who dealt exuberantly on both sides of the Atlantic, turning a patent for a rheumatism cream into a financial empire; Ronald Perelman, who put together a corporate behemoth, acquiring Revlon as the jewel of his crown; T. Boone Pickens, a Texas oil tycoon rumored to be related to another bold adventurer (Daniel Boone), who took over Mesa Petroleum and cast his nets for Texaco; and Carl Icahn, who won control of TWA.

While impoverished folk at the underbelly of the American economy continued to struggle to exist, others sloshed around in steamy self-indulgence. This was an era of meticulously calculated vulgarity in which a famous movie star presented his actress wife with a million-dollar, inch-long pearl, La Peregrina, that had been discovered four centuries previously by an African slave and worn by a succession of celebrated European queens. People lined up at Cartier's to gawk at the lavish bauble before it was shipped to its new owner. One cynic, bemused by the sight, remarked that the jewel "would have been nice for Marie Antoinette to have worn in the tumbril on her way to the guillotine."

Cash was quickly made and quickly spent. A bearded young writer in dirty jeans hit the news headlines by standing on a street corner and handing out $100 bills to anybody who caught his fancy. "We picked interesting-looking cats and spread a little sunshine," observed this Johnny Appleseed of paper money. In this breezy atmosphere high technology was hitched to pop psychology in a shotgun wedding. One deep thinker told the press he was certain computers were becoming human enough to experience typical psychiatric troubles. "Unruly memories sometimes spread through a machine as fears and fixations spread through a psychotic brain."

People turned up in the news in highly bizarre fashion. An individual, nabbed in Detroit for biting a policeman while roaring drunk, was released when it was discovered he had no teeth. A man who was arrested in Las Vegas for possessing heroin syringes argued he was selling them to support himself through Bible school. A certain George Taylor petitioned the court to change his name to Pappadapolous because his Greek friends couldn't pronounce Taylor. Oddly, as in the boom times of the 1920s, there was a strong revival of interest in the occult world. Belief in reincarnation became especially fashionable. A West Coast hypnotist announced he would demonstrate the previous lives of anyone for $25 a visit. Hostesses gave "come as you were" parties, and guests turned up as Roman legionnaires in the time of Caesar, twelfth-century queens of France, meistersingers of medieval Nuremberg. One fellow insisted he had been George Washington's horse.

Ostentatiously in evidence was a group of younger-generation Americans, the "baby boomers" or "yuppies," who flocked to Wall Street from the nation's graduate business schools to hustle for a quick dollar. Some of them, or their fathers, had passed through a turbulent radicalism of the 1960s before feeling their oats as staunch upholders of the capitalist credo. No previous generation in America had made so spectacularly rapid or quixotic a transition from a left-wing to a conservative acculturation. The "baby boomers" had been spawned in an era of the Weathermen, of black power and the Electric Circus, of communal living, peace demonstrations, and the assassinations of John F. Kennedy, Bobby Kennedy and Martin Luther King, Jr.

By the 1980s these erstwhile radicals (and their children) were no longer the counterculture bohemians, the underground iconoclasts, the *sans-culottes* of a revolutionary past. Rather they had become the rock-ribbed advocates of the Establishment. To paraphrase an old Roman proverb, for them money no longer stank. *Playboy*, the leading house organ of these radicals-turned-Sybarites, proudly pointed out in its advertising the remarkable evolution of its new-breed readers. By the 1980s they had "matured." No longer were they titillated merely by sex. The draft card burners and flower children of Chicago and San Francisco in the 1960s were now prosperous young businessmen. "Those young men who wouldn't sell out in 1967 . . . are buying [today]." According to *Playboy*, its new readers drove a Corniche and resided in a classy house because the former hippie "can afford most things now." The old electronic guitar strummer and joints smoker of Woodstock had "matured" into a "mellow" man who "buys and buys and buys" to really enjoy his existence. Enthused one *Playboy* reader in a testimonial ad, "For years, the important thing in my life was gloss; now it's texture."

Many of these "baby boomers," basking in the intoxicating rise of the stock market, took plush jobs with brokerage firms and investment banking houses and within a year or two out of Harvard Business School pulled down $100,000 a year and more. They were certain that the stock market would go up and up, innocently unaware that Wall Street was a two-way thoroughfare, that a stock market floating on iridescent fantasies was sooner or later bound to make a crash landing and that the days of wine and roses, of splurging on million-dollar condominiums, would grind to a halt.

As Wall Street entered what proved to be a memorable year, 1987, the nation's spending continued to outpace its tax revenues and it was experiencing its largest budget and trade deficits in history. It was a debtor nation, living high on the hog on money borrowed from foreigners, notably the Japanese, who were supplying much of the funds that enabled American consumers to maintain the living standards to which they were as compulsively addicted as a heroin junkie unable to kick the habit. Moreover, America was undergoing a paralysis of political leadership. It had in Washington a "lame duck" Republican President harried by the Iran-contra revelations and a Congress run by Democrats who were intent on checkmating the Administration on every front.

On Wall Street there was uneasiness among some experts. The Street had been disturbed by disclosures of widespread illegal trading operations. But, paradoxically, the stock market had entered the euphoric stage of a five-year bull rampage, during which the Dow Jones Industrials Average had pushed through the 2,000-point level to 2,700 and seemed headed toward 3,000, according to the exuberant prognoses of some forecasters. Stock prices were skyrocketing wildly out of proportion to the companies they represented, and the Averages were way out of line with the prospects of the economy, which was experiencing only a modest growth. Yields had in many cases fallen significantly below bond yields, tempting investors to move from stocks into fixed-income securities.

Concerned over the burgeoning trade deficit, the U.S. Government allowed the dollar to plummet in relationship to foreign currencies, hoping to force West Germany and other trading partners to lower their interest rates and stimulate their domestic growth, enhancing the market for U.S. exports and at the same time rendering their exports more expensive and less competitive to ours.

Meanwhile, although some market professionals pointed out that stock prices had lost touch with reality, the public kept rushing into equities. The feeling, even of sophisticated investors, seemed to be that despite all economic logic, the market had been going up, and it would be foolish to bail out while the tide was still running favorably. In short, in many respects it was 1929 all over again. Once more the dreary script of fifty-eight years ago was being played out almost to the letter, except that the exuberant new swingers, armed with their ultrasophisticated computers, were equipped potentially to wreak even more damage on themselves and others.

Oddly, the crash that followed took place in the same month, October, as the 1929 disaster, but this one wasn't centered on Wall Street. In the half century since the earlier crash, the world's economy had become more tightly intertwined. The Street was functioning only as a branch, if a highly visible one, of the world's Super Stock Exchange, plugged into the global pattern through a sophisticated communications system, interlocking currencies, and other financial developments. The 1987 Wall Street crash was part of a chain reaction that simultaneously hit the stock exchanges in Tokyo, London, Hong Kong and elsewhere.

Although Wall Street had been simmering for some time with the ingredients for a downfall, two announcements seemed to precipitate the actual event. On October 14 Washington disclosed that the nation's trade deficit was running higher than had been anticipated, considering that the U.S. dollar had been falling sharply for some time; and in an unrelated move, Congress proposed withdrawing preferential tax treatment for hostile corporate takeovers.

October 16, the Friday before "Black Monday," provided a foretaste of what was to come. The Dow Jones Industrials Average plummeted over 100 points, a new record for a single session. The following Monday, October 19, the market lurched into a freefall, dropping 508 points on a 600-million-share volume, erasing over $500 billion in stock values. This drop of the Dow Jones Industrials Average percentagewise was twice the decline suffered on the worst day of the 1929 crash, October 29.

The managers of the giant funds, the block house traders who for years had been entranced by the sorcery of the electronic brain, were appalled. As the price of stocks continued to hurtle down and down and failed to rebound at any level, the institutional gunslingers dumped block after block of their securities, and market-makers, who normally provided the outlet for such mass unloadings, reeled and collapsed under the assault. When the market was on a bull rampage everybody had rushed in to grab stocks at heady commissions from euphorically swinging fund managers. But now when the chips were down and the casino was on fire, the market-makers vanished like icebergs under a tropical sun. Blue-chip stocks that had been touted for years as supremely safe, highly liquid investments were suddenly at the mercy of wildly erratic bids.

The nation was shocked. The Chairman of the New York Stock Exchange called the crash "a financial meltdown." Officials at Wall Street brokerage houses, bombarded by orders from panicky investors to unload their stock, called in security guards to prevent their traders from being assaulted by outraged customers. Americans, unable to reach their brokers on Wall Street, frantically wired the London Stock Exchange, trying to unload their shares there.

The suddenness of the market decline resulted in a frightening display of volatility that was aggravated by the heavy use of computerized program trading by a handful of giant financial institutions. When stocks dropped to a mathematically predetermined level, the elaborate portfolio strategies that had been programmed into computers to operate on what amounted to an automatic-pilot course moved instantaneously into action, amplifying the frenzy of the decline without giving the human brain a chance to reconsider its trading options. The effect was the financial equivalent of detonating a nuclear bomb.

The devotees of the avant-garde computers had been hoisted by their own petard. The managers of the giant funds had been smugly operating under the delusion that they could move in and out of the market quickly whenever they wished to do so. They hadn't dreamed of a situation wherein market liquidity would completely vanish, as all of them stampeded for the same exit, trying to sell into a market that had no buyers. Equally chastened were the stock specialists on the floor of the exchange who traditionally stood ready to put up their own capital to match buying and selling orders and keep the market running in an orderly fashion. Caught in the tidal wave of selling orders, the financial resources of many specialists had reached the exhaustion point. Oddly, one of the specialist firms trapped in the holocaust was M. J. Meehan Company, which bore the name of the legendary Mike Meehan, who played so dramatic a role in the 1920s and who was caught in the stampede of "Black Thursday" in 1929. Now, fifty-eight years later, the Meehan firm proved that lightning really can strike twice.

In an effort to stem the tailspin, a hundred companies purchased their own stock with a fanfare of publicity, but the crisis continued. The need for capital became even more urgent when major commercial banks threatened to cut off their short-term lending to brokerage houses and market-makers for carrying on their operations. At this juncture, the Federal Reserve Board, fearing that the crisis would spread to other areas of the economy, stepped in to prevent the stock market from utterly collapsing. It used its muscle to persuade the banks to continue to lend urgently needed money, promising to pump more money into the banking system, if necessary, to maintain its liquidity.

So ended the five-year market boom. As in the 1929 disaster, the overwhelming majority of forecasters were totally oblivious of the approaching catastrophe. The psychological impact was predictable. For millions of Americans born after 1929, who had never before experienced a serious panic on Wall Street, the realization sank in that the stock market was a two-way affair, and, as any market historian could have told them, it was as capable of going disastrously down as zestfully up.

However, there were somewhat mitigating circumstances to this crash. Unlike the 1929 disaster, this market was not nearly as heavily margined; fewer investors were wiped out, and the pension funds and other financial institutions still had billions of dollars available for reinvestment when the right conditions returned.

Nevertheless, once again, as so frequently in the past, Wall Street had become the stage for dramatically humbling events. In the wake of the 1987 crash, the shades of yesterday returned to haunt America. It was along this ancient thoroughfare, wending its way from Trinity Church to the waterfront, where in October 1987 over $500 billion vanished in a single day, that ex-President Ulysses Grant, the old Civil War hero, had limped on crutches into his broker's office, trying desperately to save himself and his family from bankruptcy, and a group of cynical, hard-boiled reporters took off their hats as he walked by. Here the eccentric Claflin sisters, the first female brokers, had strolled indolently in their Parisian attire with pencils nestling saucily behind their ears, ogled by curiosity-seekers. Here in Gilpin's, a greedy group of "goldbugs" had snapped up the precious metal, betting on the defeat of the Union armies on the battlefield and the collapse of the Lincoln government. Here during the Panic of 1907, J. P. Morgan, rising from his sickbed, rode up to his banking offices as a mob surged around his carriage for assurances it would not be wiped out in a banking crash.

Here in 1920, a bombing by radical agitators took place, when a time explosive, hidden in a horse-drawn wagon, went off in front of J. P. Morgan and Company, killing and maiming over 230 people and shattering the windows of the New York Stock Exchange. Here Mike Meehan, the hyperkinetic, red-headed stock specialist for radio in the 1920s, had collapsed near the floor of the Exchange, his face bruised, his shirt torn to tatters by short sellers striving desperately to get out of the trap he had sprung for them. And it was the crumbling of his stock on this fateful Wall Street that led Robert Young, the Texas financier who had so exultantly seized control of the New York Central Railroad, to press the muzzles of a shotgun against his temple and kill himself.

Over the years the booms and busts on Wall Street have struck an overpoweringly percussive note in the hustle and bustle of America. The ups and downs of the Dow Jones Industrial Averages have uncannily reflected the nation's mood as it moved from arrogance to humility and back again. The Crash of 1987 was merely the latest swing of the pendulum.

14
WALL STREET TOMORROW

WHERE IS THE STOCK MARKET HEADED—CAN WE SAVE THE GOOSE THAT LAYS THE GOLDEN EGGS?

Today America and Wall Street are standing at the crossroads. The twentieth century opened with a mighty outpouring of national enthusiasm. But as we enter the final years of our century, the atmosphere is charged with uncertainty. Approaching the year 2000, many Americans are becoming increasingly anxious about tomorrow. They are concerned over the signs of a declining economy and a slippage of our position in the world as we continue to be hammered by soaring debt, increasing obsolescence of our industrial plant, an avalanche of imports and a rising threat of job losses to foreign workers. Once we were unquestionably the world's number one industrial superpower. What will we be tomorrow? The fears that we may sink to a second-rate status, bested by others in the competitive race, have been intensified by the 1987 stock market crash. We are concerned over the health of Wall Street and our capital markets.

For better or worse, we Americans are stuck with our stock market. We may get angry; pound the table; rage at its unpredictable, perverse behavior, but we cannot live without it, for if Wall Street were to vanish, so would our free-market economy. If the nation's business corporations were unable to raise the equity capital they so urgently require to expand and prosper, they would have to resort to heavy debt financing, which could result in sluggish growth, joblessness and depressions. The inability to raise money from the public in the stock market would especially hurt small businesses who need to go public for the capital to expand.*

We find ourselves on the horns of a dilemma. In the wake of the Crash of 1987 there have been calls for tougher regulations of Wall Street trading. The problem in assessing the need for this is that the degree of return in the stock market is inherent in the amount of risk. Our nation was built by its risk-takers. The Declaration of Independence was signed by adventurers. If Americans had played it safe, the nation's railroads would never have extended beyond the Alleghenies.

Indeed, the settlement of America was from the beginning a giant real-estate speculation. The Spanish King Ferdinand, who financed Columbus's trip, cashed in on his subject's discovery of the New World by exacting lush profits on the land titles that resulted. King George III's attempt to stop George Washington from speculating in undeveloped lands west of the Mississippi in order to make a financial killing was an important factor in the latter's becoming bitterly antiroyalist and led to his joining the war of rebellion against His British Majesty. Had Washington not chosen to lead the rebels' army, there is no telling whether the colonies would have won their independence. The city of Washington itself was built

*While some firms have recently been raising money by privately issuing their stock to pension funds and insurance companies, nothing has replaced the public stock market for offering liquidity and dynamic capital growth.

as a real-estate speculation. By selecting an undeveloped tract of wilderness along the Potomac instead of an already inhabited city for the site of America's new capital, politicians pocketed a fortune as the value of the virgin land skyrocketed upon its upgrading.

Abraham Lincoln, while President, headed a group of real-estate investors who fought to have the terminus of the Union Pacific, which formed the western branch of the nation's first continental railroad, located on land he and his friends had quietly put their money into. The nation's early banks started out in the most dubious fashion. Many regional bankers raised money by issuing inflated paper bank notes to the public and then proceeded to build their tellers' offices in the middle of woods or on swampland beyond the reach of roads so that it was difficult if not impossible for their depositors to get to them and redeem their bank notes for their equivalent in gold or silver.

However, America's banks matured eventually into more legitimate enterprises, and the nation's railroads were constructed; the steel and auto industries launched; mines dug; electric utilities organized; and telephone, radio and television given their start as a result of speculators who provided the money up front for their development. Thanks to the role of the stock market and its generous infusions of equity by the risk-takers, America's industrial production by the end of the nineteenth century topped that of any previous nation on earth.

Over the years, however, there has been a change in the nature and benefits of risk-taking. Throughout most of the nineteenth century, despite the freewheeling speculation engaged in by the Harrimans, the Morgans and the "Bet-a-Million" Gateses, Wall Street never lost sight of its primary function: to provide capital as the lifeblood of our economy. Yet when America entered the 1920s and lurched toward the Crash of 1929, the Street's role as a provider of capital became distorted in an orgy of mindless, reckless speculation that lined the pockets of profiteers while adding substantially nothing to the nation's wealth. The 1980s have experienced similar sabotaging of Wall Street's legitimate function, as speculators through dizzily leveraged buyouts fueled by junk-bond financing and insider trading manipulations have been pushing paper money around in a frenzied numbers game that has added nothing to America's industrial muscle.

Complicating the problem is the fact that since the Second World War the stock market has evolved into an arena where enormous power has fallen into the hands of giant financial institutions. These institutional game players have replaced the individual big swingers of the past—the Harrimans, the Morgans, the Livermores—and are exercising their newly won influence with the help of a formidable ally, computers. These institutions have become the major investment forces in today's stock market. Armed with billions of dollars in their portfolios, they have been maximizing their returns by massaging whole universes of stocks. The stocks within their universe are cold statistics in a high-stakes numbers game. The jobs, the joys and the agonies of the human beings whose lives are involved with the companies these stocks represent don't show up in computer calculations. Many institutions have been playing around with numbers in the manner of the old bucket shop players whose obsession with the price quotes put up on the shop board was only remotely related to the real world outside.

No one can forecast where our rampaging technology will ultimately take the stock market, any more than we can predict where it will lead the human race. We only know that technological developments have far outpaced the political, social and economic, to say nothing of the ethical development, of mankind, and as a result, society has become dangerously unbalanced.

In the years preceding the Crash of 1987, the computer had seduced many traders into a dangerous illusion of infallibility. They mesmerized themselves into believing that their computerized trading programs would protect them from the consequences of financial disaster no matter how frenetically they operated. They figured that the electronic brain was smart enough to outwit the twists and turns of destiny. However, on "Black Monday" 1987 the worshipers of the computer got a rude comeuppance. The realization was hammered home to them that the behavior of human beings cannot be predicted by computer programs; that no amount of massaging the statistics can cope with the unexpected.

It is just as well that computerized systems were subjected to this humbling experience, for if they ever managed to retain unchallenged their mystique of infallibility, this could well compel man to reevaluate the religious and moral assumptions by which much of the world has lived since the days of the old Hebrew prophets and Christ. As Norbert Wiener, a pioneer and philosopher of the computer age, pointed out, the greatest game of all—the root of Judaic-Christian theology—is a game played by God with His creatures. God is continually playing, say the theologians, with Satan for the souls of man. This is the theme of the Bible, of *Paradise Lost*, of *Faust* and other great spiritual epics. However, in the past one could always take comfort in the knowledge that the game was actually a loaded one. The devil is a creature of God and therefore has been foreordained to lose, since a creation of the Almighty can never hope to triumph over its creator. However, in recent years a disturbing new element has entered. If the computer and its systems continually prove able to outwit man, who created them, then the conflict between God and *His* creation could become one in which the outcome is terribly uncertain. God could be embarked on a struggle that He has an excellent chance of losing.

The danger of the computer wielded by powerful Wall Streeters was dramatically revealed on "Black Monday" 1987. One well-known institution dumped $1 billion worth of stock from its portfolios at the push of a button. Other funds followed suit, individually unloading hundreds of millions of dollars' worth of stock at a time. This massive dumping of funds played a critical role in turning what would have been a severe drop into an uncontrollable catastrophe, one that brought the nation's financial system to the brink of disaster.

At the turn of the century a handful of business corporations wielded dangerously unchecked power over the American economy. They were the great industrial trusts— the steel, the oil, the sugar, the tobacco cartels. President Theodore Roosevelt initiated a trust-busting policy, and the power of the cartels was broken up by the antitrust laws.

Today we have a new phenomenon, the institutional money trusts. It is true that these trusts (or funds) don't operate on the same crudely selfish principles of the old industrial trusts. They are not in the business solely to line their own pockets but to invest staggering amounts of other people's money. Nevertheless, at critical times they can virtually monopolize trading in the stock market. When the buying or selling of billions of dollars' worth of stock can be decided by the decision of a handful of traders in the twinkle of an eye and when by their action they can bring America's financial establishment to its knees, there is definite cause for concern. Rules must certainly be devised to counteract the vastly disproportionate power of these Wall Street supertraders.

As this is being written, all kinds of suggestions are being made for restructuring the stock market. Technology, some people say, must be slowed down so human beings can keep up with it. Shortly after the Crash of 1987, the New York Stock Exchange began studying the possibility, among other things, of stopping trading in individual stocks automatically if the daily rise or fall of the stocks exceeded a limit based on a predetermined percentage rate. Several brokerage firms announced plans to prohibit their employees from computerized program trading for their firms' account. NASDAQ, representing the over-the-counter stocks, advocated measures to improve its market-making capabilities. A presidential commission studying the Crash of 1987 suggested that the markets for stocks, futures and options be formally organized into what they are de facto, a single marketplace; that "circuit breakers" be applied to cushion steep swings in stock prices; and that the Federal Reserve Board be installed as a watchdog to supervise all the financial markets as a single unit. Also, there was talk of boosting margin requirements to discourage excessive speculation; curbing speculation in stock index futures by putting daily price limits on them, as they have traditionally been placed on corn, wheat and other commodities; and beefing up the capital structure of stock specialists and brokerage houses to provide greater liquidity in the market.

Obviously some degree of regulatory action is necessary to lessen the impact of mammoth trading by the powerful swingers and to encourage grass-roots investors to participate more actively in the stock market, buying shares in America's corporations instead of in statistical indexes. However, regulations by themselves will never solve the problem of preventing future crashes. People always will find ways to lose money in the stock market. Moreover, whenever one regulatory loophole is plugged, clever traders will come up with other strategies to make financial killings. The stock market has been vastly more popular in America than anywhere else; more rank-and-file investors have been involved here than in the stock exchanges of London, Tokyo, Hong Kong or Paris. This is because Americans beyond all others are obsessed with winning and therefore are willing to expose themselves to the risk of losing. According to the American credo of free enterprise, there must be losers as well as winners, and people win in the stock market by cashing in on the mistakes of others. Even if, by some miracle, the government through its regulatory action were able to ensure that no one suffered substantial losses in the market, this would at the same time virtually guarantee that no one would make significant profits, either.

There will continue to be market crashes in the future as

there have been in the past because two basic factors have remained unchanged through the ages: human gullibility and greed.

Our readers will recall how a century ago, Edward Harriman, a master at pushing up stocks in pool operations, when asked by a colleague whether he could manipulate a stock he had bought at 70 to 80, replied that he couldn't because a piddling 10-point rise wouldn't excite the imagination of the public; but, he added, he could easily boost the stock from 70 to 150 and then sell it to the public while running it down to 100, since an 80-point change would whet appetites to such an extent that he could dump almost any amount of stock he desired on a 50-point drop.

Another psychological quirk that will undoubtedly raise the speculative fever of the market tomorrow as in the past is the seemingly inexhaustible need of traders to try to guess the final inch of the top of the market to squeeze every last cent of profits, or to guess the bottom to rake in "bargains." Over the years a small army of traders has gone broke chasing the will-o'-the-wisp of market tops and bottoms. Readers will remember how after the Crash of 1929 many experts confidently proclaimed the bottom had been reached and now was the time for the public to buy stocks cheaply and cash in on the rebound sure to follow. But the market, far from reaching its bottom in the October crash, had only commenced its nosedive. For almost three years it kept dropping to eighty-six percent below the level of 1929's "Black Tuesday" before it finally struck its rock bottom. In the meantime, traders who had been astute enough to escape with profits before the Crash of 1929 and who reentered in 1930 to exploit "bargains" were ruined. Finally, by 1932, even the most hard-core optimist was convinced that the bear market was here to stay and though many stocks were selling well below the physical assets of the firms they represented, nobody would touch them. Then one day in July, when the economy was at its lowest and the nation was plunged into its deepest despair, the stock market, without any warning, started upward and within the next two months soared ninety percent in the fastest rise in history up to that point. It is frustrating to try to call the major tops or bottoms of the market with any consistent success. Yet traders get hoodwinked time after time while attempting this.

The question on the minds of many is, What lies ahead? How can we, any more than our predecessors in previous generations, recognize the signs of a coming disaster and act accordingly?

In peering ahead, one should remember that two basic trends are woven into the fabric of Wall Street history, and we should look for them today and tomorrow. Over the years, tight money, indicated by soaring interest rates, has caused market downturns and depressions, while cheap money has fueled booms. America's first major depression, after the nation embarked on a major industrial expansion following the Civil War, took place in 1873. The approaching signals were ominously tightening money, signified by a rise in interest rates and in the price of gold, which reached its highest level in three years. As interest on the U.S. dollar climbed to twenty-five percent, the stock market crumbled. The disaster spread to the industrial sector and plunged the nation into its worst depression up to that time. Similarly, the Panic of 1893, which occurred twenty years later, was heralded by tight money and a rise in interest rates. Also the money Panic of 1907, which threatened to close down the nation's banking system, was signaled by a severe money squeeze. In 1920 in the United States soaring inflation, triggered by the First World War, was followed upon the ending of hostilities by skyrocketing interest rates. During that year, a speculative spree in far-off Japan ended up in a bust that sent shock waves through the international community. Call money on Wall Street leaped to twenty-five percent. The price of Liberty Bonds, which had been issued to finance America's war effort, fell to a chilling discount, and, sure enough, a depression followed.

Along came the raging bull market of the 1920s, stroked by a rapidly increasing supply of cheap money and credit. Then the Federal Reserve Board suddenly began tightening the screws, and interest rates went up. We will recall how Billy Durant, the leader of a consortium of big swingers, paid a secret visit to the White House to warn President Hoover of the dire consequences if the Fed didn't relax its tight-money policy. Stock speculation, Durant candidly pointed out, was based on the availability of cheap money and credit and the assurance that this would continue. He and his associates, he argued, couldn't lure the public into the stocks they themselves were buying (a euphemism for their pool operations) unless credit was kept cheap and interest rates low. When Hoover refused to press the Fed and the latter continued its tight-money policy, Durant and his friends quietly withdrew $4 billion from the stock market. This became a significant factor in the ensuing market tumble that turned into a crash.

Since cheap money has meant, at least in its initial stages, good times, and tight money, hard ones, the politicians, especially after the Hoover experience and the Depression, have pressed to keep the money supply ample and its price cheap. Especially in times of crisis they have exhibited a consistent bias for printing wads of money, risking inflation and going deeper into debt rather than adopting the unpopular practice of levying taxes to foot the nation's bills. The reader will recall how long before Hoover, during the Civil War, the Lincoln Government, faced with the options of raising money to pay for the war effort by levying a stiff income tax or taking the more politically palatable tactic of printing paper money, took the easy way out. It levied a token tax and printed $450 million in greenbacks unredeemable in gold or silver. One way or another, Uncle Sam has been in the money-printing business to this day.

In view of this, it is not surprising that Americans in recent years have become obsessed with the trend of interest rates.

Rates not only affect the return on our bank savings, they also determine whether we can sell our home at a profitable price, whether the mortgage rate will enable us to buy a new one and whether the stocks we own will enjoy a favorable market environment in which to appreciate.

One thing the investor should bear in mind in protecting himself against losses is that in many markets, when the majority of stocks are either rising or declining—as distinct from out-and-out market crashes, when everything is in shambles—a handful of stocks will behave counter to the general trend. These counterbehavior stocks climb conspicuously in a market when everything else is nose-diving. For instance, after the Second World War the stocks of energy producers bucked the general downtrend and dramatically outperformed the market as a whole. In the 1960s shares of gold mining firms performed bullishly in a bear market. In the 1970s beet sugar and other agricultural stocks withstood the market downtrend and came through with flying colors for their owners. Therefore, in an uncertain market an investor might examine stocks with a countermovement history.

Looking ahead, while acknowledging that America has serious economic problems, we should put them in perspective. For instance, anxiety is being expressed over the nation's trade deficit and the fact that we have become a debtor nation. This is understandable. But at the same time it should be pointed out that during the nineteenth century, when the United States experienced the most rapid industrial expansion recorded by any society, we were a debtor nation, owing money to the world. European capital played a major role in financing our railroad industry. J. P. Morgan, who raised the money for much of America's industrial expansion, was closely affiliated with British banking interests. On the other hand, after we finally managed to graduate from the status of a debtor nation, as a result of the First World War, to become a creditor, we nevertheless were unable to stave off a market

W A L L   S T R E E T   T O M O R R O W — 355

crash and the worst depression in our history. So our task is not to eschew foreign lenders but to make wise use of them.

One thing seems certain: The shrewd, successful investor has two major allies working for him today, as in the past: basic economic conditions that will yield significant insights to the serious student of them; and the large numbers of people who will continue to guess wrong about them. Since the beginning of Wall Street, the handful of investors who have steadily guessed right have been the ones quick to foresee and to interpret at an early stage leading developments in the American economy. In the nineteenth century they made their money on the boom of canal building that linked the Eastern Seaboard with the Middle West, on the rise of the railroads and on the agglomeration of the giant trusts. In the decades before World War II they struck it rich on the boom of the automobile and the mushrooming of retail chain stores. Similarly, the astute investor is striving today to be where the action is before the majority of people are aware of its existence.

As he peers ahead, what new growth industries will capture his imagination, as it was once seized by the Union Pacific Railroad, General Motors, Xerox? For one thing, people seeking investment opportunities should be able to count on two basic trends: the world's growing need for food as its population multiplies, and a demand for new sources of energy. Moreover, while America's space program has temporarily been slowed down because of technical problems, it should pick up and gain headway and at some point begin providing major opportunities for investors in the area of space exploration and space colonization. Back on Earth, there will be a continual "graying" of America. The number of people over sixty-five will become an increasing force in the economy, and a host of products and services will be launched to meet their needs.

To handle the growing shortage of physicians, an increasing number of paramedics will be educated to do the routine medical tasks once performed by doctors. With more and more attention paid to caring for the elderly, many social workers and therapists will be trained in geriatrics. Sophisticated new drugs will sharpen the functioning of the brain and the memory, making it easier for the mentally slow to learn. There will be new, enthusiastically embraced drugs to deal with the scourge of AIDS. Already antibiotics and other forms of medication are curing or ameliorating conditions that formerly could be handled only by surgery. One powerful new therapy increasingly making the scalpel unnecessary is the laser beam, which is being used on throat tumors, cataracts and is being experimented with to unclog coronary arteries in heart patients.

At some point electrical energy, produced through nuclear fission, will become even more widespread. Robots will increasingly replace human labor in manufacturing processes. Computers, telecommunications and the sports and entertainment industries will continue their sturdy growth. Another industry already making significant headway is genetic engineering. Biologists insist that the splicing of the gene has been mankind's most significant achievement since the splitting of the atom to produce nuclear energy. A number of genetic engineering firms have already entered the lists to turn the technique to commercial uses. Work is being done in breeding wholly new forms of bacteria to sop up oil spills and to turn garbage into nutritious food. A new kind of wheat has been bred that can be grown without the need of chemical fertilizers, since it can absorb all the nitrogen it requires directly from the air. Researchers hope that at some point genetic engineering will breed powerful new viruses that will attack and kill cancer cells in the most effective way known to man.

Meanwhile, in addition to domestic opportunities, overseas markets could become increasingly alluring to American investors. To cite an example, Australia should be a promising area where Americans will be putting money into natural-resource companies for long-term asset plays. Like the United States over a century ago, Australia is underpopulated, and it has experienced an explosive industrial boom similar to ours after the Civil War. If tensions with the Soviet Union abate —and both nations seem headed toward rechanneling expenditures from building more lethal armaments into strengthening the health of our domestic economies—we and the Soviets may become active trading partners, supplying new opportunity for investors. Canada, like Australia, will become increasingly desirable for asset plays. China, if its political atmosphere becomes more liberalized, could be a major customer for our technological know-how.

As for the shape Wall Street itself may take in the years ahead, the brokerage and investment banking businesses are currently faced with the prospect of competition from commercial banks eager to enter the field, and if this transpires there will be an even greater scramble for customers, broadening stock ownership.* Women, who, as noted, already head their own investment businesses and manage the assets of major financial funds, will assume increasing influence in the Wall Street hierarchy, making the crusty old Street a growing showcase for feminine enterprise.

There are other developments lying ahead. Already the stock market is recognized to be a global one, and it could very well be structured formally into one in the future. The technology is already at hand, and the march of technology will not be halted. Since the fortunes of major exchanges around the world are heavily interrelated, it could conceivably be only a question of when (sometime during the early twenty-first century?) common trading standards and requirements will be introduced on the major exchanges to prevent any of them from triggering a global crash and a worldwide depression. To enforce these regulations, an international

*Some commercial banks are already engaging in limited underwriting activities.

agency could be established as a watchdog, supervising the functioning of the international stock exchanges in the way in which the Securities and Exchange Commission operates in the United States today. By then trades could be taking place routinely anywhere in the world wherever there are two computers hooked into a terminal. All deals will cross international boundaries as rapidly and as easily as if the traders were sitting opposite one another in a single room.

With trading being conducted under universally accepted rules, investment opportunities will become truly worldwide. The stock market averages will be global averages, weighted with industries everywhere.

But no matter what shape the future market takes, no matter how formidably efficient our technology becomes, nothing will completely eradicate the quirks of investor psychology as long as human beings continue to inhabit our planet. There will still be investors who will continue to live by the traditional folklore of the market and follow such maxims as "Don't sell short when the sap is running up the trees." Even in tomorrow's era of supertechnology we'll have our share of seat-of-the-pants risk-takers.

This generally optimistic scenario we have depicted for tomorrow has several important qualifications.

In discussing the future, we have made a major assumption that, in the wake of the Crash of 1987, the stock exchange will succeed in stabilizing the flow of its capital resources and continue to earn the confidence of its grass-roots investors.

An overriding problem that is haunting the Street is how to continue providing sufficient market liquidity to handle stock trading that already has grown to such potentially staggering proportions. The issue is one that Durant put to President Hoover during his visit to the White House in 1929, phrased crudely by him, to be sure, but essentially accurately. For, to keep the stock market prosperous and booming as the people and the politicians want it to be, there will be the

WALL STREET TOMORROW — 359

continual temptation to print whatever amount of money may be necessary to accomplish this—to use the popular expression, to prime the pump.

A future market crash, if it occurs, could be even bigger and more devastating than the Crash of 1987 because of the even heavier volume of trading propelled by even more lethal electronics technology. Should priming the pump be resorted to in an effort to save investors in their hour of need, this could result in the collapse of the U.S. dollar, driving down its value astronomically and destroying the very financial system it tried to save.

In addition to the pitfalls of the stock market, other problems are lurking. America is faced with overwhelming spending demands. As this is being written, a rising number of savings institutions, plagued by financial mismanagement, may require a major government bail out. Enormous health, environmental, drug control, national defense, education requirements are clamoring to be met. Reluctant to raise taxes significantly or dip into the surplus of the revamped Social Security fund, the politicians in coming years could be pressured into plastering the nation with inflationary money to meet America's spending needs. The consequences of an inflation running out of control have historically been grim.

In Ancient Rome the people's money, the *denarius*, a coin of virtually the purest silver, was debased by political manipulation and skyrocketing inflation into a cheap piece of copper, and along with this the civilized world was plunged into an age of barbarism. During the French Revolution, the people's money—*assignats*—drastically deteriorated in an inflationary panic. A bushel of flour that had cost the equivalent of 40 cents climbed to $45, and a cartload of wood, previously priced at $4, soared to $250. A mob broke into the government offices, smashed the presses that printed the money, and burned the *assignats* in a blazing bonfire. The economic chaos that followed helped bring on the dictator Napoleon. In Germany of the early 1920s the *deutsche mark* dropped to one trillionth of its former value and the economy collapsed, planting the seeds for the rise of Adolf Hitler and the Nazis.

While nothing like these disasters—runaway inflation causing social catastrophe—seems in the cards for America, the potential danger is clear. Our social needs definitely must be met but we cannot ignore our fiscal requirements. It appears that we must continue a perilous juggling act in order to prosper.

We commenced our story about Wall Street by comparing the stock market to Thackeray's *Vanity Fair*, with its Tom Fools and its Jack Puddings, its actors and its clowns who wiped the greasepaint from their faces when the carnival was over and the curtain came down. All too frequently when the last of the audience has exited and the lights are turned off, it is found that the stuff the actor wipes from his cheeks is not greasepaint but a tear. For tragedy continually stalks the Street.

All the characteristics of the old *Vanity Fair* are still here, the daring and the greed, the brilliance and the chicanery, the innocent optimism and the calculated cynicism. Much that has happened could in some fashion occur again but more rapidly and perhaps even more devastatingly as time goes on. Thanks to the emergence of newer generations of computers and increasingly sophisticated telecommunications systems, more money could be made and lost within a quicker time frame. And the punishment for guessing wrong will be even greater. For in today's nuclear era we are living on a breathtakingly narrow margin of survival. The very existence of the human race could well be the most highly leveraged speculation since the prehistoric Ice Age.

That is why today more than ever we must live with a strong sense of our past. By absorbing historical memories and their lessons into our own brief span of mortal experience we can hope to annihilate our greatest enemy: ignorance.

BIBLIOGRAPHY

1—"SPECULATION WIPED A TEAR ..."

The literature on Wall Street is extensive; the sources consulted by the author have been numerous. Lack of space permits mention of only the more important source material used most frequently in the preparation of this book.

For the origins and early years of Wall Street and the New York Stock Exchange, the writer has made frequent use of a definitive book, Edmund Clarence Stedman, ed., *The New York Stock Exchange. Its History* (New York Stock Exchange Historical Company, 1905), 2 vols. For these early years the writer has also made use of several other basic books, written by contemporaries of the period, notably James Knowles Medberry, *Men and Mysteries of Wall Street* (Fields, Osgood & Co., 1870); Henry Clews, *Fifty Years in Wall Street* (Irving Publishing Co., 1915); Matthew Hale Smith, *Bulls and Bears of New York* (J. B. Burr & Co., 1874). Two excellent modern books on the beginnings of the Street to which the author has referred are Frederick L. Collins, *Money Town, the Story of Manhattan Toe* (Putnam, 1946) and Robert Irving Warshow, *Story of Wall Street* (Greenberg, Publisher, 1929).

For specific facts on the Hamilton funding plan and his swap with Jefferson, the writer has referred, among other sources, to Stedman, *op. cit.*, Vol. I, p. 50. For the episode of the Congressmen's ships sailing on a voyage to buy up certificates from the farmers, reference has been made to the *Journal of William Maclay* [United States Senator for Pennsylvania, 1789–1791], introduction by Charles A. Beard (A. & C. Bonis, 1927), p. 179. Maclay's quote on speculation comes from his *Journal* and is also reported in Warshow, *op. cit.*, p. 31. Reference to the constitution that was drawn up in 1817 for the New York Stock Exchange Board comes from Stedman, pp. 63–4 and from *New York Stock Exchange Constitution and By-laws* (New York Stock Exchange, 1817–1925). For the single slowest trading day ever recorded, see Stedman, p. 85. The story about the peephole watchers spying on the Exchange is derived from Stedman, p. 146, as is the merger of the Stock Exchange with the Open Board and Government Bond Department, p. 214. Other sources cited for this period have been J. Edward Meeker, *The Work of the Stock Exchange* (Ronald Press, 1930); Thomas F. Woodcock, *The Stock Exchange and the Money Market* (Columbia University Press, 1908); and Richard D. Wycoff, *Wall Street Ventures and Adventures Through Forty Years* (Harper, 1930).

2—THE BLUE, THE GRAY AND THE GOLD

Henry Clews' advice on how to take advantage of panics comes from his invaluable reminiscences, *op. cit.* For material on the state of U.S. Treasury finances on the eve of the Civil War, the writer has drawn from the *Annual Report of the Treasury, 1860*, and the *Congressional Globe, 1860–1*, Part I, p. 42. The reference to Secretary Cobb's blunders comes from Ellis Paxson Oberholtzer, *Jay Cooke, Financier of the Civil War*, 2 vols. (G. W. Jacobs & Co., 1907), Vol. I, p. 124. The reference to Mayor Fernando Wood's suggestion that New York withdraw from the Union comes from Wood's addresses before the Common Council of New York, filed in the New York Public Library. For material on the gold speculators, reference has been made, among other sources, to Emerson David Fite, *Social and Industrial Conditions in the North During the Civil War* (Macmillan, 1910); to *American Gold Quotations* (J. C. Mersereau, 1866–1879), 6 vols.; and to Kinahan Cornwallis, *The Gold Room, and the New York Stock Exchange and Clearing House* (A. S. Barnes, 1878). The description of the Gold Room is found in William Worthington Fowler, *Ten Years in Wall Street* (Worthington, Dustin & Co., 1870). For further data on the Goldbugs, see Stedman, pp. 133, 149, 150, 153, 154 ff. For facts about Cooke's war bond drives, reference has been made to Oberholtzer, *op. cit.*, Vol. I, pp. 124 ff., 577–8, 580–3 ff. Cooke's dealings with newsmen are discussed in Oberholtzer, Vol. I, pp. 578–82. Other works referred to for the bond drive are Matthew Josephson, *The Robber Barons* (Harcourt, 1934), pp. 53–8; Henrietta Larson, *Jay Cooke, Private Banker* (Harvard University Press, 1936); and Jay Cooke, "Questions and Answers, or What People Ought to Know About the National Banks," Sandusky *Daily Register* (October 19, 1867); "Letter of Mr. Jay Cooke on Payment in Gold of the U. S. Five-Twenty Bonds," Philadelphia *Inquirer* (1868); Jay Cooke and Dr. William Elder, *How Our National Debt Can Be Paid* (Sherman & Co., 1865).

3—ULYSSES IN NIGHT TOWN

The reference to Broomhall's chart and the social significance of commodity prices comes from Cutten's privately printed auto-biography, Arthur W. Cutten and Boyden Sparkes, *The Story of a Speculator* (privately printed by students in Division of Graphic Arts, New York University, 1936); for Gould's speculation in railroads, see Clews, *op. cit.*, pp. 625 ff. A great deal of literature has been published about Gould's gold plot and Black Friday. The writer has relied chiefly on sources of the period, notably Clews, pp. 182–200, and Stedman, *op. cit.*, Vol. I, pp. 216–33. The account of the planting of Corbin's article in the New York *Times* comes from Stedman, Vol. I, p. 217. In addition, the writer has referred to the New York *Times* (September 24, 1869) and the New York *Herald Tribune* (September 25, 1869) for the scenes on the floor during Black Friday. Material has also been drawn from testimony on the Gold Conspiracy, before the James A. Garfield Congressional Committee, House Report No. 31. Forty-first Congress, Second Session. The details of Ward's swindle of Grant appear in Stedman, Vol. I, pp. 309–13 and 314–6; also in Clews, pp. 215–22, and in Alexander Dana Noyes, *The Market Place; Reminiscences of a Financial Editor* (Little, Brown, 1938), pp. 42–4; Noyes' description of Grant's visit to the broker offices comes from pp. 44–5. For Grant's illness and death, the writer has drawn from the memoirs of the attending physician, George F. Shrady, *General Grant's Last Days* (De Vinne Press, 1908). Other works referred to include a compilation of newspaper clippings, Claxton Wilstach, comp., *The Death of General U. S. Grant* (issued by compiler in Lafayette, Ind., 1885); also a personal memoir by a military colleague and friend, Adam Badeau, *Grant in Peace, from Appomattox to Mount McGregor* (S. S. Scranton & Co., 1875), and Ishbel Ross, *The General's Wife* (Dodd, Mead, 1959).

4—THE BULLS AND THE BEARS

Facts about the first railroad securities and other pioneer stocks traded in the Street have come from Stedman, *op. cit.*, pp. 87 ff. For a discussion of the psychology and strategy of speculation, the writer has referred to Stedman; to Clews, *op. cit.*; to William Lawson, *Frenzied Finance* (Ridgway-Thayer Co., 1905); and to Wycoff, *op. cit.* One especially valuable source for the psychology of the old-time speculators is by a financial writer, Edwin Lefevre, *Wall Street Stories* (McClure, Phillips & Co., 1901)—classic case studies of stock manipulation thinly disguised as fiction. Other sources the writer has referred to include John Moody, *The Art of Wall Street Investing* (Moody Corp., 1900); Warren Fayette Hickernell, *Manipulations and Market Leadership* (American Institute of Finance, 1919); Arthur Crump, *The Theory of Stock Exchange Speculation* (Longmans, Green, 1874); George Charles Selden, "Psychology of the Stock Market," *Magazine of Wall Street* (1919); Franklin C. Keyes, *Wall Street Speculation, Its Tricks and Its Tragedies* (Columbia Publishing Co., 1904); Henry Howard Harper, *The Psychology of Speculation* (Torch Press, 1926). Material on the birth of the stock ticker appears in Stedman, pp. 433–5. The source for Harriman's techniques of trading is Wycoff, pp. 165–7; the material on Keene's tape reading habits comes from Wycoff and from Clews, pp. 229–39. The description of the Stock Exchange's move into new quarters is derived from John Rodemeyer, in Stedman, Vol. I, Sect. III, pp. 411–9.

5—THE GREAT SOCIETY—YESTERDAY

For the social history of New York before the Civil War, the writer has referred to the *Diary of Philip Hone, 1828–51*, introduction by Allan Nevins, ed. (Dodd, Mead, 1936). For the Bradley Martin ball the writer has drawn from Frederick Townsend Martin,

The Passing of the Idle Rich (Doubleday, Page, 1911) and Dixon Wecter, *The Saga of American Society* (Scribner's, 1937). Also consulted has been Frederick Martin, *Things I Remember* (J. Lane Co., 1913). For additional social doings of the plungers, reference has been made to Josephson, *op. cit.*, pp. 315–46. For the section on the Claflin sisters, the writer has drawn from Emanie Sachs, *The Terrible Siren, Victoria Woodhull* (Harper, 1928) and from a fictionalized account, Beril Becker, *Whirlwind in Petticoats* (Garden City, 1947). The writer has also consulted a number of contemporary pamphlets and magazine articles, notably "Victoria C. Woodhull. A Biographical Sketch," *The Golden Age* (1871); *Two Noble Women, Nobly Planned* (Phelps Brothers, 1893); James M. Nelson, "America's Victoria," *Historical and Philosophical Society of Ohio* (October, 1958); Victoria Martin, *Speech on the Principles of Finance* (Woodhull Claflin & Co., 1871); a speech delivered in Steinway Hall, November 20, 1871, and Music Hall, Boston, January 3, 1872, Victoria Claflin Woodhull Martin, *And the Truth Shall Make You Free* (Blackfriars, Printers, 1894). Also consulted was "The Beecher-Tilton Scandal: A Complete History of the Case, from November, 1872, to the Present Time, with Mrs. Woodhull's Statement," *Woodhull & Claflin's Weekly* (November 2, 1872). Material on Howe and Hummell comes chiefly from Sachs and Richard Halworth Rovere, *Howe & Hummell, Their True and Scandalous History* (Farrar, Straus, 1947). The account of the Vanderbilt will is derived from clippings from New York newspapers, mounted and bound in the New York Public Library, 1877–8. For a discussion of marriages of Wall Street heiresses with European nobility, see William Thomas Stead, *The Americanization of the World* (H. Markley, 1902). A basic source for the personality and career of Morgan has been Herbert Livingston Satterlee, *J. Pierpont Morgan; an Intimate Portrait* (Macmillan, 1939). Other sources consulted include John K. Winkler, *Morgan the Magnificent* (Vanguard Press, 1930); Lewis Corey, *The House of Morgan* (Grosset & Dunlap, 1930). A source for Morgan's role as an art collector has been *Pierpont Morgan as Collector and Patron* (Pierpont Morgan Library, Yale University Press, 1957). Material has also been cited from Josephson, pp. 319, 320, 346; also from the following magazine articles: Joseph B. Gilder, "Mr. Morgan's Personality as Viewed by His Friends," *Century* Magazine, Vol. 86 (1913), pp. 459–66;

John Moody and George Kibbe Turner, "Morgan the Great Trustee," *McClure's Magazine*, Vol. 36 (1910); E. C. Machen, "A View of Pierpont Morgan and His Work," *Cosmopolitan*, Vol. 31 (1901).

6—BANK RUNS AND A MONEY PANIC

For a discussion of the Dow theory, the writer has referred to William Peter Hamilton, *The Stock Market Barometer; a Study of Its Forecast Value Based on Charles H. Dow's Theory of the Price Movement* (Harper, 1922). Reference has also been made to Robert Rhea, *The Dow Theory* (Barron's, 1922), which is another important contribution to the field. For a discussion of Wall Street panics, reference has been made, among other sources, to Hamilton and to David Walter Perkins, *Wall Street Panics, 1813–1930* (Utica Printing Co., 1931). The anecdotes about Travers have been taken from Clews, *op. cit.*, p. 407 ff.; the story of Gates' shutting his mill has been taken from Wycoff, *op. cit.*, pp. 77–8. Other references for short selling have been drawn from Charles Amos Dice and Wilford John Eiteman, *The Stock Market* (McGraw-Hill, 1924); Frederick Drew Bond, *Stock Movements and Speculation* (D. Appleton & Co., 1930); Algernon Ashburner Osborne, *Speculation on the New York Stock Exchange, September 1904 to March 1907* (Columbia University Press, 1913). Much source material is available on the panic of 1907. Lack of space forbids the listing of all sources referred to. A basic account of Morgan's role is found in Satterlee, *op. cit.* For a description of the bank runs and other local color stories, the writer has drawn freely from the news accounts in the New York *Times* and *Herald Tribune* for October and November, 1907. For an account of the Pujo hearings, the writer has drawn from the *Banking and Currency Committee, May 16, 1912, to February 26, 1913*, House, 62:2–3. For Morgan's role, see Satterlee, pp. 556–8. Parrington's quote on the muckrakers comes from Harold E. Stearns, ed., *America Now; an Inquiry into Civilization in the United States* (Scribner, 1938), p. 346. For a description of America's social life preceding the outbreak of the First World War, the writer has referred to the New York *Times* for the month of July, 1914, and to Walter Lord, *The Good Years* (Harper, 1960), pp. 308–14. Reference has been made to Henry Noble, *The New York Stock Exchange in the Crisis of 1914* (Garden City, 1915).

For the growth of the American Stock Exchange, reference has been made, among other sources, to *The History of the New York Curb* (Jones & Baker, 1916); Meeker, *op. cit.*; John Brooks, *The Seven Fat Years* (Doubleday, 1961), Dolphin Books, Chap. 7, pp. 178–81; *Constitution of New York Curb Exchange and Rules Adopted by the Board of Governors Pursuant thereto* (New York Curb Exchange, 1926 to date).

7—THE BULLS SEE RED

A basic reference source for American society in the 1920s has been Frederick Lewis Allen, *Only Yesterday* (Harper, 1931). The writer has also consulted Robert S. Lynd and Helen Merrell Lynd, *Middletown, a Study in Contemporary American Culture* (Harcourt, 1929) and Joseph Wood Krutch, *The Modern Temper, a Study and a Confession* (Harcourt, 1929). For the discussion of spiritualism, the writer has referred to Harry Houdini, *A Magician Among the Spirits* (Harper, 1924) and to a number of contemporary magazine articles, including "Spiritualism, Signs and Portents," *Harper's* (June, 1919); "Will a Spiritual Movement Appear?" *Collier's* (February 7, 1920); "Ghosts and Devils; New Style," *Scribner's* (April, 1922); "Crooks of Ghostland," *Saturday Evening Post* (April 24, 1920). For the Wall Street bombing, the writer has consulted Frederick Lewis Allen's excellent account, *op. cit.*, pp. 59–62, and news stories appearing in the New York *Times* and *Herald Tribune* (September 16, 17, 18, 1920). The writer has drawn additional facts from articles—"Wall Street's Bomb Mystery," *Literary Digest* (October 2, 1920); from an article written by Sidney Sutherland, in *Liberty* (April 26, 1930); and an account in the *Independent and Weekly Review* (October, 1920). For a discussion of Attorney General Palmer's Red raids, the writer has consulted Zechariah Chafee, Jr., *Freedom of Speech* (Harcourt, 1920) and Sidney Howard, "Our Professional Patriots," *New Republic* (August 20 to October 15, 1924).

8—THE BIG SWINGERS

For a discussion of trading reforms instituted by the New York Stock Exchange, the writer has referred, among other sources, to

Sidney Struble, *A Brief Review of the Changes of the 1925 Revision of the Constitution and Rules of the New York Stock Exchange* (filed in New York Public Library, 1925); also to the *New York Stock Exchange, History, Organization, Operations and Service* (New York Stock Exchange, 1926–1934). For a discussion of the shifting of the base of investment power in the United States of the 1920s, reference has been made to Dice and Eiteman, *op. cit.*, and to Robert Sobel, *The Big Board* (Free Press, 1965). For the story of Durant's career, the writer has referred to Arthur Pound, *The Turning Wheel, the Story of General Motors Through Twenty-Five Years* (Doubleday, Doran, 1934); also to Lawrence Howard Seltzer, *A Financial History of the American Auto Industry* (Houghton Mifflin, 1928). For the details of Durant's severance from General Motors, the writer has drawn from Alfred P. Sloan, Jr., *My Years with General Motors* (Doubleday, 1963), pp. 27–38. A source for the financial arrangements which GM made with Durant and the amount of money he was left with is Arthur Pound and Samuel Taylor Moore, eds., *They Told Barron's; the Notes of the Late Clarence W. Barron* (Harper, 1930). For additional material on Durant's personality and his Wall Street dealings, the writer has consulted Earl Sparling, *Mystery Men of Wall Street* (Greenberg, Publisher, 1930) and Humphrey Bancroft Neill, *The Inside Story of the Stock Exchange* (Forbes, 1950). Two articles providing additional material appeared in *Current Opinion* (November, 1924) and the *Saturday Evening Post* (February 7, 1920). For the career of the Fisher brothers, the writer has relied, among other sources, on Sparling; J. T. Flynn, "Riders of the Whirlwind," *Collier's* (January 19, 1929); an article by T. H. Gammack in *Outlook* (October 3, 1928); and contemporary newspaper accounts. The material on Cutten comes largely from his autobiography, *op. cit.* Facts on Livermore come from his book, *How to Trade in Stocks* (Duell, Sloan & Pearce, 1940). Further sources are Wycoff, *op. cit.*, pp. 252–7 and Sparling, pp. 45–76. Another valuable reference book has been Edwin Lefevre, *Reminiscences of a Stock Operator* (Doubleday, Doran, 1931); although written as fiction, the book is a thinly disguised account of Livermore's career. For a description of Livermore's trading quarters in the early 1920s, the writer has turned to Wycoff, *op. cit.*, pp. 252–3, and for details of his postwar trading strategy, reference has been made to *They Told Barron's,*

p. 47 ff. For the manipulations of the Durant consortium, the writer has consulted Sparling; Neill; Frederick Lewis Allen, *Lords of Creation* (Harper, 1935); Forrest Davis, *What Price Wall Street* (W. Goodwin, 1932). The writer has also relied on the post-crash testimony given before the Banking and Currency Committee, Senate 72:1–2. Seventy-second Congress, from April 11, 1932 to March 2, 1933.

9—PROPHETS AND PROFITS

Three books have been most frequently consulted for the stock market boom of the 1920s, John Kenneth Galbraith, *The Great Crash 1929* (Houghton Mifflin, 1955); Noyes, *op. cit.*; and Allen, *Only Yesterday*. For the reference to promoters advertising how many points favored stocks would go up each day, see Noyes, p. 328; the episode about Irving Berlin's opening the trading on the *Île de France* comes from Galbraith, p. 86. The information about the increase in numbers of ticker tape installations comes from an article in the *Literary Digest* (April 14, 1928). The reference to the increase in automobile, art buying and the nightclub business is taken from the *Literary Digest* (May 19, 1928). Eunice Fuller Barnard's article on the new wisdom of women as traders comes from "Ladies of the Ticker," *North American Review* (April 29, 1929). The anecdotes about gullible women traders derive from Elizabeth Frazer, "Did You Lose Your Shirt in the Market?" *Saturday Evening Post* (September 8, 1928). John Moody's prophecy is taken from the *Literary Digest* (May 26, 1928). Quotes from other optimistic prophets come from the *Literary Digest* (June 23, 1928) and the *Outlook* (March 28, 1928). The account of Durant's visit to the White House is based on his statement in the New York *Times* (December 14, 1929), as well as on Sparling, *op. cit.*, and Neill, *op. cit.* The facts about the Radio stock corner are based on Allen's *Lords of Creation*, Sparling, and contemporary newspaper accounts.

10—THE CRASH OF 1929

Since there is a vast amount of material on the 1929 crash, the writer can mention only several of the most frequent sources consulted. For a description of American life during the weeks before the crash, the writer has drawn from the New York *Times* (September 3 to October 24, 1929). For the story of the crash itself, data has been taken from the *Times* and the *Herald Tribune* (October 24 to October 31, 1929). In addition, the writer has consulted Galbraith, *op. cit.*; Allen, *Only Yesterday*; and Noyes, *op. cit.* In addition reference has been made to Davis, *op. cit.*; John Lloyd Parker, *Unmasking Wall Street* (Stratford Co., 1932) and to A. Newton Plummer, *The Great American Swindle, Inc.* (A. N. Plummer, 1932). Among articles of the period dealing with phases of the crash, the writer has drawn from *Current History* (December 19, 1929); *Review of Reviews* (December, 1929, and January, 1930); Edwin Lefevre's articles in the *Saturday Evening Post* (January 4 and 11, 1930). For the state of mind of Americans after the crash, material has been drawn from *Overland Monthly* (January, 1930); *Current History* (December, 1929); *Literary Digest* (November 9, 1929); *Collier's* (April 9, 1932); *Saturday Evening Post* (August 1, 1931, and January 23, 1932). For an analysis of the panic on the floor of the Exchange, the writer has drawn from "The Work of the New York Stock Exchange in the Panic of 1929," an address by Richard Whitney, the president, delivered before the Boston Association of Stock Exchange Firms on June 10, 1930. For the attitude of business leaders after the crash, the writer has consulted James Truslow Adams "Presidential Prosperity," *Harper's* (August, 1930). For post-crash anecdotes and other local color stories, the writer has consulted Edward Angly, compiler, *Oh Yeah?* (Viking Press, 1931), and Eddie Cantor, *Caught Short! A Saga of Wailing Wall Street* (Simon & Schuster, 1929). For an analysis of the 86 percent drop in stock prices after the October crash, the writer has referred among others to Noyes, *op. cit.* The material on the final years and death of Durant comes from *Newsweek* (March 27, 1939), p. 46; *Time* (March 31, 1947), p. 86; *Newsweek* (March 31, 1947). A description of Livermore's death comes from *Newsweek* and *Time* (both December 9, 1940), p. 41 and pp. 79–81 respectively. Meehan's confinement to Bloomingdale is referred to in the New York *Times* (August 3, 1937), p. 31; *Newsweek* (December 5, 1936), pp. 33–4; and *Literary Digest* (December 26, 1936), p. 37. For a description of the environment at Bloomingdale, the writer has referred to William Seabrook, *Asylum* (Harcourt, 1935).

11—THE GREAT DEPRESSION

The material on technocracy has been drawn from Allen, *Only Yesterday*, pp. 71–3, and from the writings of Howard Scott, including *Introduction to Technocracy* (John Day, 1933); *Technocracy: Science vs. Chaos* (Technocracy, Inc., 1933); *The Evolution of Statesmanship* (Technocracy, Inc., 1939). Among the magazine articles consulted have been Howard Scott, "Technology Smashes the Price System," *Harper's* (January, 1933), pp. 129–42; Howard Scott, "Technocracy Speaks," *Living Age* (December, 1932), pp. 297–303; Henry Hazlitt, "Scrambled Ergs," *Nation* (February 1, 1933), pp. 112–5. The episode of the shipboard passengers who grew panicky when the market went down was taken from Noyes, *op. cit.*, p. 343. The cases of "smart" traders who went broke after the market crash comes from a study by Edwin Lefevre, "Soaking the Rich," *Saturday Evening Post* (February 20, 1932), p. 14 ff. For the controversy over short sellers, the writer has consulted the Hearing before the Committee on the Judiciary, House of Representatives, Seventy-second Congress, First Session, 1932; also "Short Selling," a reply by William Robertson Perkins to the address of Richard Whitney before the Chamber of Commerce of Hartford, Connecticut, October 16, 1931; also D. McD. Bruner, *Short-selling the U.S.A.* (Winston, 1933). For the references to stock manipulation by the banking syndicates, the writer has drawn from the hearings before the Banking and Currency Committee, Senate 72:1–2, Seventy-second Congress, held from April 11, 1932, to March 2, 1933; from a survey by Alfred L. Bernheim, *The Security Markets* (Twentieth Century Fund, Inc., 1935); and from a book by counsel to the Banking and Currency Committee, Ferdinand Pecora, *Wall Street Under Oath, the Story of Our Modern Money Changers* (Simon & Schuster, 1939). Material on the financial dealings of the Van Sweringen brothers comes from Pecora, pp. 215–9; from Allen's *Only Yesterday*; and from contemporary newspaper articles. The episode of the auction is referred to in Brooks, *op. cit.*, in a three-part series, Matthew Josephson "The Daring Young Man of Wall Street," *Saturday Evening Post* (August 11, 1945 ff.); and in news accounts in the *Times* and *Herald Tribune*. Space prohibits listing the numerous sources consulted for the New Deal reforms of the stock market and the founding of the SEC. In addition to the standard works on Roosevelt and the New Deal, one especially useful interpretation is "Wall Street Looks at the Securities and Exchange Commission," an address delivered by Eugene L. Garey at Richmond, Virginia, on April 28, 1939, before the Legal Institute of Modern Federal Administrative Law.

12—THE CORPORATE RAIDERS

Some of the material on Wall Street since World War II comes from the author's writings on contemporaries of the business world. In addition, he has made use of a number of important books and articles of the period. A source for the changes that took place in the Stock Exchange during World War II is Neill, *op. cit.*; also Dice and Eiteman, *op. cit.* An excellent study is *Postwar Securities Markets* (National Bureau of Economic Research, 1946). One source for the section on the Very Rich is Richard Austin Smith, "The Fifty-Million Dollar Man," *Fortune* (November, 1957). Another source is the "Road to Riches" series, *Wall Street Journal* (May 16 to October 25, 1960). The reference to Getty comes from his book *How to Be Rich* (Playboy Press, 1965). For the section on Murchison, the author has relied on his own research, as well as on studies appearing in various financial publications. An excellent analysis of Murchison's strategy of leveraging debt is Freeman Lincoln, "Big Wheeler-Dealer from Dallas," *Fortune* (January and February, 1953). The description of Karr's strategy of proxy fighting is taken from his book *Fight for Control* (Ballantine Books, 1956). The material on Green's fight for Twentieth Century-Fox comes from contemporary news accounts and from the author's files. An account also appears in Karr. For the career of Young and the New York Central proxy battle, the writer has consulted several articles published in *Barron's National Business and Financial Weekly* during the 1950's, as well as his personal research. A comprehensive treatment of Young's early career is Josephson, "The Daring Young Man of Wall Street," *op. cit.* An analysis of the results of the proxy voting appeared in *Fortune* (August, 1954) and *Newsweek* (June 7, 1954).

13—THE PLUNGERS AND THE PEACOCKS TODAY

My discussion of the shift to institutional trading with accompanying statistics was developed originally in a two-part series by the author, "Unorganized Exchange," *Barron's National Business and Financial Weekly* (August 8 and 15, 1966). The section on the birth of the computer in England was suggested, among other sources, by Norbert Wiener's *Cybernetics; or, Control and Communication in the Animal and the Machine,* 2nd ed. (MIT Press, 1961). The computer revolution on Wall Street has been partly adapted from "Computers and Investors," *Barron's* (June 22, 1964) and "Calculating Risks," *Barron's* (June 28, 1965), both by Dana L. Thomas, as well as additional articles by the author in *Barron's* (August 14 and 28, 1969; August 30 and September 6, 1971). Material on the gold market is based partly on four *Barron's* articles by Dana L. Thomas (November 8, 1971; August 26 and September 2, 1974; and April 11, 1977). The discussion of Cornfeld is suggested partly by *The Bernie Cornfeld Story* by Bert Cantor (Lyle Stuart, 1970). Material on cattle breeding and Florida orange-groves investments was suggested originally by articles in *Barron's* (October 6, 1969; August 19, 1968; and October 21, 1974) by Dana L. Thomas.

14—WALL STREET TOMORROW

Observations on hyperinflation and its historical and political ramifications are based among other sources on Chapter 2, "The Historical Perspective," *Everything You Need to Know Now About Gold and Silver* by Dana L. Thomas (Arlington House, 1972), and an interview with Thomas for the *Pacific Coast Coin Exchange*. A source for the discussion of investment strategy is *How to Increase Your Income During Your Retirement* by Thomas (Doubleday, 1983).

INDEX